The Computer Comes of Age

The MIT Press Series in the History of Computing
I. Bernard Cohen, editor; William Aspray, associate editor

The Computer Comes of Age, R. Moreau, 1984

Memories That Shaped an Industry, Emerson W. Pugh, 1984

The Computer Comes of Age

The People, the Hardware, and the Software

R. Moreau

Translated by J. Howlett

The MIT Press
Cambridge, Massachusetts
London, England

Original edition copyright © 1981 by Bordas, Paris, published under the title *Ainsi naquit l'informatique.*

This book was set in Baskerville by The MIT Press Computergraphics Department and printed and bound by The Murray Printing Co. in the United States of America.

Library of Congress Cataloging in Publication Data

Moreau, René.
    The computer comes of age.

    (The MIT Press series in the history of computing)
    Translation of: Ainsi naquit l'informatique.
    Bibliography: p.
    Includes index.
    1. Computers—History. 2. Programming languages (Electronic computers)—History. I. Title. II. Series.
QA76.17.M6713 1984   001.64′09   83-9424
ISBN 0-262-13194-3

Contents

Series Foreword   *vii*

Preface   *ix*

Introduction   *1*

1
The Birth of the Computer   *4*

1
Problem Solving and Its Mechanization   4

2
Mechanical Machines   10

3
Electromechanical Machines   21

4
Electronic Machines   33

5
Conclusion   46

2
The First Generation: 1950–1959   *48*

1
1950–1954: Evolution   49

2
The Development of Other Information Supports   69

3
Conclusion   87

3

The Second Generation: 1959–1963   *89*

1
Meeting the Needs of the Users   92

2
Batch Processing   108

3
Direct-Access Shared-Use Systems   121

4
Conclusion   131

4

Programming Languages   *148*

1
The Low-Level Languages   150

2
The First High-Level Languages   159

3
Formally Defined High-Level Languages   167

4
Functional Languages   178

5
Conclusion   182

5

Conclusions   *186*

Appendix: Early Work on Computers in the USSR   *197*

Author's Notes   *203*

Translator's Notes   *209*

Bibliography   *211*

Index   *219*

Series Foreword

René Moreau's book inaugurates a new series devoted to the history of computer and data processing. Future volumes will deal with various aspects of the development of systems, hardware, and software, and there will be both general works and specialized monographs. Some works being planned for the series will be of a biographical and even autobiographical nature, and others will concentrate on either a particular development, such as magnetic memory, or the technical history of an industrial company.

The first book in the series is by René Moreau, manager of scientific development for IBM France. He is the author of a general computer-oriented work on the theory of languages (1975) and of computer-based analyses of the language of General De Gaulle and of the language used in the election campaigns by Giscard D'Estaing and Mitterrand.

The history of computers and data processing is a relatively new subject. There are numerous specialized historical presentations within this area, but this is the first book to attempt to make a synthesis of the whole subject. René Moreau has given us a technical history that centers on problems and their solutions, stage by stage, from the beginnings of this subject until the year 1963, when the IBM Series 360 computers introduced a new age in the history of technology.

In this book each of the major concepts and devices is explained or described in its historical context. Accordingly, this book should be of significance for any reader wishing to understand the development of information processing and information theory (or informatics). Rene Moreau has enlarged our understanding of the development of technology and of the role of machines in modern society. All readers will be stimulated by his fresh point of view and his deep insight into the significance of information technology.

I. Bernard Cohen
William Aspray

Preface

It is not uncommon to read that the first computer was the MARK I, or the Harvard-IBM machine, or perhaps ENIAC; but it is seldom stated that the IBM Selective Sequence-Controlled Electronic Calculator (SSEC) alone can claim this distinction. There is the same uncertainty in dating the first formulations of the main concepts of what we now call computer science—multiprogramming, operating systems, teleprocessing, programming languages, and so on. There are at least two reasons for this. The definitions of the concepts can vary from one writer to another, and it is often difficult to select from the multitude of facts relating to these concepts the one or the few that indicate the origins of the most significant developments.

It seemed to me that it would be interesting to give an account of the history of the computer and of computer science that, while addressed to the nonspecialist, would define these concepts as precisely as possible and, taking the majority view of the knowledgeable writers, would assign dates to first formulations. Thus the book is not simply a history of one particular technology; it is also an exposition of the main ideas and concepts to which this technology has given rise. As a work of popularization, it may give to the reader who does not work in the field of computers some familiarity with the subject. As a history, it may give the specialist a better feeling for the origins of this subject.

The bibliography of so broad a subject could fill several volumes; the bibliographical entries given here are works actually cited in or having a direct bearing on the text.

Translator's note: Certain conventions have been adopted for this edition. First, author's notes are cited by superscripts 1, 2, 3, . . . ; translator's notes, by superscripts a, b, c, . . . ; both author's and translator's notes appear at the back of the book. Second, text in square brackets is an insertion by the translator.

Before concluding this preface, I should like to thank all those who have given me so much help, whether in reading and criticizing my text or in providing me with documents.

The Computer Comes of Age

Introduction

Twenty years ago very few people, apart from the small number actually in the field, had ever heard of computers, let alone seen one. But in 1980 it is estimated that about 50 percent of the venture capital invested during the past few years has gone into computer hardware and software companies. In France, according to the Accountant General (Cour des Comptes) the total value of the computers and associated equipment installed was over $10,000 million. The computer has already invaded most human activities; who among us has never called upon its services, usually without knowing it, whether in running one's washing machine, checking one's wristwatch, or using the automatic cash dispenser at one's bank? Who for that matter has never seen a computer, at least in its physically smallest form, now called the microprocessor, which can be bought in the big stores or the specialist shops for a few hundred dollars? The transformation has been so rapid that it seems to have been brought about by some magician, more or less diabolical, waving a mysterious magic wand.

Twenty years ago, however, the main concepts of computer science had already been formulated, and there is no mystery about this; they were the culmination of a slow intellectual and technological evolution that began at a very early period in the history of mankind. Today's computers, of whatever shape or form, do not differ in essence from those of that time; moreover, the main kinds of uses had already been defined and the main fields of application sketched out. By the end of 1963 or the beginning of 1964 computer science had in some sense come of age.

From the point of view of the early 1980s, the period ending in 1963 can be regarded as belonging to the history of the technology with which this book is concerned. It is now possible, because of the passage of time, to see papers that up to now have been held as confidential, and thus to give a more exact account than had previously been possible of the more recent developments in computer science, still too closely linked with people still alive. This historical period is described here, together with accounts (to put it as simply as possible) of the main concepts forming the skeleton of computer science as we now know it. This history can serve therefore as an introductory course on the subject.

The first chapter deals with the "gestation" period of computer science, which stretches from the earliest times to the appearance of the first computer early in 1948. In this account of the linking of the various concepts and attempts at construction leading to the first calculating devices, then to the true calculators, and finally to the computer, I do not have the space to describe all the abaci, calculating instruments, and other machines that mathematicians, astronomers, and military engineers have built over the years for the evaluation of mathematical functions. I have dealt only with those that contribute directly to the understanding of the historical account. In the second chapter I speak of the "infancy" of computer science. Before it could be considered to be adult, the subject had to grow, and its essential device, the computer, had to develop from the research laboratories where it was born into a manufacturable product. This period lasted from 1949 to 1959; it is not fortuitous that computer specialists when describing the technology of the computer call this period the "first generation." I have chosen that title for this second chapter. The third period, from 1959 to 1963, is that of "adolescence," during which computers started to invade all human activities. It has been called the "second generation" of computers, the title and subject of the third chapter.

This division into three periods can be regarded as corresponding to three main phases of the evolution of the technology: realization of the computer in the first, development of supporting and ancillary equipment for storing information in the second, and during the third the development of operating systems for the control and exploitation of the computer's resources—systems intended for the replacement of the human operator, who was becoming incapable of reacting to the ever increasing speed of the machine.

The same division into three periods corresponds equally well to the three main phases in the development and use of the principal languages of communication between man and machine. Before 1948 the languages used were very primitive; the first of the more highly developed languages appeared during 1948–1959; and 1959–1963 saw the birth of all the languages now most in use. But because the development of languages is linked less closely to that of the machine than is the development of other technologies, I have dealt with this in a separate chapter, the fourth.

The history of this whole period is in every aspect so complex that in the interest of clarity it has been necessary to select particular events, particular pieces of hardware, and particular manufacturers. An attempt to cover everything would have been very difficult and led to a far too bulky book. It was therefore necessary to decide either not to mention this or that machine or manufacturer or not to say very much about them. Since no such choice can be made purely objectively, there will inevitably be some criticisms of those made here. It is not only the choice of facts that poses problems; there is also that of dates, for different dates for the same event can often be found in the literature. There are at least three phases in the development of a computer product: conception, announcement, and installation in a user's premises. I have usually chosen the date of announcement, which has also been done most often in the relevant literature.

1

The Birth of the Computer

Ever since the invention of numbers, humanity has tried to make instruments to help in performing calculations. There were tablets for calculating earlier than 3000 B.C., and the well-known Chinese bead frame existed well before the birth of Christ; but tablets, bead frames, and abaci are all completely nonautomatic. The idea of mechanizing calculation is very old, although it was not a practical possibility until mechanical engineering (whose finest applications had been in the design and making of clocks) became sufficiently highly developed. In the early nineteenth century the British astronomer and mathematician Charles Babbage described what could have been a machine with the ability to perform any calculation whatever; but unfortunately the mechanical-engineering technology of the time provided neither the reliability nor the speed that were necessary for the realization of his dream. The construction of the first calculators had to await the arrival of electromechanical technology, and it was the development of electronics that led to the first computers.

1 Problem Solving and Its Mechanization

If it is to carry out a calculation, a machine must know the route it has to follow. But a machine has no intrinsic knowledge and knows nothing about the external world; therefore it has to be given instructions on how to proceed in the minutest detail. The details of the method of solution of a problem that can be performed by a machine are in the form of a statement of a sequence of operations that the machine has to carry out. We call this the *process*. This way of describing a process is in fact common practice, and we use it whenever we follow what we may call an *algorithmic procedure*.

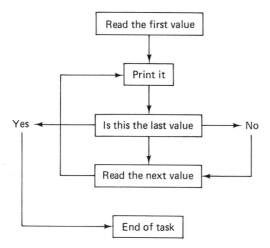

Figure 1.1
Reading a table of values.

Algorithmic Procedure

Among the problems continually presenting themselves for solution are a very large class for which the process of solution can be given in advance in terms of a finite number of exact statements of operations to be used in order to produce a specific result. Figure 1.1 illustrates this type of procedure by showing the steps that must be followed in order to read a table of values. We say that a procedure for solving a problem is *algorithmic* when it can be expressed as a sequence of statements of operations to be performed and when no knowledge or intelligence is required beyond what is strictly necessary in order to perform these operations. The statements must therefore be sufficiently clear and precise as to present no difficulties of interpretation. The diagrammatic representation of an algorithmic procedure is called a *flowchart*.

The statements in an algorithmic procedure are of two types. The first type is illustrated in Figure 1.1 by "Read the first value" or "Go from the part of the flowchart where the operation required is to print the value read to that where the operation is to check whether the last value has been read." These are what we might call imperative commands and we describe such statements as *unconditional*. The second type can be put in this general form: "*If* such-and-such a result is observed, *then* do this *else* do that." Such a statement in figure 1.1 is "*If* the value in the table that has been read is the last value, *then* the task is ended *else* read the next value." These are called *conditional* or *logical* statements.[1]

Thanks to the conditional statement there is the possibility, at any stage in a procedure, of choosing between different routes to follow from there on depending upon the conditions at that stage: for example, whether or not to read another value from the table. A procedure with no conditional statements permits of no variations at all and therefore can be used only to solve a single problem: for example, "Read a value from the table." The inclusion of conditional statements, on the contrary, allows a very much broader class of problems to be solved by making it possible to vary the procedure according to the requirements of the individual problems.

Algorithms

From now on we shall be concerned only with problems for which the process of solution, expressed as an algorithmic procedure, can be given to a machine and followed step by step by the machine until the result is obtained. To put it another way, we shall be studying only those types of algorithmic procedures corresponding to classes of problems that can be attacked with the help of a machine. We shall speak of *operations* to be performed rather than of statements, and of *algorithms* rather than of algorithmic procedures.

In general, an algorithm is constructed for the solution of a problem when it has been found, by reasoning or by experience or as a result of teaching, that a process for the solution can be described as a sequence of operations that can be performed without any need to attach meaning to them. We learn such step-by-step processes for solving certain problems from our earliest school days: for example, the addition or multiplication of numbers, finding square roots, and finding the volume of a sphere. These methods are all algorithms; they all lead from the use of a finite number of operations required to solve a particular problem (for example, the addition of 21 and 33) to their use in solving a broad class of problems (for example, the addition of *any* two numbers).

Algorithms have a long history. Those for addition, multiplication, and division were produced in prehistoric times. The Babylonians are a case in point; they devised algorithms for the solution of decidedly complex arithmetical problems posed by their studies of the movements of the stars and the planets. The word itself, however, comes from the name of the Persian mathematician Abu Ja'far Mohammed Ibn Musa Al Khowarismi, whose writings on arithmetic circa 825 A.D. influenced for centuries the development of mathematics.

Algorithmic Processing

As I have said, carrying out the sequence of operations represented by the statements forming an algorithm requires nothing more than what is necessary to understand these operations; therefore the process is essentially mechanical. Thus if a machine can be built for this special purpose, it will perform better than any human because it will follow the sequence precisely without any variation and will not tire. It is not surprising therefore that the idea of mechanizing algorithms is very old. (Rosenberg [1969], who gives attempts to mechanize algorithms before the year 1000 A.D., holds that the most typical were those made by Gerbert d'Aurillac, who became Pope Sylvester II in 999.)

What characteristics must a machine have in order to carry out such a sequence of operations, which we shall call *algorithmic processing?* At the outset, it must be able to deal with the two types of statement—unconditional and conditional respectively—defined earlier. For unconditional statements the machine must be able to perform the specific operations required by the algorithms; for example, it must have a device that can add two numbers. Such operations or transformations fall into two groups. In one are the operations of transferring information from one part of the machine to another. In the other are the operations having a single *operand*, called *unary operations* (such as the operation of changing the sign of a quantity, the quantity concerned being the operand), those having two operands, called *binary operations* (such as that of adding together two numbers, those numbers being the operands), and, further, operations having more than two operands, although these are much less common.[a] For conditional statements the machine must be able at least to perform simple tests, such as to decide whether one number is greater than another. Such operations, whether unary or binary, are called *logical operations.*

Operations of this type—transfer, unary, binary, logical—are called the *primitive operations* of the process. The elementary arithmetical and logical operations are of very great importance in any algorithmic process, as is easily seen from a consideration of a few examples. To answer the question "What is the sum of the first 10 numbers?," one needs only to make 10 additions—arithmetical operations—testing after each one to find whether that was the tenth. It is less obvious that a yes-or-no type of question can be answered by similar sequences of operations. Consider, for example, the question whether the word "greatness" occurs in a particular piece of writing of General de Gaulle's. To answer this, each word of the text must be given a code number, the same number for each occurrence of the same word and a different number for each occurrence of a different word; the text is thus

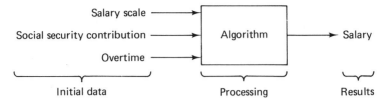

Figure 1.2
Algorithmic processing: calculating salaries.

represented by a sequence of numbers. The machine starts with the first number and subtracts from it the number representing the word "greatness"; if the result is zero, the two numbers are the same and "greatness" has been found as the first word of the text. If not, the machine moves on to the next number in the sequence and repeats the operation, and so on. If it arrives at the end of the text without recording a zero result, then the answer to the original question is no.

A machine that can carry out algorithmic processing must therefore have a number of basic operations. It must be able to perform the fundamental operations of arithmetic, and for this it must have what is called an *arithmetical unit*; similarly, it must have a *logical unit* for the logical operations. The two are often combined in one unit, called the *arithmetical-logical unit (ALU)*. Finally, the actual performance of the operations as a sequence in time must be monitored and directed, and for this there is a special unit, the control unit.

The effect of any algorithm is to transform the set of elements supplied to it at the start into the set forming the results. For the calculation of a salary, for example, the starting, or initial, set can include salary scale, hours of overtime worked, social security contribution, and so on; Figure 1.2 illustrates this.

The quantities involved in an algorithmic process can be either *numerical*—numbers, financial accounts, statistical observations—or nonnumerical—letters, phrases, pieces of text, and also, for example, music; music as a sequence of sounds can be coded by a function of the amplitude of the sound, measured at regular intervals.[2] Thus algorithmic processing can be applied to an extremely wide range of types of elements. In fact, the fields of application of algorithms are so numerous that one can say that an algorithm can be provided for any problem for which one knows a method of solution. In what follows the word *data* will be used to describe any elements that can be coded and thus subjected to algorithmic processing.

The alphabet used most frequently for coding data inside the machine is the *binary* because this is the easiest to represent in physical equipment. Hence the term *bit*, contraction of *binary digit*,[3] which can take either of only two values, represented by 0 and 1, respectively. Other forms of coding are of course possible. It seems that binary coding was not used to any great extent until after the construction in 1939 of the first Bell Laboratories machine, with which we deal shortly.

The starting values must somehow be given to the machine if it is to perform any processing on them, so there must be some device for communication between the machine and the outside world that enables this to be done; this is called the *input unit*. Similarly, the machine must be provided with some means for displaying its results, and therefore there must be an *output unit*. The two will, to a large extent, be made from the same components and are therefore usually referred to as the *input/output (I/O) units*.

We must note here that the machine carries out its processing quite independently of any meaning that the data may have; in effect, it works inside a formal world and knows nothing of any correspondence that may have been set up between data and the real world outside. Thus for the machine the word "greatness" in the de Gaulle text conveys no particular meaning. As Arsac has said [1970], "This separation of form and content characterizes all algorithmic processing." When we speak of information processing we must not forget that the word "information" is being used in a very special sense.

To sum up, an item of data has these characteristics:

1. It is coded with an alphabet of finite size.

2. So far as the machine is concerned, it carries no meaning.

Louis de Broglie wrote, "A calculating machine can provide its users with the results of its calculations, that is, with information." When it is simply a question of calculating the value of a function or the salary of an employee, or reserving a seat in a railway train or searching for a particular item in a file, or any similar task, the processing is performed with a specific end in view: given the data, to arrive at the result. For the user, who can attach whatever semantic or other significance to this result, what he gets is indeed information. The word *informatique* was coined by the French engineer Philippe Dreyfus to define the scientific activity that uses algorithms to process data in order to obtain information. The nearest English equivalent, *informatics*, has not come into general use, *data processing* being more frequent.[b]

I shall use the term machine, or information-processing machine, for any machine that can perform algorithmic processing. Such a machine can be characterized by the pair of attributes, *competence-performance*. Competence refers to the algorithm corresponding to the processing; performance, to the machine's intrinsic abilities to execute operations at speeds far greater than are possible for humans.

2 Mechanical Machines

The main components of an information-processing machine, as well as their functions, had been defined by the end of the nineteenth century, but there had been only limited success in actually constructing these at that time because the only technology available then, that of mechanical engineering, was unequal to the task.

I begin this study with a consideration of the very first machines, which were conceived and produced as aids to the most elementary algorithmic processing tasks, such as addition and subtraction. The process to be carried out was indicated by setting by hand some very simple device on the outside of the machine, and no more than about ten choices were possible. The initial data were put in by some equally simple means, such as turning a wheel or setting the position of a lever, on which also the results of the calculation could be read. These machines were, in effect, arithmetical-logical units; the speed of such a machine was of the order of that of the man who made the settings.

Once the means for performing the four operations of arithmetic have been mastered, the problem arises of how to vary the machine's competence (in the sense in which the term has just been defined) so that it can execute *any* type of algorithmic procedure. The first attack on this problem was made by Babbage, whose work is described later in this section; it was his misfortune that the mechanical-engineering technology of his time did not allow him to bring his ideas to realization. However, soon after Babbage's death it did become possible to put into practice some other basic ideas of computer science, and I end this section with an account of them.

The First Arithmetical Machines

The first difficulty to be overcome was that of mechanizing the basic operations of arithmetic. There is now little disagreement that the first calculating machine was made by Wilhelm Schickard (1592–1635) (see Flatt [1963]) who was professor of astronomy, Hebrew, and mathematics at Tübingen,[c] apparently to help him in his astronomical calculations. This machine, built in 1623, could add and subtract automatically and multiply and divide semiautomatically.

The principles of Schickard's machine derived from those of the first mechanization of logical operations made by the early clockmakers in China and later developed in the Middle East during the first millennium A.D. These depended on the use of toothed wheels (gear wheels) fitted with pins; when a wheel has turned through a certain angle, its pin meets that of a second wheel, to which it then imparts some rotation. We can describe the action of "tens carry" in Schickard's adding mechanism in terms of a conditional statement. The mechanism is made up of a number of toothed wheels, each with ten teeth. Suppose we have to add two numbers, each of a single decimal digit. A wheel—the "units wheel"—is turned one tooth at a time, counting the total one unit at a time; when it reaches the position between the teeth marked 9 and 0, its pin meets that of the next wheel, the "tens wheel," and moves this on one step. This is a translation into machinery of the conditional statement "*If* the sum of two single-digit numbers is equal to or greater than 10, *then* turn the tens wheel one unit."

Independently of Schickard, whom he probably did not know, Blaise Pascal (1623–1662) made a machine[4] in 1643 that could not only add and subtract automatically but could also convert sums of money between the different and complicated coinages of the time—*livres, sols, deniers*, and so on—and thus add and subtract these. His intention in this was to ease the burden on his father, who had recently been given the task of reorganizing the finances, and particularly the taxes, of Brittany. The fact that a machine could be given such an ability seemed at the time to have something supernatural about it; thus Pascal's sister wrote (see Perrier [1963]) that "the mind had somehow been taken over by the machine" because "it could do any kind of calculation without error, which was something extraordinary to be able to do without a pen, but even more so without even knowing arithmetic." This thought probably represents one of the first reflections on the problem of what we now call *artificial intelligence*.

It was in the same spirit that the Inquisition accused Leibniz's mother of having coupled with the Devil—for how else could she have produced a son who concerned himself with such things? Gottfried Wilhelm Leibniz (1646–1716), to ease the work of the astronomers, produced a machine that could perform the four basic operations of arithmetic—addition, subtraction, multiplication, and division—completely automatically.[5]

These three machines—Schickard's, Pascal's, and Leibniz's—had practically no direct descendants; but they were followed by a whole series of calculating machines influenced to a greater or less extent by them. There was no longer any problem in mechanizing the basic arithmetical operations when Babbage tried to build the forerunner of the modern computer. In fact, at that time a machine called the Arithometer, which performed all four operations, was being produced commercially in Europe; it was invented by Charles Xavier Thomas de Colmar (now usually known simply as Thomas de Colmar), of the insurance company Le Soleil, and was a great success, over 1,500 being sold in a period of 60 years.[6]

Babbage's Machine

The attempt made by Charles Babbage (1791–1871), the English astronomer and great mathematician,[d] to make a calculating machine was of fundamental importance. He was fascinated by technology. In his youth he was much interested in the mechanical automata based on the ideas of the Jacquemarts, which are described in the next paragraph; and after traveling in France he became equally interested in those of the Jacquard loom. He sought ways of using these two techniques in the Analytic Engine that he was planning around 1833, a machine to enable one "to solve any equation and to perform the most complex operations of mathematical analysis" (Babbage [1839]). For this, the machine would have to be able to execute complex sequences of arithmetical and logical operations, and in order to make it do so he had to overcome three difficulties. The first was to devise a mechanism for performing automatically the four basic arithmetical operations; as we have seen, this presented no problem. Next, the machine had to be able not simply to carry out one single procedure, as could all the calculators of that time, but to vary its sequences of operations from one procedure to another; this required that there be some device that could change the sequence. Finally, there had to be some means of indicating to the machine the sequence to be followed next, which implied some means of communication between the user and the machine; it was for this that Babbage employed the technique then used in the Jacquard loom.

The Jacquemarts

None of the calculating machines produced at that time could execute a long sequence of arithmetical and logical operations of the two types we have described—unconditional and conditional—characteristic of an algorithm. The first mechanism to have this ability was not a calculator, however, but an automaton. It would be going too far outside the scope of this book to deal with the history of automata, but we can say briefly that the art of clockmaking was highly developed in Europe in the fourteenth century, and that automata called Jacquemarts were built to strike the hours in many of the great clocks that still adorn our belfries. In doing this the Jacquemarts would go through a most complicated sequence of movements, all automatically.

These sequences included many logical tests. Thus, "*If* the half-hour has to be sounded, *then* make 2 strokes on the quarter-hour bell," or "*If* 3 o'clock has to be sounded, *then* make 3 strokes on the hours bell," and so on. The automata were controlled by toothed wheels or by pin-barrels; once built, these could be neither replaced nor modified, but it was possible now and again to remove or to alter some of the pins and so to make some change in the sequence of movements. Thus although these devices could perform complicated sequences of operations, they had no flexibility and it was not possible to make any significant change to the built-in sequence. Babbage used this principle but adapted it to give him the flexibility he needed.

The Jacquard Loom

As I have said, it had to be possible to instruct the machine on the sequence of operations to be followed so as to carry out the procedure required and also, at any stage in the procedure, how to use the intermediate results obtained at that stage to decide what course to follow from then on. This, I also said, required that there be some means of communication between the user and the machine that would enable the former to give the relevant instructions to the latter.

In connection with silk weaving, a technique was invented in Lyon in the eighteenth century that enabled a person to communicate to a machine a complex sequence of operations and to vary this sequence from one execution to another (Chapuis [1969]). Basile Bouchon, at the beginning of that century, had the idea of controlling the operation of a loom by means of perforated tapes. Then Joseph M. Jacquard (1752–1834) produced in 1805 his famous loom, using perforated cards; this was their first appearance, and Jacquard's cards were the ancestors of our present-day punched cards.

The method was this. Each warp (longitudinal) thread of the material being woven could be moved by its own individual hook, the movement of which was controlled by a rod; thus there was a row of rods corresponding to the row of threads across the material. If the free ends of this row of rods came against a card with perforations, the ends in line with holes would move through them, while those coming against an unperforated card would be stopped; the positions of the holes would decide which threads were to be moved for this particular weft, or line, across the material. Thus one card controlled the weaving of one weft thread; for the next a following card was used; and the weaving of a complete piece of material was controlled by a sequence of cards, which formed the *program* for the process. If the same pattern was to be repeated several times in the weaving of a single length of material, the same program or part of the program—that is, the same cards—could be used over and over again. The cards therefore provided the means of communication between the weaver and the machine. The data—the description of the pattern—were coded in terms of a binary alphabet represented by the holes and "nonholes" in the cards; thus the communication between weaver and weaving machine used a language, as all communication does, and the cards formed the channel of communication for this language.

Here again we find the competence-performance pair that characterizes the use of machines; in order to make the most of the loom's potential performance, which is its ability to weave complicated patterns quickly, the weaver supplies it, through the medium of the perforated cards, with the necessary competence, which is the sequence of instructions that cause it to weave a particular pattern selected from a large number of possibilities. In general terms, at each stage in the procedure the machine (a loom in this example) is given manually, by punched cards or other means (to be considered later), instructions for the sequence of operations to be carried out in the next stage. This was the practice for at least a century before the first computer appeared. As we shall see, the calculators that derived from Babbage's machine are distinguished from true computers by their inability to carry out, without human intervention, an entire sequence of operations required by any procedure.

The Architecture of Babbage's Machine

If a loom is to weave a patterned cloth under the control of perforated cards as has just been described, it must be provided with the necessary mechanical control and selection equipment. One might argue from this that no one machine can carry out all algorithmic procedures. There are, of course, specialized machines able to deal with only particular types of algorithms; a machine with the ability to perform any algorithmic procedure whatever can be called a *universal calculator*, and it was Babbage who first conceived the idea of such a machine and defined its structure.

Babbage's machine was made up of the input, arithmetical-logical, output, and control units described in section 1.3 in this chapter; in addition, there was what he called the store, corresponding approximately, but not exactly, to the memory of present-day computers. He saw that in order to calculate with the precision that he realized would be required, the machine would have to operate numerically, that is, digitally. Let us consider these items one by one.

The input unit   This used the idea of the pin-barrel taken from the Jacquemarts, but Babbage had to develop the device considerably in order to provide a means of giving the machine the sequence of instructions corresponding to the procedure to be carried out. Perforated cards were employed so that the pins could be pushed home so as not to project from the surface of the barrel; a card with a row of holes was brought up against a row of pins along the length of the barrel, pushing home those pins where there were no holes and leaving those pins projecting that corresponded to the perforations. The pattern of perforations on the card defined the operation to be performed, and a sequence of instructions was inputted to the machine by repeating this process with a sequence of cards, each of which had the required pattern of perforations, and turning the barrel through one angular step between each card.[c]

The arithmetical-logical unit   Babbage called this the *mill*. In his first attempts he again used pin-barrels, but as his ideas developed he replaced these more and more by mechanisms similar to those of the Jacquard loom. For logical statements he used what he called *combinatorial cards*, which "governed the repeating apparatus of the mill," and associated with these what he called *index cards*, which carried numbers used by the combinatorial cards and were thus able "to direct at certain intervals . . . the number and nature of repetitions which are to be made by those cards." This is, in fact, the control of the number of times a selected part of the program has to be repeated, and is what we now call *iteration*. This use by Babbage of the word "index" was its first appearance with this connotation; and as we shall see when we come to study the early work on computers at the University of Manchester, Babbage's index cards were the precursors of present-day index registers.

Babbage's "mill" thus provided the means for executing all the operations required by an algorithmic procedure, thus anticipating the arithmetical-logical unit of the modern computer. We know that the process of solution of a very wide class of problems, possibly infinite, can be expressed in this way; in describing his mill Babbage was probably the first to explain this. He wrote (Babbage [1864/1969]), "With the Analytic Engine any calculation whatever may be performed at one time, the choice of what is to be done being decided by conditions which we fix." He said also (Babbage [1837]) that "it is because of the sequentiality of the operations that a finite machine is able to make calculations which may be of infinite extent, the infinity of space which is needed for the solution of such a problem being replaced by an infinity of time."

The store   This was Babbage's concept; he thought of it as comprising both what we call the memory in a modern computer and the output unit. In Babbage's words (Babbage [1837]), "The Store may be considered as the place of deposit in which the numbers and quantities given by the conditions of the question are originally placed, in which all the intermediate results are provisionally preserved and in which at the termination all the required results are found." This is the role of the memory today. The anthropomorphic comparison of the place where numbers are stored with the human memory does not appear in Babbage's writings; he never uses the word memory, and the idea was certainly far from his thoughts. He compared the store more appropriately to a barn or granary where the wheat is placed before threshing, the grain and any intermediate products after this, and finally the flour at the end of the process; we have to go to the granary to get the flour when it has been produced, just as we have to go to the memory or store for the final results of our calculation.

The technology of Babbage's time required him to build his memory from toothed wheels and perforated cards. The initial numerical data for a calculation were set in advance by hand, either by turning certain wheels to required positions or with the help of perforated cards. Babbage had various ideas for the output of results that had been calculated and put into the memory. They could of course be read directly from the wheels, but he was aware of the need for permanent records. He designed equipment for perforating cards, the forerunner of the present-day card punch. There is at the Science Museum in London, together with a part of the Analytic Engine, a set of his output cards; they are rather bigger than our punched cards, and the holes are not much less than a half-inch in diameter, which seem enormous in comparison with what we are used to now. Other suggestions of his, the principles and construction of which he described in some detail, were for direct printing ("Printing Apparatus"), punching on to metal plates ("Copper Plate Punching Apparatus") and automatic curve plotting ("Curve Drawing Apparatus"). We shall consider such equipment at the end of the next chapter.

Output equipment is now considered as something separate from memory; it would therefore be better to describe the store as understood by Babbage (that is, as comprising both memory and output unit) as *information-support equipment*. This is a modern term, used to cover all the equipment involved in storing information and in communicating between the machine and the outside world, and thus including memories in the modern sense and output devices such as printers and curve plotters. However, the term "store" has been used to a significant extent by English writers as equivalent to the more restricted "memory."[f]

The control unit   Babbage took from Jacquard the fundamental principle of separating the mechanism that instructed the machine concerning which operations were to be performed from the mechanism that actually performed them. A machine that is to have the power to carry out any algorithmic procedure whatever must be able to use the intermediate results obtained at any stage to decide which of a number of possible sequences of operations to follow from then on, as required by the algorithm. The decision could be made by a human operator, but this would limit most severely the degree of automation of the process. Babbage envisaged what he called the *control unit*, which would supervise continuously the flow of operations and make these decisions automatically as required. The unit would cause the appropriate data to be extracted from the store at the appropriate time and to be transferred to the mill and intermediate or final results to be returned from the mill to the store; and by presenting to the mill, by means of perforated cards or otherwise, the statement of the operation to be performed next, it would ensure that the sequence was performed in the order required.

Analog and digital calculation   Among the brilliant people who supported Babbage was the excellent mathematician Ada, Lady Lovelace, daughter of the poet Lord Byron.[7] From accounts of the Analytic Engine given to her by Babbage, she wrote programs for calculating mathematical functions by the machine; this gave her an understanding of its architecture. From the relative difficulties she encountered in the programming, she was able to suggest various modifications to Babbage, which he found valuable. We may note in passing that these very first programs have served as models of the machine on which they were to be run; this is a feature of programs generally, to which I shall return in chapter 4. Lady Lovelace was most probably the world's first woman programmer, and it is for this reason that in 1979 her name was given to a programming language, Ada, developed in France, mainly by Jean Ichbiah, in response to an open invitation made by the US Department of Defense.

However, there were many who did not appreciate the importance of Babbage's approach in designing his machine; the entities with which it operated were all expressed in numerical form, and it was therefore what we now call a numerical, or rather a *digital*, machine. In this, Babbage was going against the current of his century, which was a period when, because of the remarkable progress being made in physics, many calculating instruments of the type we now call *analog* were being produced.

In an *analog machine* the quantities involved in the calculation are represented by physical properties. For example, we can simulate the evaluation of the (very simple) function $y = ax$ by means of an electric circuit. If a current measured by the value of x flows through a resistance a, then the potential difference across the resistance is ax and can be read on the scale of a voltmeter. There is thus an exact analog between the function and the circuit; analog calculation, in general, is made by means of continuous processes, in contrast to the discrete processes of numerical or digital calculation.[8]

Analog machines proliferated during the first half of the nineteenth century, voltmeters and ammeters especially. Moreover, in 1807 Fourier published his famous theorem, showing that a very wide range of periodic phenomena could be represented by trigonometric series, that is, as sums of terms each of which was a sine or cosine multiplied by an appropriate constant. It was known how to calculate sines and cosines analogically, and it seemed therefore that the analog approach was full of promise. Babbage, however rejected this approach, believing that it did not have the significance of the digital; and his intuition was sound, for at least three reasons, which we now consider briefly.[9]

The first reason is fundamental. It is not possible to build a single analog system that is sufficiently general to calculate any function whatever. A digital machine can be universal, but an analog machine cannot. Babbage did not state this explicitly, but it is clear that he realized it by his statement that his machine could "solve any equation and perform the most complex operations of mathematical analysis." His view was put on a firm theoretical foundation in 1935 when Turing showed that any computable function could be evaluated by means of a single digital machine—it was an abstract machine, granted, but Babbage's machine was its precursor.

The second reason is the one that led Babbage to abandon analog calculation; it is often difficult to get the required accuracy by such means. To convince oneself of this one has only to compare the reading of the hands of an ordinary mechanical watch with a digital watch, which shows the time in figures. While there need never be any error in the reading of a number, the reading of the position of a needle on the scale of an instrument will always involve an error. Further, there will also be errors in the instrument itself—for example, those arising from tolerances in the properties of its components, so that the position of the needle will itself not be precisely what it should be, and this internal error will combine with the external or reading error. A further advantage of the digital method is that in principle it can give whatever precision is desired; it has become straightforward, for example, to compute the first million decimals of π. Clearly the cost of a calculation, particularly in terms of the time needed to complete it, increases with the precision called for.[10]

The third reason concerns technology; it is difficult to store the results produced during an analog calculation, whereas this is easy in a digital machine, as we shall see later; and moreover, with a digital machine it is easy to perform logical operations on the stored information.

Babbage's Machine as the Precursor of the Computer

To sum up, Babbage's machine

1. established the architecture of all universal calculators: arithmetical-logical unit, memory, control unit, and input and output units;

2. used perforated cards as a channel of communication with the machine, the role of which is still important;

3. was a digital machine, thus showing the way to the later calculators and to computers.

Babbage's insight was remarkable; but unfortunately his plans were too ambitious for the technology of his time and his machine was never completed.

Further Progress with Mechanical Calculators

Although mechanical technology was not equal to the demands of Babbage's Analytic Engine, it did allow a number of important innovations to be made: new direct methods of multiplication; printing of output results on paper; and the development of a new and important field of application for machines, the business world.

Direct Multiplication and Division

Babbage's machine, like all those before it, treated multiplication as a series of additions. It was not until 1889 that Léon Bollée (1870–1913), when he was only 18, built a machine that multiplied not by this method but by a kind of direct method using a built-in multiplication table ingeniously represented as a matrix of needles.[11] But he was never able to achieve direct division. Only 3 models of Bollée's machine were made, and he abandoned work on calculators to help his father.[12] However, following this, O. Steiger in 1895 built a machine called the Millionaire, which used direct multiplication, of which over 1,000 models were sold in 3 years. After 1915 it was built by Hans W. Egli in Zurich, and over its total lifetime from 1894 to 1935, 4,600 models were sold. Examples of the Millionaire can now be seen at almost all the world's museums of technology. Direct division was first achieved in the machine built in 1912 in the United States by J. R. Monroe (1883–1937).

Printed-Paper Output

Until this became possible all the results produced by any of the machines had to be read directly on their various output devices, and could be preserved only by being written down by hand. Granted, Babbage had seen how equipment for permanent recording could be made, but he had never actually been able to make such equipment. The first machines to print their results on paper were the early cash registers; and the first of these was made in 1874 by the Frenchman H. Pottin, whose machine was a modification of a design due to an American, Barbour, in 1870. These modest beginnings ushered in the era of paper as a medium for the output of results and of any relevant intermediate information from calculating machinery. We are still living in that era in spite of the ever increasing competition, as we shall see later, of visual-display terminals.

First Applications to Commerce

The mechanical calculators were applied not only in scientific computation but also opened the way to the use of automatic calculation in business and commerce. The idea was certainly not new, for as we have seen, Pascal had designed his machine with the aim of easing the burdens of calculating taxes and converting currencies in connection with commercial transactions. The first machines designed and built specially for business use were developed in the United States late in the nineteenth century and by D. E. Felt and W. S. Burroughs (1857–1898). These two engineers took the view that "neither book-keeping nor the clerical staff could be better served than by machines designed to meet the special needs of book-keeping and the clerical staff." The very first of these machines was the Comptometer produced by Felt in 1885,[13] followed immediately in 1886 by a machine from Burroughs. Burroughs, the son of a mechanic, took over his father's business at the age of 24 and turned it into the American Arithmometer Company to manufacture and sell his machine. But this first model was so difficult to use that scarcely anyone but himself could do so (Eames [1973]) and in 1889, having made no sales, he threw away the 50 models he had already made.[g] However, he went on to redesign his machine, and as a result, the American Arithmometer Company had a future of astonishing success; under the name of its founder it has become one of the great computer companies of today. Burroughs called his new machine the Adding and Listing Machine. This seems to have been the first use of the term listing, now so common, in this context.

Mechanical Technology: Conclusions

The developments described so far (summarized in table 1.1) show that up to the start of World War I mechanical technology had made

Table 1.1
Stages in the mechanization of the four arithmetical operations

Addition and subtraction	Schickard	1623
	Pascal	1643
Addition and subtraction; multiplication and division by successive additions/subtractions	Leibniz	1673
First commercial machine	Thomas de Colmar	1820
Direct multiplication	Léon Bollée	1889
Direct multiplication and division	Monroe	1912

it possible for considerable progress to be made toward the realization of the universal calculator. Thanks to this technology it had been possible to formulate the basic principles underlying the automation of arithmetical and logical processing, to define the architecture of a universal calculator, and to make clear the importance of digital operation. It had also been made clear the value of printing on paper as a means of getting a permanent record of the information produced by the machines. And finally, the mechanical machines opened the way to the application of calculating equipment in those most important fields, business and commerce.

3 Electromechanical Machines

Despite these achievements, mechanical technology was too slow and too limited to allow much further progress to be made. It was the development of the new technology of electromechanical engineering that made possible the building of the first genuinely universal calculator, the Harvard-IBM machine. To show how this new stage was reached we must now return to the United States at the end of the nineteenth century.

Punched-Card Machinery
The Hollerith Machine
Hermann Hollerith (1860–1929) was an engineer who built a machine to help in the compilation of the 1890 American census. This machine was the ancestor of the whole series of electromechanical machines we now call punched-card machines, the term referring to the essential technological feature on which their method of working depends. To explain this principle and its use we quote from an account given by E. Cheysson in the French magazine *La Science Moderne* of 8 July 1893.

The problem was to record on a rectangular card all the details relating to one individual; there were altogether 210 descriptive categories, each identified by a very short conventional symbol. The notation used was indeed algebraic or chemical, one letter replacing a word or name: m—man; w—woman; rk—Roman Catholic; gk—Greek Catholic; dt—German [deutsch]; sk—Serbo-Croat;, An–illiterate; cr—cretin; and so on. . . .

With the help of a sort of pantograph, holes are punched in each card corresponding to the information on one indivdiual obtained in the census survey, so that the holes in the card give a complete and precise description of that individual. Thus all the replies collected in the census are transcribed in a precise language that can be understood by the machine, to which the cards could now be given. . . .

If one wants to extract all those cards on which a particular property is recorded, for example, all those referring to illiterates by having An, and to use these for a special study, one no longer has to search through the cards laboriously: electricity now simplifies the task. . . .

At the side of the counting machine is a row of deep boxes—the SORTING BOX—each of which is closed with a light-weight lid. An electrical connection is made between one lid and the position on the base plate of the counting machine that corresponds to the symbol An and will open when the needle of the counting machine passes through a hole in the card. Thus the operator sees that all the boxes remain closed except one, and all he has to do is to put the card, sorted automatically, into this box. . . .

Now that we have seen the role played by the machine and by the card, we can easily visualize the entire operation. All the forms filled in by the householders, sent to the central office, are given to specialist staff who translate the entries into the conventional symbols; after checking, the sheets go on to staff who punch the cards and then to others who check the perforation. The cards are then put through the machine and the SORTING BOX, which counts them and arranges them in order. Any one card can then be used for any series of processes called for by the head of the office. For example, one could use the equipment first to group the replies according to place of birth, whether or not a householder, and disabilities; and then, with the help of the SORTING BOX, form these into packets according to the two sexes and ten-year intervals in age. Each of these packets could then be submitted to the counters, which would give its numerical breakdown according to social status, educational level, and whether employer or employee. They could be further grouped by the SORT-ING BOX into packets according to profession. Finally, in a last passage each of these packets could be classified by age, sex, and profession and perhaps by social status and according to whether employer, employee, or domestic servant.

One can see how the director of the census can make liberal use of the possible combinations, which he can vary without limit. He has the power to question his cards in whatever manner seems good to him and to group the replies as he wishes. . . .

At the same time, the system has the drawback of giving more information than can be published. If one tried to use it all, a single census would provide enough to fill a large library. Thus one must keep the greater part as handwritten forms and limit oneself to publishing only summaries relating to broad classes of the population, perhaps to the entire country.

Hollerith's machine (examples of which are in a good many historical collections) made it possible for the first time in the history of American censuses to issue the results with a short enough delay for them to be still of interest. At the same time, Hollerith's system had a fundamental effect on the way work of this type was done. The *New York Herald* said in October 1890 "The field of woman's employment is steadily extending. Occupations once closed are now open to her. . . . In how many of these new spheres . . . would it appear, as in census work, that women are the superiors of men?"

In memory of the cards used by Hollerith, the punched cards used today for the input of data into a computer arc called Hollerith cards; their size and shape are rather different, but most of them have 12 rows, like the original Hollerith card. The sorting box that formed part of Hollerith's system was the ancestor of the later punched-card sorters. These were machines that, applied to entities representable by coded perforations in the cards, could perform operations of comparison that were reduceable to problems of sorting. They became automated and highly developed, so that it was no longer necessary to feed in the cards one at a time by hand. The card reader, a static device in Hollerith's system, also became automated; the cards were moved under a row of metallic brushes, so that an electrical contact was made when a hole was encountered. It was soon made possible to load the cards into the machine in batches rather than one at a time.

Hollerith's Counting Machine was the ancestor of the later punched-card tabulator, so called for its ability to print results in tabular form. These machines could also carry out some arithmetical operations. The instructions defining the sequence of operations to be performed were given to the machine by means of a connection board, or plug board; by plugging wires into sockets in the board, connections were made in the electrical circuits of the machine corresponding to the operations to be performed.

The first punched-card machines, produced to handle the problems of the census, were used later for various scientific applications; afterward the business world became the main user of the technique. But although these machines became very highly developed, they were never able, except at the cost of very time-consuming card-handling activities, to carry out the complex sequences of operations required by some algorithms.

The Beginnings of Some Industrial Companies

Hollerith left the service of the American government in 1896 to start his own company, the Tabulating Machine Company. This was very successful; his machines became very well-known and were sold all over the world. In 1911 the company merged with two others: the Computing Scale Company of America (maker of automatic weighing machines) and the International Time Recording Company (maker of time clocks). The new company was called the Computing Tabulating Recording Company (CTR), of which Thomas J. Watson (1874–1956) became the head in 1914; it then had 1,346 employees in the United States.

At that time one could have questioned the value of punched-card machinery for business use; T. J. Watson, however, foresaw the important role it would play in the future and had no hesitation, in 1917, in changing the name of the Canadian branch of the company to International Business Machines (IBM); and in 1924 he changed the name of the parent company from CTR also to IBM, now a company of more than 300,000 employees.[14]

Hollerith quarreled with the American Census Bureau, which decided to build their own machines for the 1910 census and gave the responsibility for this to James Powers. He in turn formed his own company in 1911, the Accounting and Tabulating Machines Company, for the manufacture of punched-card tabulators. As a result of a series of takeovers and mergers, notably that with the Remington Typewriter Company, the company, whose president at the time was James Rand, became Remington Rand in 1927. This merged with the Sperry Gyroscope Company in 1955 to form the present Sperry Rand. Thus two of today's great computer companies began in order to handle census data.

In Britain, the Powers Samas Company was formed in 1915 to build machines specially adapted to deal with the British currency. Although a subsidiary of American Powers, it was not involved in the merger with Remington and retained a commercial agreement with Remington Rand. We may note here that punched-card machinery did not become fully accepted in the business world until Charles Foster of Powers Samas produced a tabulator that could print letters as well as figures.

In 1920, CTR formed a British subsidiary, the British Tabulating Machines Company (BTM), which became independent in 1947. This merged with Powers Samas in 1959[15] to form the company International Computers and Tabulators (ICT).

The French company Bull also owes its origin to punched cards. A Norwegian engineer Frederick Bull (1882–1925), whose patents in this field go back to before 1914, joined with Knut Kruesen in 1922 to form a company to make punched-card machines. At the time of Bull's death in 1925 some 20 of their machines were installed in Norway, Finland, Denmark, and Switzerland. Their patents were bought by the Swiss group H. W. Egli in 1929, who formed the Egli-Bull Company. In 1932 the French group Caillies took over Egli-Bull's patents and formed the Société des Machines Bull. The first president of the new company was Colonel Rimalho (1864–1954), who was well-known in the French Artillery, especially for his design of the 75 gun used in World War I. After the war he became a specialist in industrial organization. The Bull company made a sorter based on a rotary principle; its speed, of the order of several tens of cards a minute, was comparable with that of IBM machines of the same period (Couffignal [1933]). Bull had a difficult time during World War II, but soon afterward its innovative abilities enabled it to recover. I shall discuss its subsequent success later.

To summarize: In a period of a half-century punched-card machines had created the conditions in which a market for calculators could flourish, and the manufacturing companies that designed and built these machines were later among those that played leading roles in the development of the first computers. Although the modern computer uses none of the principles of the punched-card machines, the latter were an essential step in this development; their contribution to technological innovation should not be underestimated. It is because of these machines that the perforated card of 12 rows and 80 columns came into such general use as a means of conveying information to the machine and also that sufficiently reliable equipment became available for use with later "universal calculators," in particular, plug boards and tabulators. Nevertheless, punched-card machinery could be of only limited application because its use always required a good deal of human intervention. Further, the architecture was not designed on the principles laid down by Babbage and therefore could not form the basis for a universal calculator; in particular, the sorting process was constrained by engineering considerations rather than by the logic of the problem.

The First Calculators

The route proposed by Babbage was not abandoned entirely, however; it was by following Babbage's lead that the first calculators were made.

The Difference Tabulator

After Babbage's death in 1871 his son built a part of the Analytic Engine, with which he computed a table of the first 32 multiples of π; the machine then failed. A new development occurred before World War I when the Spanish engineer Leonardo Torres y Quevedo (1852–1936) showed that Babbage's machine could be built by means of electromechanical technology and actually made, in France, several components. He might have been the first to produce a working electromechanical calculator had he been able to find the necessary financial support, but the demands for calculators were not strong enough at the time. Torres was the first to use the term *automation* for the new science which was then appearing, and to give a definition. He wrote in an article (Torres y Quevedo [1914]) that "the main aim of automation is that the automata be capable of discrimination; that at any moment they be able to take into account the impressions they are receiving, or have received up to that time, in performing the operation then required. They must imitate living beings in regulating their actions according to their impressions and in adapting their conduct to the circumstances of the time." In the same article he explained very clearly the limits of what we now call artificial intelligence; discussing the view expressed by Descartes that automata could not speak "reasonably," he said that Descartes had been "led astray by the idea that the automaton must do its own reasoning, whereas it is the builder of the automaton who does the reasoning for it." He was also the first to build a machine to play chess, which he demonstrated in Madrid in 1911.[16]

In 1929 Benjamin D. Wood, head of the Bureau of Collegiate Educational Research at Columbia University, persuaded Thomas J. Watson to contribute to the development of science and technology by helping to set up a computing laboratory at Columbia. A young scientist named Wallace J. Eckert was appointed its director, and shortly thereafter IBM delivered to the university's Astronomy Department the equipment that it thought such a laboratory would need. Eckert then connected together an IBM Type 601 punched-card multiplier, an accounting machine, and a tabulator, thus creating the first system able, without human intervention, to read cards, to compute, and to print results. This achievement led Watson in 1930 to have IBM build a machine for the laboratory based on Eckert's system; this was the Difference Tabulator.

In 1934 the laboratory was reconstituted as a non-profit-making company called the Thomas J. Watson Astronomical Computing Bureau; as we shall see shortly, this led IBM into a collaboration with

Harvard University, which resulted in what may be described as the first working universal calculator. Of the first such machines to be built in Europe and the United States after the end of the 1930s, two in particular influenced the development of computer science: the machine built in the Bell Laboratories, which was the first binary machine to be produced commercially; and the Harvard-IBM machine, which was the first complete realization of the machine planned by Babbage.

The Bell Laboratories Relay Computer: The First Binary Calculator

It was George Stibitz, a mathematician at the Bell Labs, who made the first genuinely binary calculator (Loveday [1977]). His work involved him in the use of telephone relays, and it was their "all-or-nothing" property that led him to use them in building a binary adder. In this he took up some of the ideas of the great Irish logician George Boole (1815–1864), who had expressed logical systems in terms of a very simple algebra now known as boolean algebra. This used two digits, 1 (one), representing the set of all objects, and 0 (zero), representing the empty set; and two operations, OR and AND, which may be called boolean addition and multiplication, respectively. Very little attention was paid to this when Boole first published his system, but it aroused great practical interest among the designers of the first calculators. The reason is that data coded in binary form can be represented by sets of electric contacts that are either open (0) or closed (1), so that an entire calculation can be expressed in terms of boolean algebra. This explains the success of this form of coding.

Two types of digital machine can be distinguished: those that work with numbers coded in decimal (that is, to base 10) and those that work with numbers coded in binary (to base 2); these are called decimal and binary machines, respectively. In the second chapter, when we study the computers LARC and Stretch, we shall look at the relative advantages and disadvantages of these two types.

In 1939, when little was generally known of the value of binary arithmetic in the design of calculators, the universities were showing great originality. In France Louis Couffignal (1902–1966) described in several papers and then in his doctoral thesis of 1938 (Couffignal [1938]) how a programmable binary calculator could be constructed using electromechanical technology. But the war and the German invasion put an end to all such work. It must be admitted that the climate in France was not very favorable to progress in this field; the great geometer Maurice D'Ocagne, who was to judge Couffignal's thesis, wrote a book on calculating machines (D'Ocagne [1922]) in which he rated the work of Torres y Quevedo and Couffignal as scientific curiosities (see Raymond [1969, introduction]). In Germany, on the other hand, Konrad Zuse built a binary calculator in 1938, the Z1, followed this in 1939 with a mechanical calculator Z2 and in 1941 with a relay calculator Z3.[17] But again the war intervened and prevented anything from being known about these machines outside Germany. They were destroyed in the bombing of Hamburg (Datamation [1966] and Ganzhorn [1975]). In 1939 all commercially produced machines, punched-card or otherwise, worked in decimal arithmetic.

But to return to Sibitz: He made his binary adder at home during a weekend in the summer of 1937, using a few relays rescued from the scrap heap, two pocket flashlight bulbs, and some pieces cut from a tobacco tin. The relays were wired up so that the bulbs would light if the sum was 1 and would stay unlighted if it was 0. This piece of equipment, the first able to handle elements coded in binary, started the era of machines with arithmetical-logical units, and also memories, constructed from elements that could exist in either of two stable physical states.

In his spare time Stibitz then built multipliers and dividers. He declared that he could build a complete calculator for about $50,000, but was told that no one was going to pay that amount of money just to do some calculations. However, he was able to persuade Bell Labs of their value, in particular, the value of one that could do complex arithmetic[h] automatically. An engineer, Sam Williams, whom he must have taught the theory of complex numbers, collaborated with him in 1939 on the Complex Calculator, later called the Bell Labs Relay Computer Model 1 or the Bell Telephone Labs Computer Model 1 (BTL Model 1). This was certainly the first widely known binary calculator. Data were entered into the machine on a teletype, and both the memory and the calculating units were made from telephone relays, of which there were in all about 400.

This first machine had a limited scope because although it could indeed work with complex numbers, it could perform only the four basic arithmetical operations. Stibitz therefore built a second machine that could "at least evaluate polynomials" by executing sequences of instructions now read in, as with teletypes, on punched paper tapes. This was the Bell Labs Model 2 (BTL Model 2), also called the Relay Interpolator, which appeared in 1942. This machine had a form of conditional instruction that enabled it to make complete calculations, but was too limited for the machine to be considered a universal calculator. The same applied to its successor, BTL Model 3. The first of this series of machines to rank as a universal calculator was BTL Model 5. It appeared in 1946, two years later than the Harvard-IBM machine, which up until that time had been the world's only such machine, and with which I shall deal shortly. BTL Model 5 used about 9,000 relays, weighed nearly 10 tons, and occupied a floor area of about 1,000 square feet. It needed 300 milliseconds (0.3 second) to add two numbers, each 7 decimal digits long; multiplication of these took 1 second; division, 2.2 seconds.

Other Innovations at Bell Laboratories

Bell Labs made immediate use of the Complex Calculator for their own work; they also achieved a whole series of "firsts" in computer science, of which we now consider a few. Two groups at Bell Labs with equal need for access to a machine capable of doing lengthy calculations connected two teletypes to the Complex Calculator so that each could use the machine; there were then a total of three teletypes connected, and this formed what was undoubtedly the first example of what we now call a data communication system. Sharing the machine's time among the users was organized as follows. The first teletype to request access was given access; and when its work was finished, access was transferred to whichever of the other two teletypes had been waiting the longer; and so on for subsequent requests for service.[18]

But there was better to come. In 1940, while attending a meeting of the American Mathematical Society at Dartmouth College in New Hampshire, Stibitz connected a teletype to the Bell Labs machine in New York, using an ordinary telegraph line. This made it possible for participants at the meeting to send a calculation from Hanover to the Complex Calculator and to get the result in less than a minute. This was certainly the first use of *remote job entry* and the first step along the road to what is now described as "the convergence of tele-communications and computers" (*télématique* in French, a compound of *télécommunications* and *informatique*; see Nora and Minc [1978]); after 1939 it was possible to foresee the importance of telecommunications in computer science.

Stibitz also invented, before 1942, *floating-point arithmetic*, which enabled machines to handle numbers that would otherwise have become too great. By this technique, numbers would be divided by 10, 100, 1000, etc. . . . as needed to keep their sizes manageable; these divisions would also be recorded, so that afterward the true sizes of the numbers could be restored. This technique is now used in almost all computers. However, although Stibitz's process was very successful in the Bell Labs machines, its generalization to binary calculation had to await the arrival of the computer.

The Harvard-IBM Machine

The machine built by IBM in collaboration with Harvard University was a decimal machine; it is especially interesting because it was very probably the first universal calculator.

In a paper that he did not publish at the time (but is reproduced in (Aiken [1964]), Howard H. Aiken (1900–1973) demonstrated the need for machines that would be able, among other things, to perform complete calculations entirely automatically, without any human intervention; in this they would differ from the punched-card machines. In effect, he rediscovered the principles laid down by Babbage by adding that such machines should execute the required operations in the order dictated by the mathematics of the problem and not by the engineering constraints. These views were known to T. J. Brown of Harvard, who was a member of the Board of Directors of the Thomas J. Watson Astronomical Computing Bureau at Columbia University and who spoke of them to T. J. Watson. Watson decided in 1939 to set up a joint research project between IBM and Harvard; Clair D. Lake was given the responsibility for IBM and Howard Aiken for Harvard (Aiken [1946]).[19] The project achieved its goal in 1944 with the completion of the IBM Automatic Sequence-Controlled Calculator (ASCC), better known as the Harvard-IBM machine; it was the realization of Babbage's dream.

The machine was built at IBM's Endicott (USA) laboratory. It measured 51 feet in length and 8 feet in height and was made up of 800,000 components,[20] many of which had clearly been taken from IBM punched-card machines—in particular, the input and output units and certain of the functional units. But the overall concept of the machine was essentially that of Babbage. Both addition and the transfer of quantities from one part of the machine to another used the old method based on gear wheels, which were turned by electric pulses (one complete turn for every 10 pulses). Programs were punched on paper tape, thus making it unnecessary to give the machine each instruction as it was to be executed, as had been the case with the Jacquard loom and Babbage's proposed machine. Several other devices incorporated into its design had not occurred to Babbage, but were found necessary to ensure the proper progress of calculations. One such device was a clock to synchronize the various operations.

The term *register* seems to have been used for the first time in describing this machine (Aiken [1946]). No item of information can have any existence in the machine unless there is some device in which its physical representation can be held. Such devices must include the basic components of the machine in which the fundamental units of information are held; these are what are called the registers, and the memory of a calculator is a collection of registers. The capacity of a register is normally chosen to be equal to the basic unit of information with which the machine works; we shall see later that in the case of the first machines this was what is called the machine's *word*. Subsequent to the Harvard-IBM machine, however, the term register was used more frequently to mean basic memory components belonging not to the main memory but to the arithmetical-logical unit. The registers in this sense were able to exchange information very quickly with registers in the main memory and could be used as temporary, short-term stores for items of information that would be needed again in calculations. Because the total volume of main memory in the first machines was often insufficient for the needs of a calculation, registers intended to hold the constants appearing in the calculation were often used to hold intermediate results.

A register can be used in the same way for arithmetical operations. The *accumulator* is an example of such use; at the start of an arithmetical operation it contains one of the operands, and the result is placed in it at the end. A combination of an accumulator and a calculating unit able to add and subtract is called an *adder*; for multiplication and division a second register is often provided, called the *multiplier-quotient register* or *MQ*.[i] These registers are often called *arithmetical registers*.

The main memory of the Harvard-IBM machine consisted of

60 registers designated by "for contants," each able to hold a number 23 decimal digits long and its sign ($+$ or $-$), and

72 adding registers (adders), each formed of 24 wheels with the 10 digits 0 to 9 on its periphery, which was turned electrically, as described.

The machine had a special unit for multiplication and division. The total weight of the machine was about 5 tons and an enormous amount of energy was required to drive it; the story is that several tons of ice were needed each day to cool it. The instructions forming a program were read in from perforated paper tape as needed. An addition took 0.3 second; a multiplication, 6 seconds; and a division, 11.4 seconds. Aiken reckoned that the machine was about 100 times faster than hand calculation using the desk machines of the time.

The IBM Automatic Sequence-Controlled Calculator (ASSC), the Harvard-IBM machine, later came to be called MARK I. This was because Aiken subsequently set up a computation laboratory at Harvard where he built for the US Navy, Air Force, and other branches of the armed forces machines named MARK II, MARK III, and MARK IV. The second machine built there, MARK II, was completed in 1947, although the first ideas for it had been formulated in 1944. This also was a decimal machine, which worked with numbers 10 decimal digits long; among its interesting features was its use of binary coded decimal notation to represent numbers. To explain this, consider the number 27, which is to be coded in terms of binary digits so that it can be held in registers composed of elements, such as relays and diodes, having either of two stable physical states. There are two possible ways of doing this. In decimal machines from MARK II onward each decimal digit has been coded separately, which requires at least 4 bits. The code used most frequently for this is what is called *binary coded decimal (BCD)*, in which each separate digit is represented by its binary equivalent. Thus 27 is written 0010 0111 because in binary 2 = 0010 and 7 = 0111. This enables a decimal machine like MARK II to do arithmetical operations as though it were working with decimal numbers. In a binary machine, on the other hand, decimal numbers are represented by their binary equivalents—for example, 27 is held as 11011—and the machine works directly with numbers to base 2. Another interesting feature of MARK II was that it was the second machine, after the Bell Labs, to have built-in floating-point arithmetic. In 1949 MARK II was followed by MARK III in which electromechanical technology was replaced by electronics; this new technology had become well-known by that time. But MARK III is of additional interest in that it had one of the first *drum memories*. Then in 1952 came MARK IV, with one of the first *ferrite-core memories*.

One often reads that the Harvard-IBM machine was the first computer. The machine was in fact able to perform logical operations, limited though they seem by today's standards, and so could claim to be considered the first universal calculator. But as we shall see, it could not claim to be a computer. Nevertheless, it was the most famous machine of its time and gave rise to a large, and sometimes rhapsodic, body of literature, to which even scientists contributed. L. J. Comrie[j] spoke of the "brain" of the machine when describing the perforated-paper-tape memory; and in *American Weekly* of 14 October 1944 it was said that the Harvard "robot" was a "super brain," "able to solve problems which man had no hope of solving, in physics, electronics, atomic structure and, who knows, perhaps even to solve the problem of the origin of mankind." We have treated this machine in some detail because several of its component units were reproduced in the building of the first computer. But neither MARK I and its descendants, nor the Bell Labs machine and its descendants, had the success they might have expected; they were overtaken by the electronic machines just then beginning to appear.

4 Electronic Machines

It was only natural that the researchers in calculating-machine design and construction should want to use electronic circuits for the central units and the memories because they could hope to get much higher speeds in this way. The first entirely electronic universal calculator was the ENIAC. The team that built it acquired in the process experience that enabled them to conceive of a machine in which programs would be stored in the memory and could therefore be modified by the machine itself, without any manual intervention. Before the team broke up they made their views known to a wide circle, and these views were taken up first in the United States by IBM, which made the first machine of this type, and later in Britain by the universities of Manchester and Cambridge.

ENIAC: The First Universal Electronic Calculator

In 1935 the US Army set up a laboratory for ballistics research, the Ballistics Research Laboratory (BRL)[21] at Aberdeen in Maryland. The director of the laboratory was advised by a scientific council, one member of which was the famous mathematician John von Neumann (1903–1957). One of the problems put to the laboratory was to find a means of speeding the calculation of gunnery firing tables: Hermann H. Goldstine, who was doing his military service there, pointed out that the construction of a reasonably useful firing table required the calculation of between 2,000 and 4,000 trajectories, for each of which about 750 multiplications would be needed.[22]

The Moore School of Electrical Engineering at the University of Pennsylvania in Philadelphia had worked with BRL and its predecessors since 1930. In 1941 they organized a Summer School in Electronics, financed by the laboratory, and invited John W. Mauchly (1908–1980), then head of the Physics Department at Ursinus College, Pasadena, to give a course. Mauchly, who had a personal interest in calculating machines, had done some thinking about improving the speeds at which machines performed calculations.[23] The responsibility for the summer school was in the hands of a young bachelor of science, J. Presper Eckert, whose overriding interest was electronics and who had worked on the problem of improving the reliability of vacuum tubes (thermionic valves). Mauchly and Eckert decided to collaborate on making an electronic calculator, and in September 1941 Mauchly left Ursinus College to join the Moore School. Their first work on this project became known to Goldstine, who in turn had himself assigned to the Moore School in 1942.

In June 1943 the Moore School signed a contract with BRL to build an electronic calculating machine (Goldstine [1972]). For the technology they had to choose between relays and vacuum tubes. Relays were slow but reliable; the corresponding response times for vacuum tubes were very much shorter—because it was only electrons that had to be moved, not pieces of mechanical equipment—but their reliability was very poor. It was going to be necessary to use about 18,000 tubes of 16 different types, operating at 100,000 cycles per second; and it therefore seemed certain that unless there was some major advance in vacuum-tube technology, there would be one failure every cycle if this was the choice. And as, in addition, the logical, arithmetical, and transfer circuits of the proposed machine were going to need 70,000 resistors, 10,000 capacitors, and 6,000 switches, it seemed that such a system had little chance of ever working. As Goldstine said [1972], making a wholly electronic calculator was the biggest technical challenge humanity had ever faced.

To ease the situation, on the one hand, Eckert devised new techniques for using vacuum tubes, based on methods that had been developed in nuclear-physics laboratories and in work on cosmic rays (Mauchly [1979]); and on the other, as much use as possible was made of the known, reliable techniques of punched-card machinery.[24] The resulting machine built by the Moore School, the Electronic Numerical Integrator And Computer, ENIAC, satisfied the requirements placed on it and worked in BRL at Aberdeen from 1946 to 1955. At the official inauguration on 15 February 1946 there was a demonstration of the calculation of a trajectory, the program for which had been written by Goldstine's wife Adele (Goldstine and Goldstine [1946]).

ENIAC weighed about 30 tons, covered a floor area of about 1,500 square feet, and required 160 kilowatts of power—enough to heat a block of apartments. Its denigrators had said that when it was switched on, all the lights in the western quarter of Philadelphia would go out. But it was about 500 times faster than the Harvard-IBM machine; its speed of 0.2 milliseconds for an addition and 2.8 milliseconds for a multiplication seemed extraordinary at that time—although it could not handle tasks that can be done on some of today's pocket calculators.

ENIAC had a decimal structure that was a straight translation into electronics of the toothed-wheel mechanism of the first mechanical calculators. Its counters were made up of groups of 10 tubes, the name *ring counter* making the principle clear. The number 7, for example, is represented in the ring by a pulse running through the first 6 tubes (1 to 6) and turning the seventh tube "on."[k] If then 5 is to be added, the pulse runs through the remaining 3 tubes of the ring (8 to 0), turns "on" the first tube of the "tens" ring, and continues in the "units" ring, switching "on" the second tube. The sign of a number was indicated by the state of a diode.[25]

Thus ENIAC was a decimal machine. It worked with numbers 10 decimal digits long, but could also work with numbers 20 decimal digits long. Numbers were sent to the central unit, as they were required, by a "constant transmitter" made of relays connected to an IBM card reader. Memory was provided partly by means of three "function tables" identical with those of the standard punched-card tabulators and partly by a set of relays where intermediate results could be stored. If it was necessary to store more of these latter than could be held on the relays, they could be punched on to cards and reinputted into the machine by means of the card reader and the "constant transmitter" The fast memory,[1] in fact, could hold only 20 numbers 10 decimal digits long.

A program on ENIAC was set up on a plug board as on punched-card machines; to change the program an operator had to change the plugging. If the program was at all complicated, the setting up could take several days, reducing considerably the availability of the machine. The idea of storing the program in the machine arose from the experience of this inconvenience.

The Stored-Program Computer: The Birth of the Idea

The Moore School team finished its work on ENIAC early in 1944 and started to plan a new machine, whose design and construction would take account of both the experience they had gained and the developments in technology that had taken place in the meantime. The main idea was to avoid unnecessary duplication of equipment and thus to use the same *constituent*—that is, a part of the machine dedicated to one particular function (later called a *resource*)—in every situation where its particular function was required. Thus, in contrast to ENIAC, there would be only a single arithmetic unit, which would deal with every arithmetical calculation, and if there were several input or output units, these would all be controlled by a single module.

Memory, also a resource, was to be treated in the same way. Achievements in radar had made it realistic to consider using delay lines here, whose possibilities for enhancing machine performance were on an entirely different scale from the vacuum-tube memory of ENIAC. Further, applying the principle of minimum duplication of resources, it was natural to consider storing both programs and data in the same memory because the capacity now available would permit this. The plans for the new machine, begun in April 1944, did in fact envisage holding programs in the memory.

In October 1944 the US Army offered a contract to the Moore School team requiring the latter to build a new machine; the contract's sole condition was that the machine was to be an Electronic Discrete Variable Computer, EDVAC; the team naturally wished to build the machine along the lines on which they had already been working. Von Neumann, who had always had a great interest in the theory of computability, had come to the Moore School in September 1944 to work with the computer team. Goldstine [1972] has told how this came about. One day during the summer of 1944 he was at the railway station at Aberdeen, waiting for the train to Philadelphia, where he saw von Neumann on the same platform and took courage and introduced himself. They traveled together and the conversation soon turned to what Goldstine was working on. Von Neumann put more and more searching questions to him, so that Goldstine began to feel that he was being examined for a doctorate in mathematics; afterward von Neumann had himself introduced to Mauchly and joined the team.

During a period spent at Los Alamos, von Neumann rewrote the Moore School's response to the contract offer, giving their views but expressing them in his own style. For example, fascinated as he was by the possible analogy between the machine and the human brain, he referred to the computing modules of the machine as neurons. This unfortunate anthropomorphism, coming from so distinguished a scientist, could not but give rise to echoes, often to ill effect; it certainly contributed to the spread of the name *electronic brain* for the machine.[26] The response, thus rewritten, bore so plainly the stamp of von Neumann that from then on the idea of the stored program was attributed to him.[27] Further, when this first draft of what was to be a future report was published, it carried only the name of its editor.[m] Who would have thought at the time that this publication was to be of such worldwide importance and the source of so much controversy?

Storing the program in the machine brought about a complete change of scale in processing power. We must recall that until that time the instructions to the machine were read directly from perforated paper tape or from a deck of punched cards placed in the input unit; as had been the case since Babbage or Jacquard, if some part of the program had to be repeated in the course of a calculation, the corresponding part of the tape or group of cards had to be reinserted by hand. Holding the program in the memory did away with this inconvenience.

The concept of an instruction had been made precise in the course of the development of the first calculators. We have seen that carrying out an algorithmic process involves the execution of a sequence of arithmetical or logical operations. Each of these is given to the machine in the form of a *machine instruction*, which we shall call an *elementary instruction* to distinguish it from those used in the higher-level programming languages to be discussed. The actual expression of these instructions is in the form of a numerical code; by convention the first number of the code defines the operation to be performed, the second gives the position in the memory where the operands (the quantities to be used in the operation) are to be found, and the third gives the position where the result is to be placed. This group of three numbers, in this order, can be regarded as a single number, and thus has the same form as an item of data. It was the increase in the amount of available memory that made it possible to store the program as well as the data.

The new principle had many advantages. First, it speeded up the calculation; transfers between the memory and the calculating unit now involved only the passage of electrical pulses, which is in striking contrast with the slow mechanical processes involved in, for example, reading instructions from a card. Second, and very important, because the instructions could now be treated as data, it became possible to repeat a part of a program several times, operating each time on data from different parts of the memory, so that there was no longer any need to reinput the program. To indicate the new data to be used, it was only necessary to change the number in each elementary instruction giving the *address* of the memory location where its data were to be found, that is, the number representing this location in the coded form of the instruction. The new words "to address"—to give the address of a memory location to an entity—and "addressing"—the action of giving an address—arose in this context. A third advantage was that it became possible to skip automatically over specified parts of a program.

It is easy to get an idea of the increase in flexibility that this principle brought about. All one needs to do is to use a pocket calculator to find the sum of the first 100 numbers—without using the formula $n(n+1)/2$, of course. At every step one has to enter the next number and to reenter the addition instruction, all of which would be done automatically in a stored-program machine.

The name *computer*[28] is used to mean a universal calculator in which the program is stored in the memory. A computer is able to carry out any algorithmic process given to it, under its own control and without any manual intervention, and in this it differs fundamentally from Babbage's machine and all that machine's descendants.

The control unit of a computer has to be highly developed before it can supervise the progress of the program, perform whatever modifications of addresses are required, extract from the memory the sequences of instructions to be obeyed, and so on. It is made up of subunits that coordinate the different memories, the computing circuits, and, to some extent, the equipment giving access to the machine. Its role can be contrasted with that of the arithmetical-logical unit by saying that whereas the latter at any one time is executing one program, and therefore working on a particular problem, the control unit ensures that every program, whatever may be its concern, is properly executed; thus the role of the control unit is a general one.

Two classes of computer programs can be defined. In the first are the programs that ensure the correct flow of operations by the machine, whatever the particular problem on which it is working; these are called *control programs*. In the second are the programs that give the machine the sequences of instructions required for the solution of particular problems; these are called *applications programs*. The two together are referred to as the *software*, in contrast with the *hardware*, which is the physical equipment of which the machine is built.

I have used the pair competence-performance to characterize a computer; here, performance relates to both the hardware and the programs in the first class, while competence relates to the second class of programs only. It is something of an arbitrary distinction that leads us to class together hardware—the circuits of the machine— and software—sets of instructions; I shall make it nevertheless because a machine without the programs that make it possible to utilize its resources would be of little interest. Clearly it is an arbitrary decision to say where performance ends and competence begins. At the point when data, programs, and results are all held in the memory and are all manipulable by the central processing unit, it becomes inappropriate to say that data processing is what characterizes a computer, and therefore the term *information processing* has become more commonly used.

The First Computers

Although the idea of the stored program arose in the course of the work on ENIAC, the first computer was built not by the Moore School team but by IBM. Actually, at the very beginning of the 1940s it was not only the American universities that were interested in the possibilities of electronic calculation. Well before the ENIAC project had taken shape, there were at least three private companies working in related technological fields: Radio Corporation of America (RCA), National Cash Register (NCR), and IBM. RCA tried to build numerical electronic equipment for the control of gunfire in fighter aircraft; NCR built an electronic cipher machine about which it is difficult to learn anything; and IBM's work led to the building in 1942 of a decimal electronic multiplier, the IBM 603.

IBM 603: The First IBM Electronic Calculator

The multiplier to which I have just referred was built by Byron E. Phelps. It formed the product of two numbers, each 6 decimal digits long, by a series of repeated additions. A special card punch was linked to it, the crossfooting keypunch,[n] which could add or subtract two numbers punched on the same card and punch the result also on that card. The two in combination constituted what was certainly the first wholly electronic calculator (Phelps [1980]); it was never produced commercially because there were many in IBM who doubted the reliability of vacuum tubes.

Everything changed when Thomas J. Watson, Jr., returned from the war. He had been a bomber pilot and had become convinced of the importance of electronics.[29] After the Harvard-IBM machine had been demonstrated to him he saw at once that the machine could be greatly improved by the use of electronics technology and committed IBM to make a successor. Two developments followed from this simultaneously.

One of these was that Phelps and another engineer, C. A. Bergfors, were given the task of building an electronic calculator. This resulted in the production of the IBM 603, a development of Phelps's earlier multiplier, which was able to form the product of two 6-decimal numbers and punch this on a card in the crossfooting keypunch at a speed of 100 cards per minute. The first models were demonstrated at an exhibition organized by IBM in New York in 1946. The machine was a great success, over 150 of them were ordered. Production was stopped, however, after 100 has been made because in the meantime the IBM 604, to be described later, had appeared. The other development was the construction of the IBM Selective Sequence-Controlled Electronic Calculator (IBM SSEC), designed as a stored-program machine. This was the world's first computer.

IBM SSEC: The First Computer

The SSEC was built between 1945 and 1948 by a group led by Frank Hamilton, one of the engineers who had worked on the building of the Harvard-IBM machine. In this group was Rex Sheeber, a former assistant of Aiken's who, convinced of the importance of electronics, had left the MARK I team when it decided not to adopt that technology. Wallace J. Eckert was the adviser to the group (Eckert [1948]). The SSEC was a machine in the Harvard-IBM tradition; its arithmetic unit was a modified IBM 603 that could add 3,500 numbers, each 14 decimal digits long, per second; mutliplication of two such numbers took it 20 milliseconds. The machine was thus about 100 times faster than the Harvard-IBM machine (Bowden [1953]). It had 13,500 vacuum tubes, but also 21,400 electromechanical relays, so it was not wholly electronic. The electronic memory, with access time under 1 millisecond, had locations for only 8 numbers and their signs. The relay memory had space for 150 numbers, with access time 20 milliseconds. The remainder of the memory was provided on bands of paper tape, across which rows of up to 80 holes could be perforated, so that each row was the equivalent of a standard punched card. Tables of functions, programs and subroutines, initial data, and so on could be prepunched on tapes, and there were 38 readers on which these tapes could be mounted. There were 3 tape punches, followed by 10 additional readers; this made it possible for intermediate results, modifications to programs, and so on to be punched on to tape and read back into the machine later as required.

The instructions had two addresses, thus distinguishing the SSEC from the type of machine described by von Neumann in his "First Draft Report on the EDVAC," where he advocated one address. The instructions were read into the machine from punched cards or, a row at a time, from punched paper tape. Once inside the machine they could be moved freely up or down through the hierarchy of memories — paper tapes, relays, vacuum tubes.

A difficult problem that had not been completely solved prior to the SSEC was providing a means requiring no manual intervention whereby, after completing one sequence in a program, the following sequence could be skipped over and the execution continued with a different sequence forming another part of the program. For example, after a conditional operation has been executed, it is usually necessary to "transfer" to another part of the program in order to execute the branch required by the conditions. The automation of these *transfer of control* operations was achieved for the first time in the SSEC.

In the SSEC instructions were treated as data. At a public demonstration of the machine held in New York on 27 January 1948 at IBM's headquarters, a calculation of the varying positions of the moon was made in which there was a repeated need for the sine of a certain [varying] quantity to a precision that until that time had not been available. A table of sines was stored in the relay memory, and in the

Table 1.2
Some first implementations

Arithmetical-logical unit	Schickard	1623
	Pascal	1643
	Leibniz	1673
Means for communicating different sequences of operations to the machine	Jacquard loom	1805
Instruction unit, memory, nonmanual input and output, peripheral units	Babbage's Analytic Engine (never built)	1833
Internal clock	Harvard-IBM machine	1944
Stored program	IBM SSEC	27 January 1948

instruction in the program that caused a value to be read from this table the address was left blank. Each time a value was required the machine calculated, for the specific angle whose sine was needed, the address in the table where this sine was to be found and then placed this address in the address part of the instruction. As was stated in the brochure that IBM gave to all those who attended the demonstration, "The instructions being coded in numerical form, there is no longer any distinction between these and the numerical values with which the problem is concerned. Modifications to the instructions can be calculated and made automatically in the course of the computation."[30] Thus 27 January 1948 can be taken as the birth date of the computer (and see table 1.2).

As Thomas J. Watson, Jr., had foreseen, electronics provided the means for a great step forward. The SSEC, as we have said, was about 100 times faster than the MARK I. Also, it was extremely reliable for its time; on average, it made only 1 error in 8 hours of running time, or about 1 error in every 1 million multiplications. The machine was used by IBM for their own work, but did not become a commercial product; however, IBM's work on it did lead the company later to become interested in the possibilities of the computer.[31]

The First British Computers

As we have seen, the SSEC was not a wholly electronic machine; the ENIAC, on the other hand, was. Von Neumann and Goldstine decided to make it work as a computer, by using certain function tables as memory in which to store the orders of a program and so to be able to modify these. The demonstration of ENIAC as a stored-program computer took place on 16 September 1948, with Adele Goldstine running a program for von Neumann.[32] Although the machine was greatly slowed down in this mode of use, the difficulty of programming it was so much reduced that from then on it was almost always used as a computer. But it had not been designed with this mind; in particular, its architecture was different from that specified by von Neumann and Goldstine for the future EDVAC, the concept on which the architecture of all modern computers has been based.

To operate efficiently, a computer must have at least two essential resources. First of all, as is evident, it must have a main memory of very large capacity in which instructions and data can be held. The SSEC had a fast memory of only 8 words, ENIAC only 20;° in both, the memory capacities were very small. Von Neumann therefore advocated abandoning vacuum-tube memories in favor of the delay lines used in radar, which could give much greater capacities and much higher reliability. Second, there must be a true control unit, able to organize all the transfers between the different registers, whatever the program that is being obeyed; this must thus be very different from the plug boards of the SSEC and ENIAC. All the computers designed since the publication of the "First Draft" have possessed these two resources and thus have often been called *von Neumann machines*, even if they have not had all the other features recommended by von Neumann [1945] and Goldstine (Burks, Goldstine, and von Neumann [1947]).

The EDVAC was not the first machine of von Neumann type to be completed, however. It was delivered to the Ballistics Research Laboratory in 1950, but did not start to operate until the end of 1951. (It continued to work until 1962.) After the inauguration of ENIAC in February 1946 the Moore School team broke up; Eckert and Mauchly formed their own company for the manufacture of computers; von Neumann went back to the Institute for Advanced Study (IAS) at Princeton. But before disbanding the group had publicized and lectured widely on their plans for EDVAC. Further, von Neumann and Goldstine had begun to think about a new machine, to be the IAS machine; they made their new ideas known in a report that was to become almost as famous as the "First Draft of a Report on the EDVAC" — the "Preliminary Discussion of the Logical Design of an Electronic Computing Instrument" (Burks, Goldstine, and von Neumann [1947]). They also gave many lectures on these new ideas.

The British were the first to take advantage of all this. There was great interest in Britain in calculating machinery, and the decision was taken to coordinate work in this field through the new Mathematics

Division that had been formed in the National Physical Laboratory in 1945. Two university groups, one at Manchester under M. H. A. Newman and the other at Cambridge under Maurice Wilkes, sent their students to courses at the Moore School, with which they had had close contacts.

In 1936, Alan M. Turing (1912–1954), a young mathematician holding a fellowship in King's College, Cambridge, went to Princeton for a year. At that time there were a number of people at Princeton who were later to have a great influence on the development of computers; among them were von Neumann and the great Argentinian logician Alonzo Church (1903–1937), who was leading seminars there.[33] In that year Church and Turing gave a precise meaning to the term *computability*. An algorithm is a *function*, in the mathematical sense of the word, because it transforms the elements forming the set of initial data into those forming the set of results; thus there is a sense in which an algorithm corresponds to the calculation of some function or functions. We say that a function is *computable* if there is an algorithm by means of which its values can be calculated. Turing defined an abstract machine, called a *Turing machine*, that could in theory calculate any computable function whatever. I shall not say anything more about this here, except to remark that a computer, as I have defined it, is a particular case of a Turing machine and that some have regarded Turing's papers on computability as containing the germ of the idea of the stored program machine.

Turing returned to Cambridge in 1937 and then to Princeton again in 1938. Von Neumann was greatly impressed by his work and offered him an appointment as his research assistant; Turing declined this, however, and returned to England in the summer of 1938. During World War II Turing played an important part under Newman in the highly secret work that led to the production of the machine called Colossus, designed for the deciphering of the German Army's codes, a machine using 2,000 vacuum tubes. About 10 of these machines were built. In 1945 he joined the new Mathematics Division at the National Physical Laboratory (NPL), already mentioned, where he had a strong influence on the logical design of the computer being planned there, the Automatic Computing Engine, ACE. The logic was exceptionally complicated but led to very fast operations, and the design was very ambitious. A pilot version of the ACE, called in fact Pilot ACE, was built by NPL and ran its first program in May 1950; an engineered version of this was made by the English Electric Company and sold under the name of DEUCE. One of the first models was installed in NPL in March 1955. The machine had a reasonable commercial success; about 30 were sold between 1955 and 1964. A machine of the full ACE design was built at NPL and began working at the end of 1957. This was the only one built; the machine had little influence, since it was overtaken by the new machines then appearing.

In 1946 Newman, conscious of the fact that a large-capacity memory was essential to the proper functioning of a computer, decided to try out an idea of F. C. Williams [who had come to Manchester after working on wartime applications of electronics]. Williams, familiar with the technologies used in radar, had realized that electrostatic tubes (cathode ray tubes, or CRTs) could form the basis of memories whose capacities could be much greater than those of vacuum tubes. I shall describe Williams's invention in the next chapter. Tom Kilburn, also an electronics specialist, came to Manchester with Williams, soon followed by the mathematician I. J. Good, who had worked with the Colossus project, and by Turing in 1948. Thus it is difficult to determine the paternity of the completely electronic machine that they built. A prototype was completed in 1948, with an electrostatic-tube memory of the very modest capacity of 32 words, each of 31 bits plus one bit for the sign, and with very few other resources; but it was the first completely electronic stored-program computer and in all essentials it conformed to the von Neumann specification (see figure 1.3).

The definitive machine was then built and ran its first program in June 1949. It was called the Manchester Automatic Digital Machine, or MADM. This had a memory of the same, electrostatic-tube, technology as the prototype but of much greater capacity, and also two very important innovations. The first was what its designers called the *B-Box* or *B-Register*, and what is now called the *index register*; this is the electronic successor to the index cards of Babbage's machine and greatly simplifies the process of address modification in the instructions. The other was the concept of pagination: the use of special software to simplify the use of a hierarchy of memories.[p] Some details of this are given later on.

The Manchester machine was built with only limited aims in mind; it is often said that the first true, fully electronic von Neumann machine was the EDSAC—Electronic Delay Storage Automatic Computer— built at the University of Cambridge. Maurice Wilkes had attended courses at the Moore School, and on his return to Cambridge he embarked on the design and building of this machine. This too was a fairly modest project, with ideas taken from both ENIAC and the planned IAS machine. It used about 4,000 vacuum tubes and had a memory formed of 32 ultrasonic delay lines, each able to hold 32 numbers 17 binary digits long; its organization made it possible to

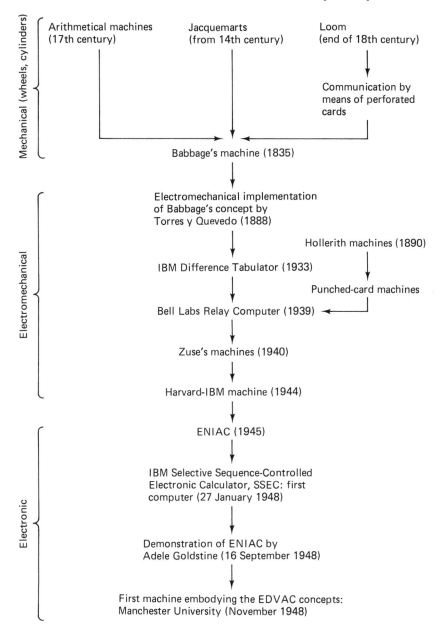

Figure 1.3
Main events in the history of the birth of the computer.

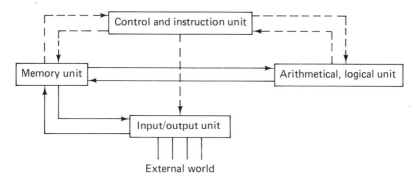

Figure 1.4
Block diagram of a computer. Solid arrow lines indicate data, instructions;
dashed arrow lines, control.

work with numbers of either 35 (including sign) or 17 bits (Wilkes
[1969]) and to hold 1,024 items of numerical data of 17 bits each. One
considerable novelty in the enterprise was the use of a new language,
designed for communication with the machine, which was much simpler
to use than any others then existing. EDSAC ran its first program on
6 May 1949: calculating a table of squares and a table of prime
numbers.

Although EDSAC is often considered to be the first wholly electronic
computer, we must recall that the first *computer* was the IBM SSEC—
which, however, was neither wholly electronic nor a von Neumann
machine. Even if we discount the Manchester machine, EDSAC has
at least two competitors for the title of first von Neumann machine,
the BINAC and the Whirlwind. But before tackling this problem, I
shall summarize the main characteristics of all the computers to be
discussed.

5 Conclusion

After Babbage's machine a century had to pass before the essential
characteristics of the computer were established and before the IBM
SSEC and then the von Neumann machines and MADM and EDSAC
were to appear. We recall the following:

1. A computer must above all be a *numerical machine* able to execute
sequences of instructions at *very high speed*. These sequences, which may
be very long, are communicated to the machine as a *program*. Once
this communication has been completed, the machine must obey the
instructions *without any human intervention*. As the machine is designed

for the processing of algorithms, and therefore for the performing of the elementary operations that such a task requires, it must have an *arithmetical unit* and a *logical unit*, which will often be combined into a single special unit, the *arithmetical-logical unit*, or ALU. In the first computers, such as EDVAC, all the operations used a single *accumulator*, or *A-register*.

2. Organization and supervision of the progress of the calculation is done by a special unit, the *control unit*. Operations are synchronized by means of a *clock*. The combination of arithmetical-logical unit and control unit forms what is called the *processor*.

3. The program and the data are held in the *memory*. For the machine to be able to execute long and complicated sequences of instructions involving large volumes of data, the memory must be of *large capacity*. All the elements of the memory must be as easily interchangeable as possible.

4. Finally, the machine must have *input and output units* (I/O) that enable it to keep contact with the outside world. It must be possible to exchange information between these units and the machine's memory.

The organization of a computer is shown schematically in figure 1.4.

The First Generation: 1950–1959

In 1950 there were about 20 automatic calculators and computers in the United States, with a total value of around $1 million. Every one of these machines was different from all the others, and each could be looked upon as a singular point on the curve of technological progress. However, from 1950 onward an increasing number of industrialists took the plunge into the computer adventure, and under their influence there developed new ideas, experiments, and successes but also failures. So strong was this influence that by 1964, which with the appearance of the IBM 360 series of computers marked the end of this historical period, most of the principal concepts of computer science as it now is had already been formulated.

Vacuum-tube technology continued to develop after 1950. The tubes became miniaturized, thus using less energy, and at the same time became more reliable. They were used for new central processing units, and the computers of which these formed part became known as the *first generation* of computers—those built from nonminiaturized tubes being considered as belonging to a *"zeroth generation."* The progress in this direction made it possible to bring efforts to bear on the development of the necessary supporting units of memory and input/output, a development that forms the framework of this chapter.

Two phases can be distinguished in this period. In the first, from 1950 to 1954 or 1955, the main problem with which the machine builders had to struggle was that of finding reliable fast memories of adequate capacity, a problem on whose solution, as von Neumann had shown, all further progress depended. As we shall see, five different technological lines were followed in the attacks on the problem in under five years. In 1955 the technique of making ferrite-core memories had been mastered, and more effort could be put into the attack on the other problems. During this second period there was the first attempt to apply software to ease the problems of handling a hierarchy of memories—the idea of paging. By 1959, marking the end of the first generation period, all these efforts had borne fruit and most of the supporting units in use today had already appeared. Thus this study of this first generation will fall into two sections. In the first I shall describe the work done between 1950 and 1955 on the development of main memory; in the second, that done between 1955 and 1959 on the other units.

I shall often speak of the two main fields of application of computers, commercial data processing and scientific computation. While the first general-purpose calculators, and then the first computers, had been made by scientists and used for scientific applications, the industrialists who built the first-generation computers were naturally more interested in the needs of the commercial and industrial worlds. I shall distinguish between computers designed primarily for commercial and industrial applications, which I shall call *business machines*, and those designed primarily for scientific applications, which I shall call *scientific machines*; the two types did not seem then to be necessarily identical.

Business data processing was usually considered to involve small amounts of calculation but very large amounts of data, the latter in decimal form; thus business computers worked in decimal rather than binary arithmetic. A machine whose arithmetical-logical unit is based on the binary scale calculates much more quickly in base 2 than in base 10; but then data in decimal form must be converted to binary, and if there is a great volume of data and the amount of calculation is not large, it will clearly be quicker to do the calculations in base 10. Scientific computation, on the contrary, was usually regarded as requiring long calculations with only small amounts of data; the time lost in converting decimal data to binary was negligible in comparison with that gained by working in binary, and hence binary machines were used for the scientific applications of the period. Further, it was often claimed that business data processing produced large volumes of results but that this was not the case in scientific work. For this reason the first business machines had equipment that could deal with large volumes of input data and print out large volumes of results, while the input/output units of the scientific machines were very primitive.

1 1950–1954: Evolution

A memory is a device in which an item of data can be stored and from which it can subsequently be recovered. The *capacity* of a memory is the maximum volume of information that it can store. Access to a memory is almost always made in groups of bits, either words or characters, and the capacity is measured in terms of one or other of these. The *memory position* is the logical entity to which access is made, and the memory to which reference is made by means of a code is called the *address*. The *access time* is the length of time required to read or to write a word or a character at a given address. It is usually the case that access to the memory is not possible for a short period immediately after a reading operation—hence the concept of the *cycle time*, which is usually twice the access time.

A consideration of even a moderately complex application will make clear the need for memories of large capacity. Take, for example, the case of a railway company offering a seat-reservation service. Suppose the company runs 500 trains per day, in each of which, on average, 200 sets can be reserved, and that it will accept reservations up to 100 days before the departure of any train; this means that a total of $500 \times 200 \times 100 = 10,000,000$ reservations have to be catered for. Each record concerning a seat—name of the traveler, address, and so on—will require, say, 50 characters of 8 bits each, so that the total amount of memory needed for this application alone is 4,000 million bits; and at even a few pennies per bit this costs a fortune. Thus ever since the first machines were produced, there has been a search for means of reducing the cost per bit of memory by using combinations of high-speed, and therefore expensive, memories of small capacity with slower but cheaper memories of large capacity. It is for this reason that there were what von Neumann called *memory hierarchies* (Burks, Goldstine, and von Neumann [1947]) in the first machines; ENIAC, for example, had at least four types of memory: cards, relays, vacuum tubes, and function tables of the type used in punched-card machines.

Memory hierarchies are organized in terms of their cycle times; in general, they fall into two classes, *main* and *secondary* memories, respectively. The main memory has as short a cycle time as can be achieved with the technology available, and so is necessarily expensive; it is the only memory that can communicate directly with the central processing unit—which is the reason for the name—and it is usually the one of smallest capacity. All information has to go through this memory in the course of the calculation; the processing unit extracts from it, one by one, the operands, the codes defining the operations, the instructions that it has to decode, and so on, and records there all the intermediate results. In view of their small capacities, therefore, the main memories of the early computers could usually hold only those instructions and data items that were of immediate need in the calculation then in progress, the remainder[1] being held in the secondary memories, which, while of much greater capacity, use technologies that are much cheaper and less demanding.

Five types of technology were used between 1950 and 1954 in building main memories: vacuum tubes, delay lines, Williams (electrostatic) tubes, magnetic drums, and, finally, in 1954, ferrite cores. Some of these were used only for the main memories in certain machines; some (in effect only magnetic drums), for both main and secondary memories; and some, only for secondary memories. I now describe these in the chronological order in which they appeared.

Delay Lines

As soon as it was decided that both the control program and the program for the calculation to be performed (the applications program) should be held in the memory, it became clear that the memory of a machine of the type of ENIAC could never be made great enough. In such a machine one bit of memory required at least one vacuum tube;[2] increasing the memory meant increasing the number of tubes and therefore lowering the reliability. Von Neumann therefore recommended the use of *delay lines*, the technology of which had been thoroughly mastered thanks to the development of radar.[3] By means of this technology, memories could be built with a hundred times the capacity that was possible with vacuum tubes, and, moreover, of much greater reliability.

Here we meet a new type of memory. In the Manchester machine MADM and its predecessors, the memories were *static*, the information being stored in devices that could remain in one or other of two stable physical states. But in EDVAC and EDSAC it was a *dynamic* memory, the information being represented by trains of pulses circulating in some suitable material and readable only when passing some particular point (see figure 2.1). These two different approaches to the concept of memory continue to exist. Dynamic memories were used in three famous machines— BINAC, Whirlwind, and UNIVAC I.

BINAC

At the end of 1946 Eckert and Mauchly left the Moore School to form their own company, the *Electronic Control Company*. They designed a machine having 512 words of delay-line memory that they called the Binary Automatic Computer, BINAC; it was four times faster than its rival EDSAC at Cambridge, England. The machine was made to the order of the Northrop Aircraft Company and was one of the first computers to be produced commercially in the United States. Machines

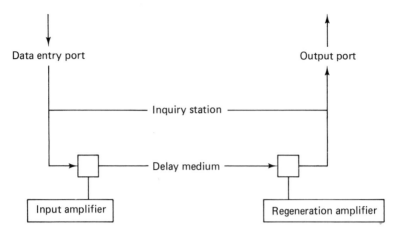

Figure 2.1
Schematic diagram of dynamic memory.

of that period were so unreliable that to ensure the correctness of the results it produced, BINAC consisted of two identical computers working simultaneously on the same calculation; intermediate results were compared periodically, and any discrepancy stopped the calculations. As it happened, the first of the two computers to be built ran a 44-hour test without a single failure, which was a remarkable achievement for the time. As this test took place in April 1949, preceding by a month the first demonstration of EDSAC, it is difficult to say which of those two machines was the first to operate.

Whirlwind

Shortly after BINAC came Whirlwind, a machine with 5,000 vacuum tubes and 11,000 diodes and a word length of 16 bits, able to multiply two 16-bit numbers in 16 microseconds. The machine was built between 1946 and 1955 in the Servomechanisms Laboratory at the Massachusetts Institute of Technology (MIT) under a contract first with the US Navy and later with the Air Force; the team was led by Jay Forrester and included Charles W. Adams, Robert Everett, and Ken Olson. Its original purpose was the control of flight simulators used in the training of pilots, but as time went on it developed into a computer that could be used for any problem requiring real-time control.

A calculator is said to work in *real time* if it is able to receive a signal from an object, carry out whatever processing of that signal is required, and send the results back to the object within a short enough time for the object to modify its behavior [in accordance with the information it has received from the computer]. For example, in order to study

Table 2.1
Some Whirlwind innovations

Magnetic-core memory
Graphical output terminal for display of results
Light pen for interaction between operator and machine
A programming language easier to use than the machine language
Software aids in putting together the constituents of a program
Diagnostic routines to identify faults and defective components
Data communication over a telephone line
Interaction with a distant terminal
Computer-run air-traffic control
Pattern recognition by computer
Automatic documentation by computer
Automatic control of machine tools by computer

the behavior of an airplane in flight, using a wind-tunnel model, the computer, having received from the model information about its position, the wind force, and so on, must be able to calculate what changes are required in the model's parameters if it is to remain in flight and send these to the model in time for these changes to be made.

Whirlwind machines were installed in the US air-defense system SAGE (Semi Automatic Ground Environment). These machines made it possible to carry out (in 1951 at Cape Cod, Massachusetts) the first simulation of SAGE, in which Whirlwind served as the central control. Whirlwind introduced a great number of innovations; the main ones are listed in table 2.1.[4]

UNIVAC I

It was the Europeans rather than the Americans who were the first in the world to make a computer as a commercial product. This was the Ferranti MARK I, built by the Ferranti company and designed in collaboration with the Manchester University group. The first model was delivered to the Royal Society Computing Machine Laboratory at the university in February 1951 and was the machine for which Turing wrote one of the first chess-playing programs, admittedly a very limited one, but even so much more advanced than the one of Torres y Quevedo (referred to in the previous chapter).

However, the first commercially produced machine to have a strong influence on the development of computers was the UNIVAC I, itself a descendant of ENIAC. Eckert and Mauchly had reorganized their company, which became the Eckert-Mauchly Computer Corporation, and were awarded a contract by the National Bureau of Standards (NBS) for the building of a new machine to process the data of the 1950 census. Eckert and Mauchly called this machine the Universal Automatic Computer (UNIVAC); we should note that once again it was the needs of the American census that led to an important step being taken in the development of computers.

The Eckert-Mauchly Computer Corporation was not set up without problems. Before awarding the contract NBS had sought the advice of several experts of impeccable reputation, including Aiken, Stibitz, and von Neumann, all of whom gave unfavorable responses. Nancy Stern [1981] gives some of the reasons: In Aiken's view there was no need for more than one or two machines of this type, and in any case he had never appreciated the importance of the stored-program principle. For Stibitz, too many things in the project were unclear. And for von Neumann, the proposed UNIVAC had nothing new about it when compared with EDVAC, which was true enough because it was designed as an EDVAC-type machine. Further, the company had run into various difficulties. Getting the machine to work took longer than the founders had foreseen; the banker who had financed them was killed in an air accident; and the machine was costing much more to make than its $250,000 price. The consequence of all this was that in March 1950 Eckert and Mauchly had to agree to the takeover of their company by Remington Rand, which in so doing formed a special division called the Univac Division for the production and sale of computers. The UNIVAC I was launched in 1951 as a commercial product; it was the world's first business computer.[5]

UNIVAC I was a decimal machine. It used 5,000 vacuum tubes, its central processing unit was about 8 feet high and 15 feet long, covered a floor area of about 220 square feet and weighed about 5 tons; cooling was by forced air, at a rate of 300 cubic feet per minute. It could perform an addition in 0.5 millisecond, a multiplication in 2.5; up to the end of the 1960s it had the best error-detection system of any computer.

As a machine intended for business use, it had to be able to handle very large volumes of data; Eckert and Mauchly therefore attached to it, for the first time for any computer, a magnetic-tape system. When an item of information has to be read from or written onto such a tape, the tape has to be wound or unwound until the appropriate place is found. To speed this process Eckert and Mauchly placed a *buffer memory* between the tape and the machine that could be filled or emptied at the speed of transfer of information to or from the tape without any need for this information to go through the processor.

The latter could therefore continue to execute the program on which it was working until it needed the information that had been read from the tape, which could then be transferred at high speed into the main memory. Magnetic tape and buffer memories were quickly adopted by all the manufacturers.

UNIVAC I was not without its defects, however. The main memory was provided by a group of 100 mercury delay lines; each line held 10 numbers, and each number was 12 decimal digits long; the buffer memory was 12 such lines, used as registers. This was certainly a large-capacity memory for that time, but it was slow, having an access time of several hundred milliseconds; it was necessary to wait until the relevant pulses arrived in order to read any particular item of data. Further, the first UNIVACs had few means for communication with the outside world; it was possible to write information directly onto the UNIVAC I magnetic tapes by typing on a keyboard, but this was very slow. (This method of direct input did not come into use again until much later—in fact, not until time-sharing systems were developed.) It is a curious fact that the specially designed equipment used by Eckert and Mauchly for writing information onto magnetic tapes from punched cards could handle only 80-column cards of IBM standard and did not accept Remington Rand cards, which at that time had 90 columns. Finally, results were printed out on a form of typewriter, which also was very slow. But to remove this defect Univac produced in 1953 the first high-speed printer of the computer era; it could print lines of 120 characters each at a rate of 600 per minute.

Fifteen models of UNIVAC I were sold. In November 1952 Remington Rand collaborated with the American CBS television network in conducting a poll of voters for the presidential election; by using UNIVAC I to analyze the data gathered by this poll, they were able, shortly after the close of the voting and well before the official results were declared, to predict that Eisenhower would be elected. By this means they drew wide public attention to the possibilities opened up by the computer.

Limitations of Delay Lines

The increases in capacity and reliability of memories made possible by the use of delay lines led to a considerable enlargement of the field of application of the computer, notably into that of commercial data processing, which within two decades became the dominant computer market and showed that despite the high cost of this machine, there were buyers for it. Many new techniques and technologies were brought into action with the delay-line computers—magnetic tapes, fast line printers and so forth—but also the first of the higher-level languages, which were later to ease the process of communication with the machines. Nevertheless memories of this type suffered from an intrinsic handicap; their dynamic structure meant that they were too slow. They vanished quickly from the scene after other technologies had been developed for making memories of at least the same capacity but higher speed. We may note that interest in the dynamic structure has been revived recently with the appearance of the magnetic-bubble memory.

Electrostatic Tubes

What replaced delay lines as main memories were the Williams electrostatic tubes, which, as I have mentioned, were first used in the Manchester machine. The principle is simple, and is easily understood if one considers in some detail the operation of a television tube. Here a beam of electrons (the cathode beam) impinges on the screen and causes it to fluoresce at the point of impact; under certain conditions this fluorescence can be maintained for a time on the order of 1/10 second; consequently, if the electrostatic charge thus created is regenerated every 1/30 second, say, a permanent memory is achieved. The charge can be detected in a very short time by means of a special electrode placed close to the screen; if the screen is divided up into a number of small areas and an electrode placed in front of each, the location of any charge can be determined.[6] This partitioning of the screen, however, limits the memory capacity of the tube, so that a number of tubes must be used in parallel in order to provide the capacity needed.[7] Williams-tube memories were not only fast, their access time being of the order of 25 microseconds; they were also inexpensive for the period.

The IBM 701

It was for the reasons just given—high speed and low cost—that IBM used the Williams tube in its first commercially produced computer. As we have seen [section 4.3 in chapter 1], IBM, spurred by Thomas J. Watson, Jr. had designed and built the world's first true computer, the SSEC; but it made no attempt to develop this into a commercial product. By contrast, it had enjoyed great commercial success with its IBM 603 electronic calculator. Watson therefore asked R. L. Palmer to set up a group whose task would be to develop an electronic machine more powerful than the IBM 603. The group included B. E. Phelps and J. A. Haddad. The machine in question was the IBM 604 Electronic Calculating Punch. Like all punched-card machines it was controlled by means of a plug board, but its use of vacuum-tube circuits, in which there were 1,400 tubes, gave it much higher speed. Its memory capacity of 50 decimal digits was double that of the IBM 603, and while the latter did not divide automatically, the IBM 604 could perform all the four basic arithmetical operations at a speed of 100 cards per minute. It could make transfers from one part of the program to another and could organize repetitions of sequences of instructions. This was the first machine in which the circuits were mounted on removable boards, so that a faulty circuit could be easily replaced simply by changing a board—thus greatly easing the task of repair; this idea of removable boards was adopted later by all the other manufacturers. The IBM 604 was launched in the autumn of 1948, and altogether 5,000 were sold—a great success, and at a time when almost all other manufacturers were still questioning the importance of electronics.

In the same year an elaboration of the IBM 604, the IBM 605, was produced, and an IBM 402 accounting machine was connected to it so as to improve its input and output facilities and to give it an additional electromechanical memory of 480 decimal digits. This combination became the IBM Card Programmed Calculator (CPC), of which 700 were sold.

But several IBM directors did not want their company to manufacture computers (Rosen [1969]). They felt that a balanced machine could not be designed with data input from magnetic tape. And what, they wondered, was to become of all these punched-card machines on which the success of IBM had been based? Further, in their view magnetic tape seemed an unreliable medium, whereas punched cards were well understood and safe. However, T. J. Watson, Jr., persisted, and on his advice, IBM, on the one hand, offered von Neumann a contract as consultant in October 1951 and, on the other hand, began to study the possibilities of magnetic tape.

Von Neumann had returned to the Institute for Advanced Study at Princeton (IAS) at the end of 1946, where he was rejoined by Goldstine. There they built a machine, called the IAS, using Williams tubes for the memory.[8] This machine was not completed until 1951 and was inaugurated only in 1952. But between 1946 and 1952 von Neumann published many papers on computer architecture. We have seen how one of these, the report by Burks, Goldstine, and von Neumann [1946] influenced the designers of EDSAC; the IBM 701, the first computer to be built commercially by IBM, was strongly influenced by the IAS.

The IBM 701 was designed by one of the two teams set up by IBM, as a result of the persistence of Thomas J. Watson, Jr., to study the use of magnetic tape in conjunction with computers. For this team the tape was to be simply a means of increasing the memory in a

Table 2.2
Characteristics of the IBM 701

Version produced 1953	Addition time: 62 microseconds
	Multiplication time: 500 microseconds
	Word length: 36 bits, 2 instructions per word
	Williams-tube memory: 2,048 words (36 bits)
	Secondary memory Magnetic drum: 8,192 words Magnetic tape: IBM 727 drives, using plastic tape, no buffer memory
	Input/output Card reader: 150 cards per minute, connected directly to the machine
	Printer: 75 lines per minute, 120 characters per line, directly connected to the machine
Version produced 1956	Same characteristics but having ferrite-core memory (IBM 701M)

scientific computer. The other team's purpose was, rather, to make possible the construction of memories of very great capacity, able to hold most of the data required for the running of a commercial or industrial company. This second team produced the IBM 702. The IBM 701 was thus the first scientific machine with magnetic tape. The tape units, the IBM 726, used reels of tape each of which could hold the equivalent of 15,000 punched cards; I shall describe these later. They were used for the first time with the IBM 701, both for input and output and as auxiliary memory.

The production of the machine, directed by J. A. Haddad and N. Rochester, was begun at the time of the Korean War in response to a request from the US Department of Defense; thus it was first known as the Defense Calculator. It was a binary machine, with a speed of 16,000 additions per second (62 microseconds for one addition) and 2,000 multiplications per second (500 microseconds for one multiplication). The main memory, on Williams tubes, was of 2,048 words of 36 bits each, with access time of 30 microseconds. It had a high-speed card reader, a card punch, and a line printer (Stevens [1953]). Data and instructions could be read, punched, or printed in either binary or the standard IBM card code, a subroutine doing the conversion to or from binary. The first IBM 701 was demonstrated on 7 April 1953 and a total of 19 were made (Goldstine [1972]). See table 2.2 for a summary of the characteristics of the IBM 701.

The IBM 702

While the IBM 701, aimed at scientific applications, was a binary machine, the IBM 702 was aimed at business data processing and was a decimal machine. The IBM team that undertook the study of the application of magnetic tape in this field was directed by B. E. Phelps and included among its engineers C. J. Bashe. One customer, the Social Security Center in Washington, DC, had put to IBM the problem of finding a means of storing very large volumes of information in a form that was at the same time compact and easy to access. The team attacked this problem by developing a system that used the IBM 726 tape units and in 1952 gave the first demonstration of what was called the Tape Processing Machine (TPM). The main memory of this machine was on Williams tubes and, what was a great novelty, was organized in terms of characters. Its capacity was 10,000 characters with an access time of 23 microseconds for one character; thus an instruction made up of 5 characters could be read in 115 microseconds. The memory hierarchy included a magnetic drum holding 5,000 decimal digits and a group of 5 tape units with a capacity of 250,000 digits [each]. The peripheral equipment included a card reader, a card punch, and a fast line printer, and there was a typewriter for communication with the machine. (An improved version of the TPM was marketed by IBM in September 1953 as the IBM 702 business data-processing machine, of which about 15 were sold; see Bashe, Buchholz, and Rochester [1954]).

Word Machines and Character Machines

The IBM 702 was the first "character" machine. What does that mean? Up to that time computers had been "word" machines. The *word* is the unit of information with which the arithmetical-logical unit of the machine works; all the words in one machine are the same size, and thus a word is a unit of fixed length and, depending on the particular machine, can represent a sequence of between 10 and 20 decimal digits. The longer the word length, the higher the precision with which a calculation can be performed.

Business applications require the processing of a different type of information. Some of the data are quantitative and are given in numerical form, such as prices or quantities, and therefore are coded in terms of numerical digits; others are qualitative, such as names of customers, and are given as groups of letters and therefore are coded in terms of alphabetic characters. We can say that a *character* is a group of a fixed number of bits in a specified order; it could be called a word were it not that it is much shorter in length than is usual for a word and that a word is often made up of a sequence of characters. With the group of bits forming the characters, we can code an *alpha-numeric alphabet*. In previous sections we saw the first appearance of numerical characters with the Harvard MARK II and of alphanumerical characters with UNIVAC I.

The code that Hollerith devised for his punched cards used 12 bits for a character; this allows one to have an alphabet of $2^{12} = 4,096$ different characters, but Hollerith used only 12—the 10 decimal digits and 2 control characters.[9] In the early 1930s this alphabet was increased to 39 characters to meet the needs of punched-card machinery: the 26 letters, the 10 digits and 3 special characters—the minus sign, the asterisk, and the ampersand. The introduction of computers and their use in business applications led to the appearance of further characters—for example, % (percentage). IBM estimated that there was a need for at least 48 characters. As the use of a 12-bit code—or worse, a code of the same length as the machine's word—leads to a waste of physical resources in the construction of the machine's registers, a 6-bit code was used for these 48 characters in the IBM 702 and thereafter.[10] This 6-bit code was used also in the IBM 705 and in the IBM 1401, and it became popular as a consequence of this latter use.[11]

Further features of the IBM 702 were, first, that the programmer could "address" directly a single character in a piece of text held in the memory and, second, that for the first time strings of any number of characters could be handled. In business applications it is most often the case that the basic items of information to be recorded are not of fixed length and must therefore be represented by sequences of characters that can themselves be of variable length.

The ability to access any single character and to work with strings of arbitrary length are the two main distinguishing features of what are called character machines; in word machines, in contrast, the unit of information is of fixed length, and in order to make access to an individual character, the whole word in which this is contained must be extracted.

Limitations of Electrostatic Tubes

I have said that about 15 models of each machine using Williams tubes for main memory were made. Thus a market was beginning to develop for computers. However, these tubes were very sensitive to electromagnetic disturbances and were not very reliable; for the IBM 701, for example, the mean time between errors in reading the memory was 20 minutes. Further, their lifetime was very short, between 50 and 100 hours. Their use in computer memories ended completely after 1954; but we may note that the principle embodied in them reappeared in more modern form in what are called *charge-coupled devices* (CCD).

Magnetic Drums

Because of these disadvantages of electrostatic memories, there was a need for an alternative that would make possible the provision of large capacities with ease of access and at the same time be reliable and, if possible, cheap. A natural course to take was to look into the possibilities offered by magnetic media; and the first device to be produced using this property was the *magnetic drum*.

The First Drums

A magnetic drum is simply a cylinder whose surface is coated with a material that can be magnetized at discrete points along the generators. This technology provides large-capacity memories that are cheap in comparison with delay lines and Williams tubes and have short access times, from 5 to 25 milliseconds. When used for main memory the drums made it possible to build low-cost computers and thus to open up a new market. Alternatively, when used for secondary memory in large computers, as, for example, in the IBM 701, they brought about a considerable reduction in the cost per bit.

The basic idea of the magnetic drum had been put forward in 1946 at the Princeton Institute for Advanced Study as a means of alleviating the IAS's constraint of 1,024 words of memory. It was taken up later by a group of engineers that included C. B. Tompkins, J. H. Wakelin and W. W. Stifler Jr., who, shortly after the war, had formed the company Electronics Research Associates, ERA. The machine they designed for the Georgia Institute of Technology seems to have been the first computer to use a magnetic drum for its main memory; this was the ERA 1101, delivered in 1950.[12] It multiplied two numbers in 260 microseconds. ERA was taken over by Univac in April 1952; the company had by then produced a scientific computer with electrostatic memory, the ERA 1103, which was offered as a commercial product in September 1953 with the name UNIVAC 1103.[a]

The Birth and Death of Some Industrial Companies

It has been noted that the magnetic drum, used for main memory, made possible the production of low-cost computers; it was in fact used in this way in several low-power machines. Many companies were formed in the United States for building medium-scale computers. On the West Coast Computer Research Association made CADAC, using a drum memory with access time of 12.5 milliseconds; CRA was taken over by NCR, which marketed CADAC under the name of NCR 102A and developed a decimal version for the business market, the NCR 102D, which had a magnetic tape unit. On the East Coast the Electronic Computer Corporation made a small machine, the ELE-COM 100; this sold badly and the company went out of business. The

Consolidated Engineering Corporation formed a computer division, which built the CEC 201, a more powerful machine than the CADAC with a drum memory of 4,000 words and access time of 8.5 milliseconds plus a small dynamic memory of 80 words and 10 time the speed that held the instructions to be obeyed next; the first deliveries of this machine were in 1953. This division later became the Electro Data Corporation and the CEC 201 was renamed the Datatron; among other innovative features it had, first, an index register; later, floating-point arithmetic; and finally, means for reading information from magnetic tape. Electro Data was taken over by Burroughs in 1956, and from this grew the Burroughs 200, a medium-scale machine put on the market in 1958; it was the success of this machine that ensured Burroughs's later importance in the computer field. As we have seen in chapter 1, Burroughs was an American company that, prior to World War II, had been a successful manufacturer of office machines. The company formed a Research Division in 1948 and gave it the task of building computers. By 1956, before the takeover of Electro Data, all that had been produced was the E101, a small calculator strongly influenced by office machinery; although this was intended for business applications, it used perforated paper tape as input and output and was therefore ill adapted to the needs of the time.

The IBM 650

It seemed to be the case that the small machines were produced by small pioneering companies set up for that purpose and that these small companies most often failed and disappeared from the scene. But at the end of 1953 IBM also produced and marketed a medium-scale machine with drum memory, the IBM 650. According to Saul Rosen [1969] IBM had no great faith in this machine and did not expect to make more than about 50; but in fact it became the first machine in the world with sales exceeding 1,000.

The 650 was a fairly fast machine, having a multiplication time of 2 milliseconds, and was essentially a scientific computer. Originally it had only punched cards for input and output, while some of its competitors were better equipped for communication with the users; paradoxically this acted in IBM's favor, because, with its high reputation for punched-card machinery, users felt they were safer with this equipment than with other, less well proven, devices. What is particularly interesting is that the IBM 650 was a decimal machine, which shows that there was by no means unanimous support for the view that arithmetic to base 2 was the best for scientific computation. Thanks to its decimal arithmetic, the machine sold in large numbers to business users.

The 650 developed as time passed. Magnetic-tape input and output units were added; the capacity of the drum was increased to 4,000 words; a core store of 60 words was added; and floating-point arithmetic, index registers, and other features were provided.

The First French Computers

Magnetic drums were used also in the first French machines. The first of all among these was the CUBA, Calculateur Universel Binaire de l'Armement. This was not only the first French computer but also the first to be made by the Societé d'Electronique et d'Automatisme, SEA; the founder of this company, the exceedingly energetic and inventive F. H. Raymond, had made it possible for France since the 1950s to hold a strong international position in the computer field and to be the source of many innovations. The CUBA was commissioned by the Laboratoire de Calcul de l'Armement at the request of Ingénieur Général Nicolau and was delivered in 1952. In designing CUBA Raymond had been influenced by the Burks, Goldstine, and von Neumann report and also by the machine built in America for the National Bureau of Standards, the SEAC (Standards Eastern Automatic Computer). This was an older machine with mercury delay lines for main memory, but the modular organization of its basic circuits made it easy to change the architecture of these, and this was taken over to some extent in CUBA. The instructions [in CUBA] used three addresses. SEA made many other computers during the period 1950–1955, such as the CAB 2000 and the CAB 3000. I shall discuss these later.

The first computer to be produced by the Compagnie des Machines Bull [see section 3.1 in chapter 1] was a drum machine, the Gamma Extension Tambour, better known as the Gamma ET; although it was first marketed in 1958 it used delay lines for main memory, with the drum for secondary memory. Since 1950 the Bull Company, in response to pressure from Franklin Maurice, director of research, and Bruno Leclerc, head of the Electronic Calculators Department, had produced a series of calculators that had made the company's name famous, especially in Europe. The technology expert in the team that produced these was Henri Feissel, and the architect of the logical structure was Pierre Chenus; another important member was Philippe Dreyfus, the inventor of the word *informatique* [see note b in chapter 1]. The prototype for this machine was the Gamma 2, shown at the international exhibition in Paris in 1951. This was a calculator, with a delay-line memory for 48 bits, equivalent to 12 decimal digits, and logical circuits using germanium diodes; the machine was linked to a tabulator that printed at 150 lines per minute and was programmed by means of a plug board. Gamma 2 was followed by Gamma 3 in 1952, a machine using the same technology but with a memory capacity for 7 words of 12 decimal digits each and an access time of 170 microseconds. It had connections for a tabulator and for a card reader and card punch; these latter ran at 120 cards per minute. Gamma 3 was an excellent machine and a great commercial success, over 1,000 being sold.[13] An extended version was produced in 1955, with a memory capacity of 32 words of 12 decimal digits each, floating-point arithmetic, and arrangements for subroutines.

Gamma ET, the Bull Company's first computer, was produced in 1958 and therefore at the end of the first-generation period. Its central units were based on the Gamma 3, but the memory capacity was greatly increased by the addition of a further 64 delay lines and, above all, by a drum—the origin of the name—holding 8,192 words, again of 12 digits, on 128 tracks of 64 words each.

Computers with Several Drums

It was inevitable that several drums would be put on one computer, it was done for the first time on the GE 210. The General Electric Company, GE, had collaborated with NCR in building the electronics for several computers produced by that company. In 1955 they set up a division in Phoenix, Arizona, for the specific purpose of building a banking system called ERMA—Electronic Recording Method for Accounting—to a design produced by Stanford Research Institute for Bank of America. The computer in this system had a high-speed memory using two drums, 8,000 vacuum tubes, and 12 magnetic-tape controllers. Later GE decided to market a descendant of ERMA, and did so in 1959 under the name GE 210.[14]

Limitations of Magnetic Drums

Magnetic drums made it possible to store large amounts of information—800,000 bits on Gamma ET, 150,000 on the IBM 650—and to access this quickly. To reduce the access time drums were made with very high rotational speeds; on the IBM 650, this was 12,500 revolutions per minute, which was at least three times faster than that of any of its competitors and gave the machine a considerable advantage despite the small capacity (only 2,000 words of 10 decimal digits) of the first models. The speed of the Gamma ET's drum was 3,000 revolutions per minute.

Even so, the use of magnetic drums for main memory could not be a permanent solution; however high their speed of rotation, their mechanical construction made it impossible for their access time to compete with what was attainable by means of purely electronic devices. Further, their capacity was limited by the possible dimensions of the cylinder forming the drum; that on the IBM 650 had a diameter of

4.5 inches and a length of 16 inches, and the storage was organized into 40 bands of 5 tracks each, with the information written at a density of 50 bits per inch. Drums were not in fact used for main memory after 1964, and they have continued to be used less and less for secondary memory; they are yielding ground to the disks, which will be described later on.

Ferrite-Core Memories and the IBM 704

A *ferrite core* is a small ring of a ferrite material whose hysteresis loop is practically rectangular; if wires are threaded through the central hole, then by means of pulses sent along these the state of magnetization of the material can be detected or changed. This property makes it possible to construct a computer memory that suffers from neither the inconveniences of electrostatic tubes nor the slowness of magnetic drums. According to H. Boucher [1966] the first attempts in this direction were made by Eckert and Chu in 1945, using more ordinary material; the first use of ferrite cores was made by Forrester, for Whirlwind, in 1949.[15] Memories of this type appeared again with Radio Corporation of America (RCA) in 1952, which used a sintered ceramic material based on a magnetic oxide. RCA's research department had specialized in memory technologies, and the company quickly developed an interest in computers. The IAS machine was to have used a special RCA electrostatic tube called the Selectron for memory (Rachjman [1948]), but RCA was never able to make this work, and in the event the IAS memory was based on Williams tubes. Later RCA took up the study of ferrite cores and was able to make certain advances in this technology; in 1952 they decided to build a core-memory machine, the BIZMAC, to be described later. The machine was not marketed until 1958.

The first machine to be marketed with a core memory was the UNIVAC 1103A in 1954, which was 50 times faster than the UNIVAC 1101; but it was undoubtedly the IBM 704, marketed in 1954 and the first really powerful computer with core memory, that typified the technology of the time. The first IBM 704s were delivered in 1955. The concept of the machine was due to Gene Amdahl.[16] The core memory had a cycle time of about 12 microseconds and a capacity initially of 4,096 (4K, 2^{12}) words of 36 bits, which was raised first to 8,192 (8K, 2^{13}) in 1956 and then to 32,768 (32K, 2^{15}) in 1957;[b] such a capacity seemed then to be immense, and indeed several users thought it too big—how could they have guessed that 20 years later there would be users who thought a memory of 100 times this capacity was too small?

The large memory, high-speed processor, and high reliability combined to make it possible for many innovations to be incorporated into the IBM 704: floating-point arithmetic, index registers, the Monitor program, and the FORTRAN language.

Floating-point arithmetic   This was provided on the IBM 704 for the first time on a commercially produced machine;[17] after this it was provided on almost all scientific machines. To explain the concept, consider first *fixed-point arithmetic*, in which all the numbers entering into a calculation—operands and results—are expressed in a standard form (p,q), meaning that the total number of decimal digits in any operand or result is p and that there are q digits after the decimal point. The numbers p,q are decided when the machine is designed and are then fixed. Thus suppose $p = 7$, $q = 3$, meaning that the machine works with 7-digit numbers with 3 digits after the decimal point. If we form the sum of $A = 9327.3$ and $B = 2151.3715$, we shall get the wrong answer, 1478.671, instead of the correct sum 11478.6715. Not only has the final 5 been lost in the rounding but also the leading 1 of the sum has been lost by "overflow." This is obviously very dangerous. The floating point gets rid of the problem; numbers are expressed in terms of a *mantissa* and an *exponent*. In the above case, for example, the result could be given as 1147867E05, meaning 0.1147867×10^5. (E05 is an IBM convention.) The hardware operates with all numbers in this form, converting data automatically.

Index registers   It is also thanks to the IBM 704, which had 3 index registers, that this concept first found in Babbage's "index cards" became adopted widely. Their prime aim is to ease the progress of a calculation in which the same sequence of operations has to be repeated a stated number of times; a count of the number of repetitions as they are made is kept in the register, and when this equals the required number, the process is stopped.[c] We may recall that index registers first appeared on the Manchester machine [under the name of B-lines] and that the concept was soon adopted by all other manufacturers. The first machine to be marketed in the United States with an index register was the Datatron, made, as we have seen, by the Electronic Data Corporation of Pasadena, California. Machines like the UNIVAC 1103A had built-in functions for the "counting-down" type of process just described; this gave them advantages over the IBM 701 and IBM 702, but they did not have the flexibility of the index-register approach.

Monitor system   The first steps toward the development of an *operating system* to make the best use of the machine's resources were taken with the IBM 704. A program, written for this machine by Bob Patrick, an engineer with General Motors, controlled automatically the input of the data, the progress of the calculation, and the output of the results. This was the first true *monitor* program. I shall take up the question of the value of such software later on.

FORTRAN   Finally, it was with the IBM 704 that the FORTRAN language for communiction with machines came into use, marking an important date in the history of computer science. This is examined in chapter 4.

See table 2.3 for a summary of computer developments in the period 1939 (relays) to 1954 (ferrite cores).

The IBM 709

The 704 was a very reliable machine for its time. Its mean time between failures was 8 days. Repair after a failure was often easy; it was necessary only to note which indicator light was extinguished and to change the corresponding component (McLaughlin [1975]). This reliability, together with its speed, three times that of the IBM 701, gained for it new classes of users. It is amusing to recall that the first IBM 704s were often underused because the machine was so powerful that there seemed no possibility of saturating it. Today the total computing power installed in Europe is equivalent to several tens of thousands of 704s.

The IBM 704 was the start of a very important line of IBM computers. Its immediate descendant was the *IBM 709*, first delivered in 1958 with the same core memory and instruction set as the IBM 704 but differing on account of at least two innovations. The first was *indirect addressing*, by which an address can refer not to the location of an item of data but to a location where the address of that item is to be found. The other was a new system for input and output, which I shall describe in the discussion of *channels*, and which to some extent marked the start of the second generation.

Longevity of the Core Memory

The reliability of the core memory was excellent compared with that of the preceding technologies. Moreover, the cycle time was from the beginning very short, of the order of 10 microseconds. Consequently its use spread rapidly to the majority of computers. But at the same time these memories were expensive (about $1 per bit), and for this reason there would often be both core and drum memory on the same machine, the latter costing about ten times less than the former. Table 2.4 summarizes the characteristics of several machines that used

Table 2.3
Some machines of the period 1939–1954

Type of memory	Date	Name of machine	Fast-memory capacity	Access time (seconds)	Word length	Addition time (seconds)
Electromechanical machines						
Relay	1939	Bell Labs[a]	400 bits	0.5	7 decimal digits	0.3
	1944	Harvard-IBM[b]	60 words	0.5	23 decimal digits	0.6
Vacuum-tube machines						
Flip-flop	1946	ENIAC[a]	20 words	0.001	10 decimal digits	0.0002
	1948	IBM SSEC[b]	8 words	0.001	14 decimal digits	0.0008
Williams tubes	1948	MADM[b] prototype	32 words	0.0001	32 bits	
Computers with miniaturized vacuum tubes						
Delay lines	1951	UNIVAC I	1,000 words	0.0003	12 decimal digits	0.0005
Williams tubes	1953	IBM 701	2,048 words	0.00003	36 bits	0.00006
Ferrite cores	1953	UNIVAC 1103	1,024 words	0.00001	36 bits	0.00003
	1954	IBM 704	8,192 words	0.00001	36 bits	0.000024
	1954	CAB 2000	128 words	0.00001	22 bits	0.00046[c]

a. Calculator.
b. Computer.
c. The discrepancy between the access time and the addition time is due to the fact that what was called the secondary memory was actually the main memory.

core memories; the IBM 650 is included because a small core memory was added to this machine in 1956.

It was not until the end of the 1960s that ferrite cores began to disappear as computer memories and to be replaced by a technology that was identical with that used to make the central circuits of the machines and therefore gave a better match between the speeds of the different parts. But there are still some computers in operation which have core memories.[18]

2 The Development of Other Information Supports

In 1955 the machine builders found themselves in possession of a technology for the construction of memories on which they could rely, that of ferrite cores; they could therefore turn their efforts to the development of other information supports [using the term as defined in section 2.2 in chapter 1]. They concerned themselves first with secondary memories [or backing stores as these are often called], using several lines of attack on the problems that these presented. One line of attack was to develop special software to improve the efficiency of use of the hierarchy of memories; the concept of *paging* arises here. Another was to improve the technology. Attention was given also to means of improving communication between the user and the machine, by developing both programming languages that were easier to use and equipment that allowed easier access to the machine and more conveniently presented results. In this section I shall describe, first, the concept and use of paging, then the development of certain support equipment, and, finally, the access devices. I deal with programming languages in chapter 4.

Paging

Whatever technology was used, the cost of main memory was such that special software for the efficient exploitation of a hierarchy of memories was going to be needed if small-scale machines, at the bottom of manufacturer's range, were to be produced that were not too costly but had adequate fast memories. The University of Manchester was the first to take up this problem.

It is clear that in any machine having a hierarchy of memories, the fast memory must at any moment contain the instruction to be executed next, and often the neighboring instructions in the program also. This presents difficult problems concerning placing instructions in the fast memory because it requires finding a part of the memory that is empty of instructions and has the capacity to hold the sequence to

Table 2.4
Some commercially produced computers of 1958

	UNIVAC II	IBM 704	IBM 705	IBM 650	Datamatic 1000	CAB 2000
Word length						
Alphabetic	12 characters		Variable		8 characters	
Numerical	11 decimals	36 bits		10 decimals	11 decimals	22 bits
Number of instructions	48	91	35	89	32	
Memory capacity	2,000–10,000	Up to 32k words	20k characters	60 words	104,000 bits, 2,000 words	128 words
Memory access time (microseconds)	40	12	17/character	96	14/character	10
Drum		Up to 16k words	300k characters/section	1,000–2,000		8k words
Add time						
Fixed point	200 microseconds	24 microseconds		0.63	0.25 milliseconds	0.46 milliseconds
Floating point		84 microseconds	$34 + 17c$ microseconds[a]			
Magnetic tape: transfer rate (characters/second)	25k	15k	15k	15k	20k	
Card/reader (cards/minute)	240	150	250	150–200		
Card punch (cards/minute)	120	100	100	100	100	
Printer (lines/minute)	600	150	500–1,000	IBM Tabulator	500–1,000	

a. c = number of characters.

be placed there. Professor Williams and his team at Manchester developed a system in which instructions were transferred between the drum and the fast memory in blocks of fixed size, which they called *pages*. By this means it was only a question of moving into the fast memory a group consisting of a fixed number of instructions, which would take the place of another group of exactly the same number. This would pose no problem. If the instruction to be executed next was not already in the fast memory, the system caused the page in which it occurred to be transferred to it from the drum and also caused space to be found for it in the fast memory by transferring from it to the drum another page, which was selected according to various criteria. It seemed to the user, therefore, that the entire program was "virtually" in the fast memory, although the level of performance — the memory access time, in particular — was lowered somewhat.

The CAB Series

The idea of the page structure was taken up and developed in France by SEA, a company that, in response to the drive of F. H. Raymond, always showed great liveliness and enterprise. SEA was aiming to build computers of medium scale for the period but whose fast memory would be used to the maximum. These were the Calculatrices Arithmetiques Binaires, CAB. In designing these Raymond was influenced by the SEAC, by the Burks, Goldstine, and von Neumann report, and by the ideas that had been developed in Britain.

The CAB 2000 series was announced at the end of 1954. The main memory was of ferrite cores; it was thanks to SEA that France was thus one of the first countries in the world to build computers with memories of this type.[19] These machines were the first to have several *accumulators*, or *arithmetical registers*: 2 registers, each of one 22-bit word in the CAB 2022, and of one 24-bit word in the CAB 2024. This practice was adopted gradually by other manufacturers, and soon several tens of registers were to be found on a single machine; in machines of the IBM 360 series, for example, there were 20, of which 16 were for floating-point arithmetic and the remaining 4 for fixed point. The CAB 2000 machines were scientific computers and accordingly, as was usual at the time, had rather poor input/output equipment. Input was by means of 5-track punched paper tape, read at 200 characters per second; output was punched on paper tape at 15 characters per second and printed on a teleprinter at 7 characters per second. The central processor, by contrast, was fast; an addition took 0.46 millisecond; a multiplication, 5.5 milliseconds.

The ferrite-core memory of the CAB 2022 was composed of two groups each of 64 words (22 bits) with an access time of 10 microseconds;

the secondary memory was a drum with 8,192 words and an access time of 15 milliseconds. As on the Manchester machine, both data and programs were held on the drum, and a rather complex algorithm transferred them into the main memory in blocks of 64 words, the data going into one group and the instructions into the other. When the main memory no longer held the instructions to be executed next, the block was returned to the drum and a new block, containing those instructions, was transferred into its place.

The system was developed further in the CAB 3000, marketed in 1957. Here the fast memory was of either 8 or 16 blocks, corresponding to 64 and 128 words, respectively, and the program was similarly divided into pages [of 8 words]. A register was associated with each block of the memory in which the number of the page of the program in that block was written; a process involving the use of certain tables made it possible to find any individual word in a page in the fast memory. This was a characteristic of the SEA computers before it was taken up by the majority of manufacturers.

These first French machines were very reliable; a CAB 3000 delivered to the Comptoir Français des Produits Siderurgiques [Metals Exhange Company] in 1958 was still working ten years later. But on account of an inadequate attack on the commercial world and with no government support, they had only a very small market. Raymond reported in 1960 that by that time only two of the CAB 2022 had been sold and only three of the CAB 3000 (Raymond [1960]).

Virtual Memory

This is a concept very closely related to that of the page, and once again it is one that originated at the University of Manchester. It was brought into operation in the Atlas computer (Kilburn et al. [1962]), built by Ferranti in 1961 in a collaboration with Manchester of which I have already spoken. Based on the use of pages, it offered the possibility of providing a main memory of much greater capacity than the actual real main memory of the machine—hence the name *virtual memory*. The organization of the paging was very different from that in the SEA machines. As we have seen, the page containing the next instruction to be executed must be in the main memory at that time. The Ferranti engineers devised a novel system based on the hypothesis that it was the pages that had already been used most that were most likely to be used again, and that therefore they were to be given preference in choosing the pages to be held in the main memory. But in spite of these innovations only a few models of Atlas were sold, and Ferranti did not continue the use of paging in their next machines.

There is a detailed bibliography of the first virtual-memory machines in Denning [1970].[d]

The first French machine with virtual memory was the SEA CAB 1500, in 1963. This employed what SEA called *generalized names*. The idea of paging spread very widely. It was taken up by IBM in some of the 360 series machines, and later, at the beginning of the 1970s, by the majority of manufacturers of large-scale machines.

Development of Support Equipment

The use of software was not the only line of attack on the problem of how to improve the use of the memory hierarchies; because of the increased reliability resulting from the use of ferrite-core technology for the building of computer memories, serious attention could also be given to the development of hardware devices with this aim. We may recall what had been said by Babbage, that in a calculator the flow of information between the outside world and the machine's main memory involves a variety of supporting devices. We have just been studying the development of the main memory and turn now to those items of support equipment now classed as access devices, although, as was the case with magnetic tapes and disks, this was not their original purpose, nor has it always been their role.

The purpose of an access device is to enable a user to make contact with the machine in order to communicate data and programs to it and to get from it the results of any processing. Such devices fall into two main classes: those in which the information is held in such a form that it can be read into the machine again on a later occasion, and those in which this is not possible. The first class includes punched cards, punched paper tape, magnetic tape, and magnetic disks; the second, to be dealt with later, includes printers, visual display screens, and keyboards. Devices of the first class can function as memories, and these again fall into two classes: those in which a location can be selected in which to store an item of information, and those in which this cannot be done. The first are called *addressable* devices and can be considered as *auxiliary memories*; the principal ones are magnetic tapes, magnetic disks, and so on. The second are *nonaddressable*; the principal ones are punched cards, punched paper tape, and so on. Let us start with the latter.

Nonaddressable Support Equipment

These are now of rapidly decreasing importance, but they were much used during the historical period under study.

Punched cards   These go back to Babbage, or even to Jacquard, and although their disappearance from the scene is now in sight, they are still used to some extent. A card can be regarded as a line of text, usually of 80 characters,[20] although smaller cards have been used with some recent machines. As we have seen, peripheral equipment has been produced by means of which the computer can read the information on the card—called *card readers*. Most frequently the same type of equipment is used also for punching the results of a calculation on to cards—the method for output used in Babbage's machine—and the combined device is called a (card) *reader/punch*.

Clearly, it is not necessary that whoever punches the input information onto the cards know the punching code; if that were necessary, computers could not have developed to the extent that they have. Actually, to ease the process of checking the punching, most punches print the line just punched along the top edge of the card, which is then said to be *interpreted*; this eases also the task of finding any particular card in a file. This use of the word "interpretation," meaning the translation of the punched code into clear text, must not be confused with its use for the translation of the instructions in which a program is written into the form executable by the machine.

Punched paper tape   Stibitz, as we have seen, was using punched paper tape as memory in the Bell Labs machine in 1939. The idea of paper tape came from its use in accounting machines—especially, teletypewriters; it was the medium in use throughout the whole of this first computer generation. But paper tape is weak and easily torn, and tape readers are necessarily slow, their speed being limited by the fact that the tape is likely to break if too strong a force is applied in order to increase the speed. Also, it cannot be addressed with the aim of recording an item in, or selecting one from, a given location. The effect of these disadvantages was that the use of paper tape declined as time went on and has now practically ceased.

Addressable Support Equipment
It was during the early years of the first computer generation that awareness of the impossibility of referring directly to an item of information in nonaddressable memory stimulated the search for alternatives that would be both addressable and less bulky. The outcome was the development of magnetic-tape and magnetic disk memories, the use of which brought about a great reduction in the use of cards and the virtual disappearance of paper tape.

Magnetic tape   This is very similar to what is used in a tape recorder, and the method of use is based on the same principle: The items of information written on the tape must be read in sequence, whether one is looking for a specific item or for a place in which to write another item. Hence the name *sequential-access memory* sometimes used.

Magnetic tapes had been used in connection with calculators before the appearance of the computer. UNIVAC I, the first business-oriented computer, had magnetic tapes, but these were of steel; such tapes often broke during winding or unwinding, a disadvantage overcome only when IBM made a system that operated in vacuum. It seems that the first plastic tapes were those on the RAYDAC, the machine designed by Louis Fem and built in 1951 for the Raytheon Corporation (Yasaki [1976]); but the first robust enough to give trouble-free operation at the high speeds of winding and unwinding necessary for their use as secondary memory were those used with the IBM 726 tape transports, the units which, as has been described, were developed for the IBM 701 computer. These could record information at a density of 100 characters per inch along the tape, and the units could read information into the computer at 7,500 characters per second; this speed is only 20 times less than that of a modern unit, but the price/performance ratio has improved by a factor of 100.

It was the Hurricane, a computer with delay-line memory, that introduced the organization of the data on the tape into blocks of fixed length, each block composed of the same number of words and the boundaries of the blocks fixed by special characters.[21] Use of magnetic tape as memory does give rise to difficult problems in addressing items of information. The solution adopted in Hurricane was that on the tape only the block could be addressed, the words in the block becoming individually addressable only when the block was in the main memory; alternate blocks were used for reading and writing, respectively. The tape could thus be used as secondary memory.

Hurricane had several other novel features; one, in particular, was the hardware for binary-to-decimal conversion, and vice versa, from which the designers of the IBM Stretch drew their ideas. But the machine was obsolete as soon as it was built, and according to Rosen [1969] only one was built.

The Honeywell Corporation of Minneapolis wanted to diversify into computer manufacture and accordingly in 1954 joined with Raytheon in forming the Datamatic Corporation; subsequently Raytheon sold its share to Honeywell, and Datamatic became the Computer Division of Honeywell.

The IBM 705   It was a natural step to connect several magnetic tapes to a single machine at the same time. The IBM 702 was the first machine to have such an arrangement, but the system here was of very limited scope. However, even before the first IBM 702s had been delivered, the IBM group under Phelps had devised another system for handling the tapes, the Tape Record Coordinator, TRC. This had a buffer for 1,024 characters on ferrite cores and, most important, logic circuits for controlling tape movement and writing into the buffer that formed one of the first attempts, perhaps the very first, to relieve the central processor of some of the task of organizing input and output; this was thus one of the first steps toward the development of what are called the *channels*, which I shall describe later.

The IBM 702 was succeeded by the IBM 705, announced in 1954; and in 1955 the machine 705 Model II appeared, to which several TRCs could be connected, making it a very powerful commercial data-processing machine.[22] The IBM 705's processor was rather slow, but the machine's memory capacity was large; as well as the magnetic tape system it had a main memory of 20,000 characters on ferrite cores, organized into groups of 5 characters with an access time of 17 microseconds for a 5-character instruction. The Model II had a main memory of 40,000 characters. The main memory [on both models] was backed by a drum of 300,000 characters capacity. The IBM 705 was the first business machine to have a real commercial success, over 100 being on order early in 1956. According to R. A. McLaughlin [1975] 175 were sold, at an average price of $1.6 million. The Datamatic 1000, which I shall describe later, was announced in 1958 and was aimed at the same market as the IBM 705; it was the first machine produced by the Honeywell Computer Division. The UNIVAC II, a machine with a core memory of 180,000 bits, 5,200 vacuum tubes, and 18,000 diodes (Dahl [1978]) had a similar aim. But these machines were more costly than the IBM 705 and arrived two years later; thus IBM gathered the fruits of the Watsons' policies.

Compatibility between Different Computers

The instruction sets of the IBM 702 and IBM 705 were very similar, but differed sufficiently for programs written for the 702 not to run on the 705. There was a similar incompatibility between the IBM 704 and the IBM 705, but in spite of the difference, IBM found it necessary to try to use the same input and output equipment on the two machines. The reason was that since the views of the early 1950s on what was required in a scientific computer were still in force, IBM had provided the IBM 704 with the same card reader and the same printer as the IBM 701, aware that these were slow; but the IBM 704 brought about very quickly a change in the whole scale of scientific computation, and it was clear that the old reader and printer were inadequate. IBM therefore sought to use the reader and printer provided for the IBM 705—a first indication that scientific and commercial computation have requirements in common. However, there were difficulties. The

IBM 704 and the IBM 705 had been designed independently, and they used different codes for the alphabetic characters; translation between the two had therefore to be provided. This gave added support to those who had already foreseen the need to design series of machines in which at least the basic codes were compatible.

The lesson was remembered when the need for a replacement for the IBM 705 arose. Actually, during the second generation IBM produced a series of machines, the IBM 7070s, which were intended as replacements for the IBM 705 but were not compatible with this and, what was strange, were word oriented, in contrast to the IBM 705's character orientation. The IBM 7070s were not successful. IBM then produced the IBM 7080, a development of the IBM 705 using transistorized circuits. According to McLaughlin [1975] 80 of these were sold, at $2.2 million each; this success was due to the fact that the IBM 7080 could run any program written for the IBM 705 and the machine could therefore replace the latter without the user having to rewrite the programs. By the end of the first generation it had become clear that all the machines made by the same manufacturer must be compatible.

The BIZMAC

But to come back to magnetic tapes, these very soon began to be used for storing information away from the computer, for which purpose they had several great advantges over punched cards: they were much less bulky; they could be used as secondary memory during the processing; and the information held on them could be changed. Commercial organizations were therefore soon building up libraries of data on magnetic tape much more compact than their equivalent in cards and much easier to read and to write. It was the scientific users who were the first to assemble libraries of *programs* on tape.

However, the need to find the particular tape reel containing the information required, to mount it on the machine, and to disconnect it after use involved manual intervention that slowed the processing; a natural step was to seek a way of using magnetic tape to provide a secondary memory of sufficiently great capacity that all the information likely to be of use could be held there, thus eliminating the need for manual operations. The first such system was developed for the BIZMAC machine.

On this machine the characters were represented by 6 bits, plus extra bits for error detection and correction. There were 22 instructions in the set, of 3-address form and each occupying 16 characters. The fast memory was of 4,096 characters on ferrite cores with an access time of 20 microseconds, and there was a drum holding 4,096 characters on each of 8 tracks, rotating at 10.24 revolutions per second.[e] The magnetic tapes were written at a density of 125 characters per inch, had a linear speed of 6.5 feet per second, and could record information from cards at 150 cards per minute.

RCA, which had designed and built the BIZMAC, claimed that it was the most powerful computer in the world. Its designers had aimed at meeting the needs of the business world by providing a means of making all the information that a company might need directly accessible by way of a machine's central processor; and for this they had developed a system in which up to 200 magnetic tape units could be connected to the machine at the same time. Given this, there should be no need for any manual operations involving the tapes, whatever processing might prove to be required in the course of the company's activities. It was a very original concept, and very modern in its attitude.

In order to ease the process of getting access to the information required and to relieve the central processor of many small tasks, several small satellite computers, dedicated to special tasks, were used. One of the most difficult problems in using magnetic tape arises in the need to sort the data that it holds; IBM had previously built a special machine, the IBM 703, for this purpose, but later abandoned the project when, with the development of the technology, it became possible to achieve adequate speeds without the need for special equipment. The BIZMAC's satellite computers were all interconnected, and each was directed by the central processor to the relevant tape unit and given instructions concerning the [sorting] task to be performed.[f] Here again, with a *network* of satellite computers organized around a powerful central machine, we meet an idea very modern in its attitude.

In spite of these innovations, however, BIZMAC seems to have had little success. One was installed at the US Army tank automotive plant in Detroit, and a few smaller-scale systems were built. There were several reasons for this. As we have seen, RCA, wishing to take advantage of the advances they had made in ferrite-core technology, had decided to build BIZMAC in 1952. This technology was still evolving at the time and was expensive. Thus the designers provided for a core memory of only small capacity, and both data and programs had to be stored on the drum. Since the concept of paging was then unknown, instructions were transferred from the drum to the core memory in blocks of lengths varying from 1 to 32 instructions, which posed problems of location that proved difficult to solve. Another difficulty arose because the BIZMAC was designed before the concept of a character-oriented machine had been fully formulated and because although aimed at business data processing, it was a word-oriented machine.

Nevertheless it boasted a very interesting business-oriented innovation: the capacity to handle records of variable length. Words could be strung together one after the other so as to give the required length, with a special symbol (1, for example) marking the end of the record. A scheme of this type was used later in the IBM Stretch and is used in all modern machines.

Further, the satellites in BIZMAC were low-powered machines and were able to perform only limited tasks, so that the central processor had to devote much of its time to looking after them; consequently there was an imbalance between what was for its time the enormous volume of information directly accessible to the processor and the extent to which this could actually be used. As we shall see, it was not until much later that problems of this type were solved satisfactorily.

The BIZMAC was one of the very first machines for which the idea of a *data base* was developed, that is, a structured set of files of information relating to a particular application. Its designers, however, encountered a difficulty that has never been fully overcome, although it has become somewhat less acute as a consequence of the computer's increasingly higher speed. The process of executing a program in a machine of von Neumann type is such that single items of information have to be located in, and extracted from, the memory, one at a time, in sequence; but the use of a data base requires that very large bodies of data be taken into account at the same time and immediately upon being called for. Before it could start to search for an item of data in the memory, the BIZMAC, like all von Neumann machines, had to spend a significant amount of time interpreting the instructions given to it; afterward it lost much time in moving the data to be processed from the secondary to the main memory and from there to the processor (Hsiao [1979]).

Thus the BIZMAC's designers and builders were faced with so many novel problems that their machine was not put on the market until 1958, by which time ferrite-core technology had been greatly developed. The access time for its hierarchy of memories then seemed long, and the combination of a small-core memory backed by a drum was more characteristic of a medium-scale machine. It was not until the start of the 1980s that the availability of other memory systems, including magnetic disks, made it possible to have all the information required in the running of a business directly and permanently connected to a machine.

One other reason for the lack of success of BIZMAC was that it appeared two years after the launch of the IBM 305, the first machine with magnetic disks: I shall describe it shortly.

Limitations of Magnetic Tape

We must not forget that, from their first introduction, magnetic tapes offered many advantages. The density of information that they could carry, even initially of the order of several tens of characters per inch, enabled several hundred thousand characters to be stored on a single tape; and the speed at which this could be read was very much higher than that of punched cards. To give an example, the IBM tape units available at the end of this first generation made it possible to exchange between the tape and the computer memory in one second a quantity of information equivalent to the contents of 1,100 cards, representing about a 100-fold increase in speed of reading or writing over card machinery.

On the other hand, there was the disadvantage that the tape had to be wound or unwound in order either to find a particular item or to write a result. Consequently, although tape was the most widely used medium for large-capacity secondary memory during the period now under discussion, it was soon in serious competition with the magnetic disk, which did not suffer from this disadvantage. Its role became gradually reduced to that of a medium for fallback storage in case of disaster, for holding archives, and for exchange of information between computer centers.

Magnetic disks   The idea of using as memory a disk coated on both surfaces with a magnetizable material was sufficiently attractive for several groups to work simultaneously on the development of such a device. The first attempts were made in 1948, with the aim of increasing the memory capacity of EDVAC. In these, information was written around the circumferences of concentric circles (which became known as *tracks*), but difficulties arose: first, those resulting from the variation in the linear density of the information as the distance of the track from the center varied, and second, those resulting from the problems of locating and regulating the distance of the reading heads from the disk surfaces. If the distance was too great, reading was impaired; if it was too small, there was the risk, of rubbing on the surface. These difficulties were only partially overcome during the period.

During the 1950s, two types of disk appeared. The first were rigid disks, produced by the American company Autonetics for the calculator built into the Minuteman ballistic missile. Flexible disks made of a plastic with a magnetic coating appeared subsequently; the rigidity necessary for their operation was produced by the centrifugal forces generated by the rotation. The patent for these was taken out in 1952 by the Laboratory for Electronics. The early flexible disks presented difficulties, and they fell out of use, but returned with steadily increasing success at the beginning of the 1970s.

First fixed disks   These first attempts involved the use of a single disk, usually readable on the two surfaces; a decisive advance was made in 1956 when IBM announced the coupling of its IBM 305 business machine—a machine having a core memory for only 100 characters—with a new product, the RAMAC, Random Access Method of Accounting and Control; RAMAC was delivered also with the IBM 704 and the IBM 680, and later with two machines that I shall describe, the IBM 7070 and the IBM 1401. It looked like a stack of 50 huge gramophone records on an enormous turntable, rotating at 1,200 revolutions per minute. Each disk was of aluminium coated with a magnetic substance; information was written around 100 tracks, the total capacity being 5 million characters. An arm with a reading/ writing head could be moved, first vertically so as to locate it correctly with respect to the disk from which the information was to be read, or on which it was to be written, and then horizontally along the radius of the disk, the latter spinning all the time until the required track was found. This type of action is called *direct access*, as opposed to the *sequential access* necessary with tape; the effect is [as the name implies] that access can be made directly to an item of information or to a location without any need to scan preceding items. The time required for the search is therefore much reduced; with RAMAC this was the sum of the times for the mechanical process and the reading from the track; it averaged 0.61 second, about 125 times less than the access time for information on the magnetic tapes of the period.[23] Four RAMACS could be attached to a single IBM 305, giving a total capacity of 20 million characters. Although the IBM 305 was marketed two years before the BIZMAC, it had, apart from its high-capacity, direct-access disk memory, several key advantages over the latter machine. Most important, it could be used from four access terminals, and one version was provided with one of the very first multiprocessing systems. As Thomas J. Watson, Jr., said when announcing the system in 1956, these innovations made the introduction of the IBM 305 one of the great events in the history of IBM. And in spite of its high price and relatively low speed, over 1,500 were sold (Morris [1981]).

Dispacs   In 1960 studies began to be made of a new type of information-support device that in time displaced most of the others: the exchangeable disk store. IBM, in connection with its work on the Stretch computer, had been led to consider a different configuration of the disk stack that would remove the need for the vertical movement of the read/write head. In this, a separate arm with its own head would be provided for each disk, so that each would need only to be moved radially between the disks. This was the origin of the *exchangeable disk pack*, or *dispac*, in which the stack of disks is packaged together in such a way that it can be mounted on or removed from the machine as required. Its first commercial appearance was the IBM 1311 in 1962, on the IBM 1440 small-business machine, and the idea was taken up later by all manufacturers. The IBM 1311 dispac comprised a stack of 6 disks, with 10 of the 12 surfaces used for storage of information, and 200 tracks on each surface, giving a total capacity of 3 million characters; on the IBM 1440 these packs rotated at several thousand revolutions per minute, and it was possible to have 15 million characters of information on line to the machine. Dispacs began immediately to rival magnetic tape both as information-support equipment and as the storage medium for data banks. (Figure 2.2 gives a pictorial representation of the evolution of IBM's magnetic-disk technology.)

Development of Secondary Memories: Conclusions

Addressable information supports were developed with three objectives. First of all, magnetic tapes and disks were originally produced for the sole purpose of providing large-capacity secondary memories and for this reason were often called *mass memories*. We may note in passing that the interpretation of this term has changed with time; some of the "mass memories" of this period had a capacity below some of today's main memories, while what are now called mass memories have several hundred times the capacity of the early examples.[24]

Next, once the first successful devices had been made, the idea arose of using them for storing information in libraries or data banks. Up to then punched cards had been used for this purpose; tapes and disks would not only reduce very considerably the volume and the weight but would also make it a great deal easier to perform any operations with the information stored.

Finally, it was very soon realized that by using these mass memories, all the information needed by an organization in the course of its activities could be held permanently connected to the computer, and that the time otherwise wasted by the operators in manual handling of the tapes could be recovered for useful work.

These three objectives are still relevant today.

Access Devices Not Usable as Memory

The great increase in memory capacity would have been of little value had it not been accompanied by the development of increasingly fast

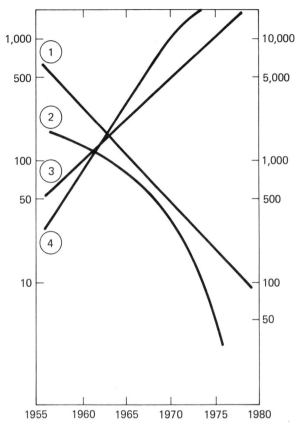

Figure 2.2
Evolution of IBM magnetic-disk technology. Legend: ①, access time in microseconds; ②, cost of storage ($) per month per megabit; ③, number of tracks per
centimeter radially; ④, number of bits per centimeter along the track.

and powerful equipment for the display of results: in effect, fast printers and visual-display screens, which are the devices still most in use.

Printers

Paper has been the main medium for the communication of results from the machine ever since William Burroughs made his Adding and Listing Machine. But the ever increasing volume and speed of production of the output have made it necessary to build special printing machinery. Machines of the classical type could not serve because they were designed with the object of first setting up a single page and then printing a large number of copies, while what is needed for computer output is the printing of a single copy of each of many different pages. To get the required speed, the output document must be composed at the pace of the computer as it produces the results, which implies what is called *dynamical printing* [or printing "on the fly"], character by character rather than page by page. This clearly has to be done at very high speed so as not to hold up the computer.

Impact printing   The first techniques to be used, called impact techniques, derived evidently from those of the typewriters that had been in use since the end of the nineteenth century. Their essential feature is that they make an impression on the paper by a hammer, or hammers, striking either a preengraved character or a set of points that together form the character, selected from a matrix.

The equipment that printed the output from the first calculators used type bars carrying preengraved characters. In this they were like typewriters. But the speed obtainable with such equipment is only a few tens of characters per second, which is ill matched to the speed of the computer; and therefore, although typewriterlike peripherals continued to be used for input of information into the machine, and are still used for this purpose, the need arose very soon for much faster equipment. The principal devices developed were the *printers*, in which both the number of type bars and the number of hammers were much increased over those in the early machines. The first printers were derived from the tabulators and could print lines of from 70 to 180 characters at speeds of a few hundreds of lines per minute; but already by 1953 the printer on the UNIVAC I printed 120-character lines at 600 lines per minute.

In some printers the characters were engraved along the generators of a cylinder or drum, the number of characters in each line being equal to maximum length, in characters, of the printed line. [Thus if the line length were 120 characters, there would be a line of 120 As, followed by 120 Bs, and so on.] As the drum turned, the hammers were positioned and struck the required characters as they passed by [so that, for example, all the As in a line were struck simultaneously, then all the Bs, and so on until the complete line was printed].

In 1960 IBM announced the IBM 1403 printer, associated with the 1401 computer. This had an endless chain engraved with five complete alphabets of characters, rotating at very high speed in front of the paper, and with 132 hammers located at each printing position and controlled so as to strike the required character in the required position. The reliability, speed, and low price for its time of this printer was undoubtedly one of the reasons for the success of the IBM 1401: the many IBM 1403s still working in many parts of the world are proof of its robustness.

In 1962 IBM produced a modification of the IBM 1403 in which the chain was replaced by an oscillating bar on which the characters were engraved. With this it was possible to change the character set simply by changing the bar, and even to increase the speed by using a shorter bar. This was the IBM 1443; it too had a great success, in spite of the low speed that resulted from the mechanical limitations imposed by the oscillatory movement of the bar.

In order to increase the number and variety of character sets, what are called *matrix printers* were developed. A matrix of dots was used and each character—whether a letter, a figure, or any other symbol or graphic element—was formed by causing very fine hammers to strike the appropriate selection of dots. The first such printers were made by IBM toward the end of the 1940s, as output units for calculators; but what was considered the most typical of this class was the IBM 730 printer, produced in 1957, with a speed of up to 1,000 lines per minute. It was considered a marvel of mechanical engineering at the time; thousands of steel wires and cams were used to build up a character one dot at a time. But it was a delicate and expensive piece of equipment.

Nonimpact printing   Impact techniques, which are intrinsically slow because of their dependence on the movement of many pieces of mechanical equipment, such as hammers, chains, bars, and so on, began to lose some of their importance when new techniques based on electronics appeared. Much higher printing speeds became possible with these latter—for example, 30 pages per second, each 12 inches in width of line of type, with the IBM 3800, in contrast to only one such page per second for the IBM 1403. Further, the reliability of such printers was much greater than the mechanical types and the power consumption much less. Two main types are now in use, laser printers and ink-jet printers. They are very expensive, however; Myers [1971] has suggested that, other things being equal, the day will come when a free computer will be offered with each purchase of a printer—but that is not yet.

There are several million printers today around the world.

Visual Display Screens

A modern fast printer can pour out as much as 2 miles of paper an hour. But very often a user wants to know results that are of only momentary interest and does not want to keep a record of these. Thus it soon seemed desirable to find some other way to communicate these results. Cathode ray tubes (CRTs), much used since 1945 in laboratory oscilloscopes and radar scanning equiment, formed the basis for this and were being used as visual display screens on the earliest computers. Thus on EDSAC, oscilloscopes were used to display the contents of the delay-line memory; and in the Whirlwind computer incorporated into the SAGE air-defense system, a radar screen enabled enemy aircraft to be identified as such by comparing the information picked up by SAGE with that on the flight plans of friendly aircraft stored in the computer memory.

Such screens were soon used to ease the task of the operator of the computer, who has to watch the progress of a calculation and may have to intervene from the machine's *console*. It seems that IBM was the first to do this in the Naval Ordnance Research Calculator (NORC), a machine built specially for the US Navy and inaugurated on 2 December 1954 by von Neumann. This had what was actually a television screen to help the console operator. Visual display screens are now found on the majority of computer operating stations. From these display screens have developed the *graphic terminals*, the use of which is growing continuously.

To conclude this discussion of the attempts made to reduce the volume of paper produced by the computer, we may note that in France in 1963, which is during the second computer generation, SEA explored the use of photographic film as an output medium. They designed what they called the *numerograph*, a piece of apparatus that converted the binary numbers provided by the computer into decimal and wrote these on a CRT at the rate of 6 digits or symbols per millisecond; these images could be photographed by a motion-picture camera mounted on the frame of the CRT. Unfortunately this all came too soon and only two were built.

3 Conclusion

By the end of the first generation the efforts made toward developing the various types of information-support equipment had clearly borne fruit. In 1948 both ENIAC and the IBM SSEC had main memories of a few hundred bits capacity; in 1957 the IBM 704 had a million bits, and from then on memory capacity was measured not in bits but in words or characters. Auxiliary memory capacities had by then increased from some thousands of bits to several hundred million.

Similarly the first attempts had then been made to use software to improve the exploitation of memory hierarchies. Paging was the first step taken in this direction, and with its use the hierarchy could be made to appear to the user as one single memory with a continuous address system. We should recall that in a paged machine the page containing the instructions next to be executed was transferred automatically into the main memory from the less expensive secondary memory, where it was held when not needed.

At this stage memories had become fast and reliable enough for it to be realistic to embark on new applications of the computer and for the first attempts to be made at setting up what we now call data bases. The very modern idea arose of making all the information that might be needed by a business organization permanently and directly available to the machine; but unfortunately the attempts made in this direction with the BIZMAC machine were held back by the inadequacy of the technology of the time and of the techniques then available for handling input and output. As we shall see, it was not until the start of the 1960s that adequate techniques in this field began to be developed.

But it was not only memories that benefited from these efforts; as we have seen, important progress was made also in the development of output equipment, such as printers and visual-display screens. We should note also that in the history of computers the period 1950–1959 was the most fruitful for the development of programming languages; we shall not say anything more about this here, but have devoted the whole of chapter 4 to this particular subject.

These efforts did not lead to any slackening of the development of the central processing units; the technology may not have changed fundamentally, but the performance improved steadily, as is shown in table 2.3.

If we take the time for an addition as a measure of the speed of the processor we see that for the two Univac machines this speed rose during the first generation from 500 microseconds (2,000 additions per second) for UNIVAC I to 30 microseconds (33,000 additions per second) for UNIVAC III. If we use the multiplication time, we see that MARK I needed 3 seconds to multiply two numbers of 10 decimal digits, the IBM 650 about 2 milliseconds, the IBM 701 about 450 microseconds, and the ERA 1101 260 microseconds. The NORC in 1954 took 30 microseconds. Thus by this measure there was an increase of 100,000 in 10 years; and the increase has continued ever since, as figure 5.1 in the concluding chapter shows.

Thanks to this progress, the field of applications of computers broadened to take in regions that previously had been looked on as being on an intellectual plane beyond their reach: for example, artificial intelligence, games, character recognition, and proof of theorems. In 1952 Turing wrote a chess-playing program for the Ferranti MARK I. In the same year a machine was built that for the first time could recognize shapes. This was the work of Jack Rabinowitz of the National Bureau of Standards; it was completed by the Diamond Ordnance Fuze Laboratory.[25] And it was still during the first generation that the Americans Allen Newell, J. C. Shaw, and Herbert A. Simon, with their Logic Theory Machine, gave the first demonstrations of automatic proofs of mathematical theorems.

The effect of all these improvements was above all that it became possible to offer machines to the business world that were adapted to its needs and could be used with confidence. From the start, business machines had as many users as scientific machines, as is shown by comparing the IBM 701 with the UNIVAC I and the IBM 702. Subsequently, business use rapidly outstripped scientific use.

By the end of the first generation, the manufacture of calculators had ceased to develop, but the growth in the manufacture of computers was in full flood. It has only been by using the technologies and the architecture of the computer that the calculator has returned, in the form of the pocket electronic calculator of today.

This technological progress, however, demanded more and more massive financial investment, and consequently became more and more the province of industry. The universities, lacking these financial resources, turned more and more toward research and development and consultation and advice. By 1959 the computer industry, which had developed from work done in the universities, was firmly established. The day of the one-of-a-kind computer had gone.

3

The Second Generation: 1959–1963

Thanks to the speed and reliability of ferrite-core memories, effort could be turned to the improvement of the throughput of computers. Processing speed was increased by the use of transistors as circuit elements in the central processors (a useful criterion for distinguishing between machines of the first and second generations). Even miniaturized vacuum tubes made the central processors of first-generation machines less reliable, heavier in energy consumption, and physically larger, and were therefore displaced by the new transistor technology, which did not suffer from these faults.

Since the beginning of the 1930s physicists had been aware that certain crystals conduct electricity in only one direction. The commonest of these is lead. Others, such as germanium and selenium, have electric properties intermediate between those of conductors like copper and nonconductors like quartz, and accordingly may be called *semiconductors*. Around 1945 it was found that amplifiers could be made in solid semiconducting materials by forming, by means of impurities, zones having either a surplus of electrons (and thus able to act as what were called *emitters* or *collectors*) or a deficit of electrons (thus forming what was called the *base*); amplification was achieved by modifying the polarization of the emitter-base junction and hence its level of electron deficiency.

Three physicists at the Bell Labs, J. Bardeen, W. Brattain, and W. Shockley, using germanium and very fine metallic point contacts, made the first transistor and gave a presentation to management on 27 January 1947. This was a fundamental invention. It was already 200 times smaller than even a miniaturized vacuum tube and, being made of solid material, was much more robust. Further, as there was no need for the hot cathode as a source of electrons, which was an inescapable cause of deterioration, it was also much more reliable.

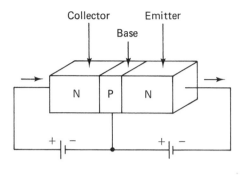

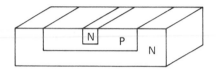

Figure 3.1
Structure of a planar transistor: (top) principle of NPN transistor; (bottom) planar
structure of NPN transistor.

Finally, it not only consumed much less energy but also dissipated
much less heat. From 1947 to 1957 the material most used for transistors was germanium; this was then gradually replaced by silicon,
which had the advantage of forming a surface layer of quartz when
heated in an atmosphere of oxygen. This layer not only provided
electrical isolation but also protected the device from the environment
by encapsulating it in a very thin covering.

At the beginning of the 1960s *planar technology* began to appear, in
which the emitter, base, and collector zones were formed as plane
regions within the silicon (see figure 3.1). Small regions of impurities
were formed by injecting, for example, phosphorous through holes
in the quartz layer, and electric contacts were made by depositing
very fine layers of aluminum in channels engraved in the quartz. While
the first circuits were made from germanium transistors and diodes
attached with the necessary resistors and capacitors to single-sided
printed circuit boards, it was now possible to make many transistors
side by side on a single silicon substrate. Thus as it developed the
planar technology enabled very complex circuits to be formed on
silicon with components of microscopic size, called *integrated circuits*.
This was the origin of *microelectronics*, thanks to which the volume of
the cirucits has since 1948 been reduced by a factor of 10 every 5
years—a rate that, far from slackening, is only increasing.

The first computer to use transistors was the SEAC, which was working in 1950, but in which the soldered connections always gave trouble. It was used mainly for meteorology. Apart from transistors it had 750 vacuum tubes and about 10,000 diodes; all of its logic was in germanium diodes. The second was made by the Philco Corporation, which in 1954 had produced what was called the surface-barrier transistor, the first step toward the transistors used in the second-generation machines. Shortly afterward, under a contract with the National Security Agency, they built a computer using these transistors, the TRANSAC S-1000; and then in 1956, under a contract with the US Navy, a second transistorized machine, the CXPQ. The Philco directors, aware of having made an important technological advance, decided in 1957 to put on the market a TRANSAC 2000, of which the CXPQ was the prototype. This machine, often known as the Philco 2000, was directly inspired by the Institute of Advanced Studies and, further, had a very well-developed magnetic-tape system. It had some commercial success, but the first deliveries to customers were not made until 1960, after the announcement of the IBM 7090, which we shall study later. Philco then made great efforts to produce a computer with a central processor using faster transistors. This was the Philco 212, first delivered to customers in 1963, which was able to compete with the IBM 7094 and the CDC 3600, which I shall discuss later. But the Philco Corporation lacked financial resources and had to look for help; it was bought by the Ford Motor Company, which later closed down the computer branch. The third transistor computer was undoubtedly the Atlas Guidance Computer Model 1, built in 1956–1957, which was used at Cape Canaveral from 1958 to 1961 to control the launching of communications satellites and also the first American intercontinental ballistic missiles.[1]

At almost the same time there appeared another transistorized computer, the Control Data 1604 (CDC 1604), made by a company formed by a group of engineers from Remington Rand who had previously been involved in the formation of ERA. The president of this company, named Control Data Corporation, was William C. Norris; the design of the CDC 1604 was the work of the founding members, Seymour Cray.[2] The CDC 1604 was offered as a commercial product from 1958 onward; its arithmetical-logical unit contained 25,000 transistors and 5,000 diodes, and its ferrite-core memory was 32,768 words of 48 bits each. It was sold with practically no software. Control Data offered very low prices to universities, which were stimulated by the idea of a machine for which they had to write the programs. It is possible that this first market influenced CDC's later development, for it was to become famous for its large-scale scientific machines.

Apart from these first transistorized machines, several first-generation computers, notably, the UNIVAC 1103 and the IBM 650, were using this technology at the ends of their developments. Nevertheless the second generation is considered to have begun in 1959, when several companies announced their first wholly transistorized machines.[3] These were, in chronological order from June 1959 on: GE 210, IBM 1401, IBM 1620, IBM 7090, NCR 304, and RCA 501.

Given large-capacity memories, thanks to ferrite cores, and central processors with fast and reliable circuits, thanks to transistors, designers could concentrate their efforts on improving the productivity of the machines of the second generation. This was achieved chiefly in three ways. First, there was a better adaptation of the machines to the needs of the users, with the production, on the one hand, of machines of greater and greater power and wider and wider fields of application, and, on the other hand, of smaller and simpler machines for more specific applications. One begins to speak now of specialized machines, understanding by this term machines designed to handle particular classes of problem. Then throughput was increased by the development of what were called batch-processing systems, which reduced the time wasted between separate jobs. Finally, computers were made more readily accessible to users by the development of systems that enabled their resources to be shared by numbers of simultaneous users.

1 Meeting the Needs of the Users

The first line of machines to be announced that belonged to the second generation included not only powerful universal computers, such as the IBM 7090, but also less powerful, more specialized machines such as the IBM 1620, intended for the types of scientific application encountered in engineering design offices, and the IBM 1401, which was intended for small-scale commercial enterprises that up to then had used punched-card machinery. This diversity only became greater as time passed.

The Very Powerful Machines

It was the requirements of the American government that led to the building of the most powerful computers of the period. In 1956 the US Atomic Energy Commission (AEC) invited tenders for a machine 100 times faster than any then existing and with a very low failure rate. IBM and Univac responded to this challenge, which implied producing circuits having a signal propagation time of 50 nanoseconds; the standard was on the order of half a microsecond. Only by using transistors could such a leap forward in speed be achieved, and this would at the same time give a great increase in reliability. Univac offered the LARC (Livermore Automatic Research Computer)[4] in 1959 and IBM the IBM 7030, called Stretch, in 1960. Others entered the race so as not to be left behind, for example, Bull in France with the Gamma 60. LARC, Stretch, and Gamma 60 were three pioneering machines that made innovations in many fields; I shall describe them shortly. Soon after this AEC tender a second American government agency, the Department of Defense (DOD), invited offers for equally powerful machines; IBM again responded, this time with the IBM 7090, a machine that was more evolutionary than revolutionary, and which also will be described.

The Three Pioneering Machines: LARC, Stretch, and Gamma 60

LARC, Stretch, and Gamma 60 were required for scientific applications in which the volumes of data to be handled were large and the calculations complex; their architectures had therefore to be adapted to these needs. The requirement of large data volumes poses several problems, not all of which have been solved even now. For example, should the machine be binary or decimal? What kinds of auxiliary memory should it have? How should the input/output units—which must be increasingly numerous and increasingly fast as greater demands arise—be controlled? The responses made to these questions have had a determining effect on the whole course of the history of computer development.

While general agreement had been reached in the business world that business computers should be character based, and if possible decimal, in the scientific world, in contrast, the rival partisans of binary and decimal bases never ceased to press their respective cases. Thus it is not surprising that LARC and Stretch represented the two different views. Both machines had long word lengths in order to give the necessary high arithmetical precision, but LARC had decimal words of 12 digits, while Stretch had binary words of 64 bits.

In opting for the decimal word the designers of LARC had taken two considerations into account. The first was that scientific computations could well involve the handling of much larger volumes of data than had been generally supposed and also could produce much larger volumes of output. Consequently the time lost in converting between binary and decimal would cancel out that gained by working in binary rather than in decimal. The second was that it was difficult to calculate the rounding errors introduced in these conversions. The

Stretch designers spent a long time weighing the pros and cons of the two systems of arithmetic before deciding on binary. The advantages of that choice were clear: simplification of the structure by making the machine wholly binary, greater ease of control, more compact representation of the information, and faster computation. The disadvantages, equally clear, were those just described; but they were greatly reduced by the provision of special hardware for decimal/binary and binary/decimal conversion, which removed much of the force of the arguments about the relative merits of the two systems. The effect of making this provision was so satisfactory that after Stretch the majority of computers have worked in binary.

The structure of the Stretch word was highly original. It was based on the realization that any machine intended for scientific applications above the trivial level must be able to perform both numerical operations (on numbers) and nonnumerical operations (on more general characters). The designers therefore produced a compromise between word organization and character organization in which the basic word, while indeed binary and of 64 bits, was made up of 8 elements each of 8 bits, later called *bytes*. Knowing that the more recent programming languages, ALGOL, for example, could already use alphabets of up to about 100 characters, they felt it necessary to plan for an alphabet that would include the 48 characters of the existing 6-bit code, the 26 upper-case letters, the commonest punctuation marks, certain logical and mathematical symbols, and possibly other characters—say, for about 150 to 160 characters in total. This would make it necessary to use an 8-bit character code [which would provide for up to 256 characters]. Actually, Stretch for the most part used a set of only 120 characters, for reasons connected with the design of its printer.

It was with the advent of the IBM 360 series of computers that the 8-bit byte became the basic element of both word and character machines. On these it was possible to do the arithmetical work either with "single-length" words of 4 bytes or with "double-length" words of 8 bytes, according to the precision required. On Stretch nonnumerical processing could be done with strings of characters (that is, bytes) of arbitrary lengths, though always a multiple of 8 characters: all that was necessary was to place the required number of 64-bit words together end to end, as had been done on BIZMAC.

We shall see later that a similar idea had arisen in France at about the same time in connection with the Bull Gamma 60. Here the element was the 24-bit *catène* (chain), but was less successful, being too short to be used as the basic word and too long to be used to code the characters.

To handle the large volumes of data required auxiliary memories. Stretch was richly supplied with these. We have seen already that it was the first machine to use a disk memory in the form of a stack of disks with a read/write arm for each disk. In addition a magnetic tape system called TRACTOR was adapted for its use. This could handle up to 640 tapes, each of which could hold 60 million characters, equivalent to several thousand pages of a normal book, and could read or write information at a rate of 1.5 million characters per second. Thus the distinction made in the early 1950s between business and scientific computers, which held that the first needed to be able to handle large volumes of data while the second did not, had not stood up to practical experience.

The large volumes of data also required adequate input and output units. In order to control these without overloading the central processor, LARC had what was called an *input/output controller* (*IOC*), which was itself a genuine computer—an innovation soon found in the majority of computers.

The Stretch introduced a large number of innovations into computer architecture. I have already mentioned several and shall be describing others in the course of this history; here I shall recall some of the most important. First, the addressing system. The organization into words, bytes, and bits greatly simplified the problems associated with addressing and, as I have said, has been adopted on all modern machines. Stretch addresses could be up to 24 bits long. Second, the arithmetic. This could be done either in decimal, for simple processing of data, or in binary, for more extensive calculations. Much care had been taken in the design of the floating-point operations, especially in the control of precision. Multiple precision was provided by means of a special set of instructions. Finally, the powerful interrupt-control system. This made multiprocessing possible. I shall return to this point later.

Several tens of thousands of circuits had to be used in order to provide the computational power of these three pioneering machines, and the problem then arose of how to design the connections between the members of such a large assembly. The IBM and Univac engineers attacked this problem with the aid of computers, writing special programs to lay out the connections. This was undoubtedly the first example, at least on such a scale, of what is now called *computer-aided design* (*CAD*).

Recovery from failures also presented very difficult problems. To aid in this both LARC and Stretch had, in addition to the *operators' console*, which was used to control the normal running of the machine, an *engineers' console*, where among other things information concerning incidents could be recorded; this was for the exclusive use of the team of maintenance engineers. Special diagnostic programs made it possible to identify the type of fault and the area of the machine, or the defective component, in which it had occurred. It was even possible to effect certain repairs from the engineers' console without having to stop the machine or disturb the operator or user; this was done by making appropriate disconnections and reconnections of redundant units. Here IBM had drawn on and extended the experience they had gained in designing the means for detection and immediate repair of faults in the AN/FSQ7 computer incorporated into the SAGE air-defense system. This was a real-time computer designed by MIT for the processing of the information gathered by a radar network; it had to be of very high reliability because, in spite of using 50,000 vacuum tubes, it had to work 24 hours a day continuously. The way to the automatic diagnosis of faults, which is now the standard practice, was by this time open.[5]

As well as being powerful (in the sense of having large-scale resources), the machines we are discussing had to be fast. Thus alongside the classical von Neumann architecture based on the single processing unit there began to appear an architecture oriented toward *multiprocessing*, in which several units operated simultaneously on one or a number of programs, each unit having access to common resources (such as memory). The first experiments along these lines seem to have been made at the US National Bureau of Standards in 1954, where two normally independent computers were linked together in such a way that either could act as input/output to the other.

The first commercially produced machine to have a multiprocessing capability was the IBM 305, in 1956. A pair of IBM 305s could share a single RAMAC memory, each having its own read/write arm; as was clearly necessary, there was an instruction that prevented either arm from attempting to read from a location already being used by the other. But the machines that were most famous for this activity were the LARC and the Gamma 60, on which for the first time on such a scale different processors shared the same resources, especially memory.

In the LARC multiprocessing took place at two levels. First, there was a separate computer for handling all input and output activities, which went on while the central processor was carrying out other tasks; I shall return to this problem when considering input/output processing. Second, at the level of processing in the truer sense of the term, LARC had two units that could work independently of each other; the aim was to increase the overall processing speed by a factor of up to 2 by a suitable sharing of the work between the two processors. This was to be done automatically without any intervention by a human operator, and the two parts were to work simultaneously; but the task of actually doing this proved so difficult that the right balance between the two units was seldom achieved. The organization of LARC is shown schematically in figure 3.2, where we see the various lines that carry the information flows between the different units that make up the machine; these are called BUS in figure 3.2

Multiprocessing was not confined to Univac machines, however. Just at the time of the Department of Defense's invitation, the Bull company was aiming to get into the top league in computer production with a machine that would be able to process several programs, independent or otherwise, simultaneously; this was to be achieved by sharing the work among several units specialized to deal with certain tasks and capable of working independently. The machine was the Gamma 60, the central units of which were formed of transistor circuits (Davous, Bataille, and Harrand [1960]).

The architecture of Gamma 60 provided for three main activities: (1) organization of the main memory; (2) multiprocessing; (3) coordination between processes and allocation of resources. We consider these separately.

Main memory   This was of from 1 to 8 blocks of 4,000 words each, each word being 27 bits, of which 3 were for control purposes. It had a very original organization, similar to that of byte-organized memories. Here, instead of the byte (8-bit), the organization was into *catènes*, chains of 24 bits, which could represent a 24-bit binary number, 6 decimal digits, or 4 6-bit characters from an alphabet of 64. The cycle time was 10 microseconds. The memory would hold at any moment not only the information used by the program then being executed but also the information transmitted between the various functional units as was required to meet the needs of the multiprocessing.

Multiprocessing   This was made possible on a scale not achieved on any previous machine by means of the independent functional units; among these were the following:

1. Equipment concerned with the input and output of information, able to take control of, and later release, input/output units. (These latter were card readers and punches, paper tape readers and punches, printers, typewriters and inquiry keyboards.)

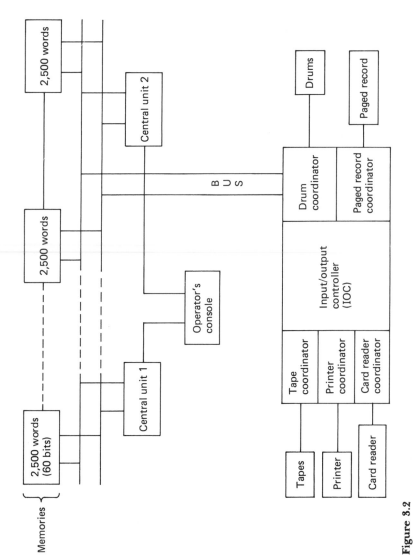

Figure 3.2
Block diagram for LARC.

2. The actual processing units. An arithmetical unit carried out arithmetical calculations to base 10; this was checked by calculating the residues modulo 7, which was a very original idea.

3. A logical unit, which analyzed instruction codes and logical statements.

4. A translator, which performed translations between codes, packing of information, page layout, and display.

All these pieces of equipment could work independently; to make this possible, each was provided with the necessary control circuits, instruction processors, and memories to ensure its total autonomy and to enable it to exchange with the main memory whatever information it needed.

Coordination   Special circuits provided the coordination between the various processing units (see figure 3.3). The functional units were linked to the main memory and to the coordination circuits, respectively, by two bus lines called *channels* by Gamma 60 designers, the term not having acquired at that time the sense in which it is now used in connection with the handling of input and output. The first bus, which we may call a collector, took information from the functional units to the central units of the machine, that is, the main memory and the coordinating circuits; the second, from these central units to the functional units.

Requests by the functional units to access the main memory were handled by two circuits that included selection mechanisms. One dealt with input data, called "quantities" by Gamma 60's builders, and gave the lowest priority to those coming from the slowest input units (typewriters, for example) because these could be made to wait without risk of loss of time. The second dealt with requests made by programs in course of execution, and the relative priorities here were set by the user.

Gamma 60 was not without its defects. First, a minor defect was that it used an enormous amount of power. Second, users had to study in advance the courses their calculations would take so as to find out which processes could be performed simultaneously; this was a difficult task, made more so by the lack of a high-level programming language. Gamma 60 was put on the market with a language scarcely at the level of an assembler. By the start of the 1960s, most computer manufacturers had provided highly developed languages, such as FORTRAN and COBOL, with their machines, whereas Bull did not provide compilers for ALGOL and COBOL until the end of 1962.[6] Finally, the

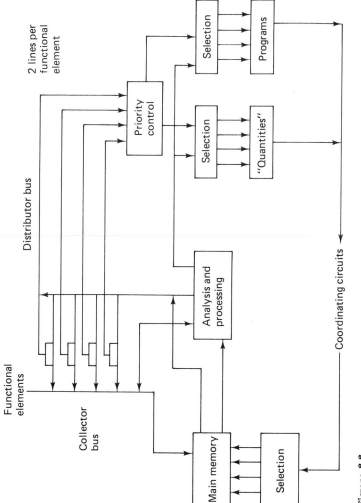

Figure 3.3
Block diagram for Gamma 60.

solution represented by Gamma 60 was not entirely satisfactory; there was an imbalance between the needs that had to be met in the course of handling a problem and the capabilities of the hardware, with the result that often much of this was idle, although the needs were not being met.

Gamma 60 was innovative in almost every field; consequently, bringing it to a satisfactory state of operation was difficult, and it was not marketed until 1960, a year later, it was said, than had been planned. Further, it seems that Bull did not have the financial resources to develop simultaneously the machine, the advanced operating system that it required, and the programming languages. The French government did nothing to help, and only a dozen machines were built. One may speculate on the course the French Plan Calcul might have taken if it had been designed around SEA and Bull, with their high technical standards and Bull's strong commercial position in Europe.

According to S. Rosen [1969] only two models of LARC were sold, one each to the US AEC and Navy at $6 million each; and 8 of Stretch — one to the French Commisariat à l'Energie Atomique — at $8 million each. The fact is that LARC and Stretch came up against the same difficulties as do all machines in which both the technology and the architecture are completely new and for which the benefit of prior experience is lacking.

The IBM 7090 Series

With its IBM 7090, IBM avoided the need to make innovations in all fields. This machine, almost as powerful as LARC or Stretch, was developed in response to the invitation for tenders issued by the US Department of Defense in 1958. The requirement was for machines that could analyze very quickly the data provided by the antimissile defense system, Ballistic Missile Early Warning System (BMEWS). As the delivery times were very short and the penalties for delay were very high, IBM seemed to be in a poor position for this business because its Stretch was much too costly and was unlikely to be produced in time; nevertheless, IBM accepted the challenge and undertook to deliver before November 1959 a machine based on the IBM 709 but five times as fast and more precise. It was called the IBM 709TX.

In making these commitments IBM took into account the studies they had made for Stretch, particularly those concerning the development of very fast transistor-circuit central processors and core stores with cycle times less than 2 microseconds. The required precision could be obtained by using the Stretch word of 64 bits together with its additional 8 bits for error detection and correction, either as two 36-bit words or, if need be, as one double-length word of 72 bits. IBM won the contract by offering to develop the BMEWS programs in advance for the IBM 709, so that the IBM 709TX machines could be used immediately after installation—a striking demonstration of the value of compatible machines.

Thus began one of the grandest races against time in the history of the computer. In November 1959 the difficulties seemed not to have been overcome, and the IBM 709TX was not entirely ready. However, at that period the time needed to install a machine was on the order of several weeks. IBM delivered the machines to the site on the required day, and with them there arrived a team of engineers (20 according to one account, or 200 according to another—the extra zero is of some importance) for the task of finishing the work. This was done with complete success. This success raised other problems however. The first IBM 709s had just been delivered to customers, mostly on rental; if IBM was to include the 709TX in its catalogue, it would run the risk of having its customers give up the 709 in favor of the new machine. But at the same time other transistor machines, faster than the 709, were being offered, in particular the CDC 1604. IBM therefore decided to take the risk and offered the 709TX as a commercial product, with the name of the IBM 7090. The result showed that this was the right decision; the IBM 7090 was a truly remarkable machine, and in particular, was very reliable. Over 400 of them were made at an average price of $3 million (McLaughlin [1975]). We may note that it was cooled by water, and not by oil, as were the IBM 704 and the IBM 709.

In 1962 IBM developed the IBM 7090 into the IBM 7094, a slightly faster machine differing mainly from the IBM 7090 in having 7 index registers; this may seem a surprising number, but one must remember that while the number of such registers provided in various machines varies over a wide range, it is usually of the form $b^n - 1$, where b is the base of the machine's number system and n is an integer. Thus for binary machines there are usually 1, 3, 7, . . . , and for decimal machines 9 or 99. Index registers became the standard means for modifying addresses in instructions and were provided in increasing numbers; thus with IBM's scientific machines there were 3 on the IBMs 650, 704, 709, and 7090, and then 7 on the IBM 7094. When the number became considerably greater, they were grouped together in a single memory unit, as was the case with the 99 registers of the decimal IBM 7070.

Before finishing this account of the 7090 I must mention two related machines, the IBM 7040 and the IBM 7044, first delivered in 1962–1963; these were less powerful than the IBM 7090 but also much cheaper, and became very popular. Several modifications of the IBM 7090 were made in order to reduce the price; one, in the basic version of the IBM 7040, was to provide only indirect addressing for address modification, which enabled the same manipulations of addresses to be performed as with index registers, but less conveniently. Index registers could be provided as an optional extra. The IBM 7040 and IBM 7044 were used either as independent computers or in conjunction with the IBM 7094; one special arrangement for this latter use provided a memory-to-memory link between the two machines, so that the IBM 7040 handled all the input/output traffic, while the IBM 7094 carried out the processing tasks transmitted to it by the IBM 7040.

Influence of the Top-of-the-Line Machines
After the second generation, such features as engineers' consoles, channels, bytes, and multiprocessing were found on the majority of machines. These were not the only innovations; the software written to exploit the resources of the second-generation machines was the forerunner of the operating systems of today's machines. I shall take up these points again shortly, after a consideration of ways in which these general-purpose machines were adapted to meet the special needs of certain classes of users.

Three Bottom-of-the-Line Machines
The adaptation just mentioned was brought about by the manufacturers providing machines at the bottom of their lines, which, in contrast to the universal machines at the top, were intended for particular applications. I shall consider only three of these, all of which became very popular in varying degrees: the business machine IBM 1401, the real-time machine PDP 1, and the scientific machine CAB 500.

The IBM 1401
The ideas for this machine were formed in IBM's development laboratory at La Gaude in Alpes-Maritimes, France; the aim was to ease the introduction of computers into business enterprises that up to then had been using punched-card office machinery. A prototype was produced in the form of a calculator linked to an IBM 1402 high-speed card reader/punch for input and output, and thus no longer using a plug board for that purpose. The development of this into a stored-program machine was done in the United States.

The IBM 1401 took over the basic character-oriented structure of the IBM 702, but with the addition of many special features. One of these was the *word mark*; one bit of the 8 in which the IBM 1401's characters were coded was reserved for the indication of whether this was the last character of a sequence and thus could indicate the end of a record forming an item of input data.[a] Another was the provision of variable-length instructions, the importance of which will be seen in the next chapter; some of these simplified the specification of the layout of printed results. The minimal version was called the card IBM 1401, a very simple machine having only the IBM 1402 card reader/punch as I/O unit and neither magnetic tapes nor disks; the attraction of this machine was its relatively low price. Its great success undoubtedly started the move to the use of computer equipment in the business world.

The power of the card IBM 1401 could be increased by the addition of magnetic tapes, it being possible to connect up to 10 transports; as a result, the IBM 1401 was often used as an auxiliary machine in a large system. The tapes could be read or written at speeds ranging from 20,000 to 62,000 characters per second. A third version could have magnetic disks with capacities of 10 or 20 million alphanumeric characters with an average access time of half a second (Masson [1960]).

The IBM 1401's memory was on ferrite cores, the capacity being originally between 1,400 and 4,000 characters and later increased to 16,000; all transfers to or from the memory were done character by character at a speed of 11.5 microseconds per character. The machine was fairly fast, with speeds of 2,500 additions of 8-digit numbers per second, 520 multiplications of either 6-digit or 4-digit numbers, and 4,200 logical decisions per second.[7] As I have said, data-processing devices aimed at the medium-scale business world had a very great success; the IBM 1401 was the first computer of which over 10,000 were sold.

Two successors to the IBM 1401 were the IBM 1440 and the IBM 1460. These had the same architecture and the same memory capacity as the IBM 1401 but used faster circuits. The IBM 1440, with a memory cycle time of 11.1 microseconds, was less powerful than the IBM 1401 because of its simpler and more limited input/output equiment; the IBM 1460, with a cycle time of 6 microseconds, was rather more powerful. These were followed by the IBM 1410, again with the same architecture but much more powerful; it had a cycle time of 4.5 microseconds and a memory capacity that could go up to 80,000 characters.

The PDP 1

Another important field for which specially adapted computers were developed was that of real-time operation. One of the very first companies to build computers for this field of applications was the Digital Equipment Corporation (DEC), formed in 1962 and now one of the world's most important computer manufacturers; it was founded by

Table 3.1
Characteristics of the first two PDP computers

	PDP 1	PDP 4
Project leader	Benjamin Gurley	Gordon Hall
Starting date	Summer 1959	November 1961
First deliveries	November 1960	July 1962
Word length	18 bits	Same as PDP 1
Memory capacity	4,096–32,768 words	Same as PDP 1
Memory cycle	5 microseconds	8 microseconds
Computing speed	100,000 instructions per second	Same as PDP 1
Number of components	3,500 transistors, 4,300 diodes	
Instruction format	Operation code 5 bits, 1st address 12 bits, 2nd address 15 bits	Same as PDP 1
Power consumption	2,160 watts	1,125 watts
Languages	Editor, macroassembler, DECAL (ALGOL compiler)	Assembler, editor, FORTRAN
Number built	50	65
Price (4,096 words memory, paper tape reader, IBM typewriter)	$120,000	$65,000

Ken Olson, who had worked at MIT on Whirlwind, and his brother Sam in association with their friend Harland Anderson. DEC at first made what were considered minicomputers, the name being applied because, apart from their small size, they did not need an air-conditioned environment. They were marketed under the name PDP [Programmed Digital Processor] followed by a serial number; the PDP 1, designed by Benjamin Gurley in collaboration with John McCarthy, was produced in 1962 for the Bolt, Beranek & Newman Company. Table 3.1 gives some of its characteristics, together with those of its successor, the PDP 4.[8]

The PDP 1 had the best cost/performance ratio of any real-time computer of its period, a fact that underlay its success. It was also the first commercially produced computer with a graphical display screen— which was abandoned in the PDP 4. The PDP 1 had an ingenious means of direct access to the memory, the *high-speed channel*, found also on the PDP 4; the reason for this was that sequential access was too slow for real-time applications, and disks, which would have avoided this difficulty, were not yet in sufficiently general use.

The main uses of the PDP 1 and PDP 4 were in the fields of laboratory experiments, data processing in connection with industrial design, and message switching.

The CAB 500

It was in the field of scientific applications that the first true minicomputers appeared. Mainly for reasons of cost, the personal, exclusive use of the computer by a single individual had ceased by the beginning of the 1960s, except for the relatively cheap machines at the bottom of the manufacturers' lines. These were the minicomputers, so named to contrast them with the top-of-the-line machines. They were physically small for the period, needed only very modest air conditioning, and could be installed in an ordinary-sized room—hence the name office-size computers. The machines most characteristic of the type were the IBM 1620 and the CAB 500, the latter being designed by Raymond and made in France by SEA. I shall describe only the CAB 500 because this, like all the machines produced by SEA, had many original features.

The CAB 500 was built with transistor circuits and had for main memory a drum with 128 tracks, each holding 128 binary words; the word length was 33 bits, of which 1 bit was for error detection. Calculations were done in a group of 17 ferrite-core registers having an access time of 2.5 microseconds. Input and output were by means of a Teletype, which could be used in two modes:

1. Direct communication between the keyboard and the computer, in which mode the user could input programs and data and could receive, in clear text, responses to questions. This was called *office machine mode* at the time, and is what we should now call *conversational mode*.

2. Indirect communication by means of punched paper tape, which carried the programs and data and was read into the computer by the Teletype's reader. Correspondingly, output could be punched on to the tape and printed on the Teletype.

A high-level language, PAF, was developed for conversational use of the machine by D. Starynkevitch.

Another interesting feature of CAB 500 was that it was both microprogrammed and microprogrammable. As we know, a computer has specialized units that perform the primitive operations of which every algorithmic process is composed—transfer operations, operations on one or more operands, and so forth. These units are not normally accessible to the user. There is a basic language, called *machine language*, in terms of which the manufacturer builds up more complex operations, called elementary operations, from sequences of primitive operations;

it is usual to give the name *code* to the set of elementary operations expressed in the machine language. Since the days of the first computers, every elementary operation was realized by means of circuits that, under the direction of the control unit, activated the appropriate primitive operations. Thus the machine-language code consisted of a set of elementary operations, represented in material form by a set of circuits.

In 1951 Wilkes [1969] suggested a means of simplifying the control unit by the use of what he called *microinstructions*, corresponding to the primitive instructions; we now call the set of microinstructions the *microcode*. Programs for complex operations could be written in terms of these microinstructions and stored in the memory; Wilkes called such programs *microprograms*. This would give programmers a certain amount of freedom to design their own machine language and thus to avoid being totally dependent on the manufacturer's choice of code. Some scientific users were in face beginning to feel uneasy about the small size of the code in several machines (see table 3.3). In addition to this advantage, microprogramming could enable the computer to be adapted more specifically to the application for which it was being used.

Although microprogramming was described in 1951, it was only rarely incorporated into computers during the 1950s (Rosin [1969]), for several reasons. First, the technical reasons. With the wired-in elementary instructions just described [that is, these instructions represented by circuits], the process of executing an instruction starts with the reading of the relevant code from the memory and placing it in the control unit, where it is decoded into a sequence of control instructions. These then, one by one, activate the logical elements of the circuits that correspond to the relevant primitive instructions. In a microprogrammed computer, on the contrary, there are in principle no wired-in elementary instructions; all the microinstructions are held in the memory, and the task of the control unit is simplified to transferring control from register to register as required by the microprogram for the complex operation. However, for this to be of value, the access time to the memory must not be too long; otherwise too much time is lost in reading one microinstruction after another in order to build up the required operation. For this reason there was no significant development of microprogramming until after 1964, when, especially with the IBM 360 series[9] main memory was built with ferrite cores for which the access time, while certainly greater than the times taken by the control circuits, was comparable with these.

There were also reasons that were almost ideological. For example, hardware specialists believed that there was an essential difference between microprogramming and ordinary programming. The former, they held, required different skills from those of the good programmer in the usual sense of the term; in particular, it required close attention to problems of synchronization of operations and a knowledge of the properties of the hardware so that these could be exploited most effectively.

The widespread use of microprogramming did not come about until the manufacturers, driven by the need for compatibility among their machines, began to develop *emulators*, that is, microprograms that enabled one machine to perform the machine-language operations of another, possibly of a different manufacturer. One of the first examples of this was the Honeywell 800, which was microprogrammed to emulate the IBM 1401; this contributed to the success the Honeywell machine had when the IBM 1401 was replaced by the IBM 360 series.

In the CAB 500 the microprograms were held on the drums along with the other programs, and the machine gained great flexibility from the fact that the two could be used in identical ways. The production of this microprogrammed and microprogrammable machine as early as 1960 was one more proof that there was then already in France an industry that, if not ahead of the Americans, at least was not systematically behind. Unfortunately, although the CAB 500 had some success and about 50 were made, it disappeared with the demise of SEA.

Microprogramming, however, formed only a small part of the effort put into the adaptation of the machine to the particular needs of the user; as we have already seen, this adaptation was achieved mainly by the development of a variety of architectures, on the basis of which machines ranging from special to general purpose could be built.

2 Batch Processing

This tailoring of computer architecture to the users' needs could not itself have ensured the growth of computers if it had not been accompanied by the development of software that both improved the throughput of the machines and eased the tasks of the programmers, who up to this time had to write themselves all the instructions needed to control the running of their applications programs. The components of the *batch-processing systems* [which took over these tasks] were the following, in the order in which they appeared: monitors, parallel processing, interrupt control, input/output processing, and, finally, multiprogramming.

Monitor Systems

In order to make it possible for a computer to work, a basic program has first to be put into the memory, which can then, in turn, initiate the reading of more complex programs and their data from the input units and control the placement of these in the memory. This basic program is called the *loader*, and the intructions that read it into the memory are necessarily wired into the machine. This was done for the first time on EDSAC, the loader for which occupied 31 locations in the memory.

Programmers wishing to use EDSAC would first punch their programs in binary code onto paper tape, and to this they would add, in the appropriate places, further lengths of tape punched with subroutines. They would then check that the previous user had not left anything in the machine and would set the various control switches to the states required. And finally, given that the loader was already in the machine, they would read in the programs and start their execution by pressing the appropriate buttons. Clearly a corresponding set of actions would have to be gone through in the case of a machine using punched cards as input medium. It is evident that with such a procedure the amount of time lost between one program and the next is considerable; this loss became unacceptable as the speeds of the central processors increased.

There was already on the Harvard-IBM machine a programming system that made it possible to introduce subroutines into a program punched onto a consecutive set of cards; this enabled programs for elementary algorithms, written independently of the main program, to be used without rewriting. Also Wilkes [1969] and his team had advocated the formation of libraries of subroutines as the fundamental need in all programming work; and on EDSAC the symbolic address notation made it possible for the addresses of the memory locations into which the subroutine instructions were to be placed to be assigned automatically (see chapter 4).

However, manually changing from one program to the next slowed down the use of the machine and was the source of many errors. It was with the aim of making this change automatically without any need to clear the machine and then reload the next program that link-monitors were devised, the first of which, as we have seen, appeared on the IBM 704. The tasks to be performed were now batched together one after the other, and the monitor processed them on the

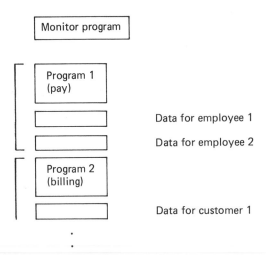

Figure 3.4
Monitor system.

principle of "first come first served"; it had the capability of abandoning
a program when an error was encountered during its execution and
passing on to the next, so that this did not stop the machine (see
figure 3.4)

By reducing the amount of dead time between programs, this primitive batch-processing system reduced the average time between the
submission of a job and the output of the results; also, it increased
the percentage utilization of the machine's resources. Thus it increased
the throughput of work. But it also reduced the number of operator
errors because it reduced the number of manual operations that had
to be made. For all these reasons such systems were very much used
from 1955 onward and were provided on almost all machines after
the end of the first generation.

Even so, these first monitors had their drawbacks. For example,
they required the jobs to be grouped together in such a way that it
was difficult to insert an urgent one, no matter with what flexibility
the work had been planned. These drawbacks disappeared only gradually during the decade 1964–1974.

Concurrency
Batch processing alone would not have given sufficient improvement
in the utilization of machines' resources without the development of
software that made it possible, to some extent, for different tasks to

be performed simultaneously. The first computers worked almost entirely sequentially and in general did only one thing at a time; thus the fastest constituent, meaning usually the processor, was fed by a single slower unit, such as an input device, and was badly underused. To alleviate this constraint sharing the work between the fast and the slow units was arranged so that the two groups could operate simultaneously. This concurrency led to a better utilization of machines' resources by reducing their idle times; resource sharing and parallelism are thus two aspects of the same problem.

We can distinguish between local and nonlocal concurrency. *Local concurrency* refers to the partially or wholly simultaneous execution of an instruction together with some number of its neighbors in the program. An example is *look-ahead*, which consists of the simultaneous decoding, during the execution of a program, of an instruction and some number of those that follow it; it appeared for the first time on the IBM SSEC, which could deal with three instructions at a time, but was abandoned in the von Neumann machines. It required that the logical elements in the control circuits be faster than the memories. Local concurrency did not appear again until the second generation, on LARC, Philco 212, and Stretch, when transistors were used for the circuits of the central units. Look-ahead on Stretch was achieved by dividing the main memory into separate parts that could be accessed separately and simultaneously, and took in six consecutive instructions.

Nonlocal concurrency refers to the simultaneous execution of instructions that need not be neighbors in a program and that may belong to completely independent programs. It can be provided only on machines with units—processors, input/output units, and so forth—that can operate simultaneously and independently. I have already given examples of such concurrency in describing the arrangements for multiprogramming on LARC and Gamma 60, and so shall not discuss that type of implementation further.

E. F. Codd, the IBM engineer now very well known for his work on relational data bases (Codd [1962]), has described the operation of nonlocal concurrency by comparing it to a workshop where there are several machines (equivalent to the separate units of the computer) and several jobs to be done (equivalent to the programs to be executed). Each job (program) is composed of a number of tasks. Several tasks can be carried out simultaneously on several machines, and at any given instant the tasks being carried out on the different machines can belong either to the same job (program) or to different ones. It is not difficult to see that if it is possible to carry out tasks belonging to different jobs at the same time, it will be easier to balance the load on the workshop as a whole than if this is not possible.

Achieving such a balance poses difficult problems. For example, unless special precautions are taken, it is virtually certain that, sooner or later, an error in one program will result in some unexpected change in another. Also, it imposes a whole set of constraints on any system of concurrent processing, in particular, the following:

It must be possible to suspend the running of any program, at any time; this implies that there must be an *interrupt-control* system.

The input/output-processing system must be able to share the services of these units between the different programs according to their needs.

When multiprogramming is provided, there must be no possibility of interference between programs, especially when several can run at the same time.

I shall now study how these conditions were partially satisfied; for this I shall describe successively the development of interrupt control, input/output processing, and, finally, the first multiprogramming systems.

Interrupt Control
The normal running of a program may be interrupted unpredictably for a number of reasons; this can occur, for example, because the program needs an item of data that has to be read from a peripheral, it needs to call a subroutine, or a program of higher priority has to be executed. Such occurrences are called *exceptions*, every one of which leads to some modification of the course of the program being executed. If the occurrence of the exception leads to the halting of this program and its transfer to another part of the memory, the address of which is in some way linked with the occurrence, this is called an *interrupt*. One of the earliest machines to be equipped with program interruption was the UNIVAC I in order to process arithmetic overflow.

As a matter of fact an interrupt always results in a delay to the processing. On the first machines the majority of the exceptions, especially those requiring some human intervention, such as the mounting of a magnetic-tape reel, involved stopping the machine; but from the ERA 1103 onward machine-state indicators were provided that made it possible for each exception to be handled by a specially written program without human intervention. The main program could then be taken up again and continued from the point at which it had been interrupted.

The essential requirement was that any program that had been interrupted could resume its normal course after the cause of the interrupt had been removed; this was the aim of the first system to be built for handling interrupts, which was developed at the Lincoln Laboratory, mainly by Wesley Clarke, and appeared on the MIT machine TX2 in 1954. Upon interruption, control was given to one of 25 possible programs written to handle special interruption cases. The first extensive use of interrupt control in commercially produced machines was on the IBM 7090 and IBM 7070 and was derived from the work done for Stretch. This last machine had in fact the first full system for handling interrupts, from which all modern systems are derived. It provided, for example, a great deal of protection to the central processor from risks arising from input and output operations. Among other innovations it introduced the *mask*, a collection of bits by means of which programmers could specify the conditions under which the exceptions could interrupt the running of their programs.

Input/Output Processing Systems
The first software was written with the objective of easing the programmer's task in overlapping input/output operations with each other and with operations of the processing units: for example, to enable a number of records scattered over several magnetic tapes to be consolidated into a single block or a program to issue an instruction to read or write and then to continue running. But in spite of this the tasks remained burdensome until the end of the 1950s because the manufacturers had not until then provided adequate systems for handling input and output.

The Need for Such Systems
In the course of input or output operations a great deal more information than merely the data items is exchanged between the computer and the I/O units; there are many control signals, and as the speed of computers has increased, the volumes of these have become considerable. Thus it is necessary, among other things,

to specify the peripheral to be used,

to check whether it is available, and if not, for what reason,

to start the transmission of the message, character by character, checking that no errors occur,

to check that the end of the message has been reached, or if not, to find the cause of the difficulty,

to assemble the message into words, and

to find the memory locations where these words are to be stored.

For most of their time the first computers had only paper-tape readers and punches for I/O peripherals, usually connected directly to the machine. An instruction to connect to one of these peripherals would be issued by a program during its execution, in order to read data items or to write results.[10] In the MARK I machine such operations were done through the accumulator and therefore could not be done at the same time as any other operation; also, to preserve the correct sequence, if an instruction called for the reading of data from a card or tape, then no other instruction could be obeyed until after this reading had been completed. In general, once a program had issued a read or write instruction and the connection to the relevant peripheral had been made, it had to halt and wait for the operation to be completed.

In these first machines all the input and output operations were controlled directly by the central processor. This reduced its throughput of work, not only because it had to devote a significant amount of its time to this activity but also because the peripherals were much slower than itself. Users tried to improve the situation by incorporating instructions into their programs that allowed some computation to be done while a read or write operation was going on; but this was a difficult task for the average programmer, and in any case it increased the time needed for writing the program. It also made editing and checking a program more difficult because the extra detailed instructions that had to be written could amount to over 50 percent of the total.

As the number and variety of peripherals increased, the constraints imposed by the input and output operations would have held back the development of computers had not three innovations been made. One was the increase in the speed with which information could be exchanged between the computer and its peripherals, brought about partly by a certain amount of automation of the operator's functions and partly by increases in speeds of the peripherals themselves. Another was the reduction of the load on the central processor, brought about by a modification of the machine's architecture following the introduction of what is now called the *channel*. And third, an overlapping between the running of some programs and the operation of the peripherals was brought about by the development of systems for the control of peripherals that relieved the programmer of more and more of this task.

Speeding Up the Transfers

Initially the users of the first computers had to supervise for themselves the majority of the operations involved, such as putting their programs and subroutines in the appropriate places or connecting and disconnecting such peripherals as readers for magnetic tapes, paper tapes, or cards. These tasks were soon handed over to operators, who carried them out in accordance with instructions written by the programmer; the latter would need to help when the work became too complicated. Some of these tasks had become partially automated by the end of the 1950s, mainly because libraries of programs were then available on tape and loader programs had been developed that could find the required routines and read them into the machine at the right moment.

At the beginning of the 1960s it was realized that printing results or reading cards by means of *on-line*—that is, directly connected— peripherals slowed the machine; the practice therefore developed of using an *off-line*—that is, independent—computer for the purpose of transferring information from cards or paper tape to magnetic tape, which was then loaded [at much higher speed] into the main computer [and correspondingly for printing results written by the main computer on magnetic tape]. These operations were referred to as card to tape, paper tape to magnetic tape [tape to printer], and so on. The IBM 1401 was often used in this way, as noted previously. A machine as powerful as the IBM 7090 would often have as many as three IBM 1401s associated with it for organizing input and printing output; IBM had adopted a uniform coding scheme for characters on all its machines, so as to avoid the problems that arose in connecting the peripherals of the IBM 704 on the IBM 705 (see section 2.2). The throughput of the peripherals themselves was increased also, by increasing the speeds of reading and writing. For example, the IBM 1402 card reader used with the IBM 1401 had a speed of 850 cards per minute.

Thus while in 1954 a computing installation would consist of a computer with a small number of directly connected peripherals for input and output, by the end of the second generation the amount of off-line equipment had become so great that from the point of view of cost, space occupied, power consumption, and so on, the central machine was no longer the most important component. From then on the totality of the central machine and its peripheral equipment became known as a *computer system.*

Development of the Channel

Speeding up the peripherals was not enough to meet the needs, however, and buffer memories were introduced in which input could be held without needing to go through the machine's central registers: as we have seen, this was first done in the UNIVAC I. The program then communicated with the buffers instead of with the peripheral, and the information there was copied into the main memory at the access speed of the buffers. Of course, if at that moment the buffer had not received all the information, the program had to wait and thus was slowed down; but in practice most of the time otherwise lost in input was regained.

Buffer memories are still used a great deal today, particularly in printers. Nevertheless there are drawbacks, quite apart from cost, and in spite of everything the procedure does delay the central processor, for the reason that this is occupied exclusively with controlling the transfer between buffer and main memory during the entire time required by this transfer, and cannot do anything else in this interval. It was to reduce this loss that the idea of the *simultaneous channel* was formed. With this, if a program needs data, or to put out results, the central processor puts all the information relevant to the required transfer into a special unit, the channel: for example, the address of the word to be output or received, the number of words to be transferred. The channel then takes over from the central processor the whole task of organizing the transfer. It is *simultaneous* because, having received its instructions, it carries them out independently of the central processor, which meanwhile can continue with other work.

As we have seen, the first use of special processors for handling input and output was on the IBM TRC; but this was only the first step toward the development of the channel. It seems probable that the first experimental channel was made in 1954 by a young IBM engineer Bob Evans for a 704 in connection with work on the control of intercontinental ballistic missiles (ICBMs). In the same year IBM installed a channel in the AN/FSQ7 computer of the SAGE air-defense system; and in 1958, for the first time anywhere, IBM offered the channel as a commercial product with the IBM 709. Up to 6 channels could be attached, making it possible to load or unload the fast memory while processing continued. Further, when a channel became available it was possible to say which of the devices connected to it and waiting to use it should have the highest priority.

This achievement of a significant measure of independence between the processing of programs and the handling of input and output was one of the main characteristics of the 1954–1964 period. It is often said that if the term second generation has any real meaning, it must be with reference to the period that began with the appearance of the channel.

Input/Output Control System (IOCS)

However, there were such stringent constraints associated with the use of channels that it was difficult for programmers to take advantage of them. There was no real reason why programmers should concern themselves with what was in fact a routine task, and it was in order to relieve them of this necessity that input/output control systems—

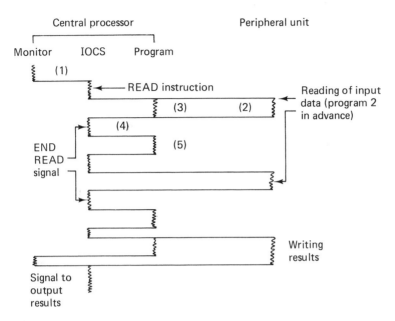

Figure 3.5
IBM monitor and IBSYS I/O control system.

IOCS—were developed for most computers; these were general programs that organized the simultaneous running of input/output operations with some of the processing. Further, they improved the reliability of computed results by performing systematic checks on input and output and could correct some types of error, a task that programmers usually found too burdensome to undertake.

The IBM System IBSYS

A further step in this direction was made by IBM with the IBSYS system for the IBM 7094. With this, the monitor, before handing control to a program, gave this first to the IOCS—see (1) on figure 3.5—which then instructed the appropriate peripheral to read in the data (2); IOCS then allowed the program to start (3). When all the data had been read and were in the memory, the peripheral signalled this to IOCS (4) and control reverted to the program (5).

Input/Output Controllers

As channel processing developed, it became necessary to make use of ancillary computers, which, although small in comparison with the machines to which they were linked, were nevertheless of significant size in comparison with the general run of machines of the time. The first such use was in connection with real-time applications of the IBM 7094, to which a "satellite" computer, usually an IBM 7040 or IBM

7044, was connected to form what was called a direct coupled system, (DCS); the same was done later with the IBM 7074, the satellite in this case being the IBM 1401.

Univac engineers had included an input/output controller in LARC. This was a small ancillary computer that, apparently, communicated directly with the central processor and controlled 8 channels to which were connected 4 magnetic tape units, 5 drums, card readers and punches, fast printers, and so on. Subsequently almost all machines had similar facilities, the ancillary computer or computers being either incorporated into the main machine or separate from and external to it. This reduced the load on the central processor arising from the needs of input and output to a few general tasks, such as optimizing the sharing of memory between the channels, the sharing of work among peripherals—for example, assigning a magnetic-tape unit when the programmer has not specified which is to be used—and dealing with special cases.

Multiprogramming

In spite of all these improvements computer throughput continued to lag behind need; the next advance to be made came from multiprogramming. It can happen that a program needs a large amount of data and that the input operation, initiated by IOCS, is not completed by the time the information is wanted, so that the machine has to wait. One way of avoiding wasting time in this way is to start a second program—that is, to resort to *multiprogramming*. The term seems to have been used for the first time by N. Rochester [1955] to describe a way in which the tape record coordinator in the IBM 705 might be used to cause data to be read from a tape while the processor works on another task; it was used later to describe simultaneous input/output and processor operations. The related term *multiprocessing* was used for the first time apparently in a description of LARC. While in multiprocessing several units of the machine are working simultaneously on instructions belonging either to a single program or to several, all of which are able to access the memory or other common resources, in multiprogramming several programs are worked on in turn by a single central processor while other operations are being carried out by other units of the machine (for example, the input/output units). Thus the utilization of the central processor is increased because it shares its activities among several programs at the same time as slower operations are going on elsewhere in the machine.

The essential aim of multiprogramming is thus to bring about non-local concurrencies—between either input/output operations and run-

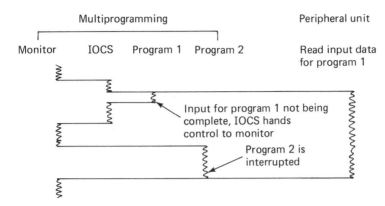

Figure 3.6
Multiprogramming.

ning a program by the central processor or handling several independent tasks by the various units of the system. In figure 3.6 there is certainly multiprogramming because the processing of a program and several input and output operations are going on at the same time; but it is more multiprocessing than multiprogramming. Although there are similarities between these two activities, the latter term is used to mean that each in turn of several programs has the attention of a single central processor.[11]

Machine Architecture and Special Software
A computer must be specially designed for multiprogramming to be possible. It must have, for example, a main memory large enough to hold all the programs that are to be run together and also their data; and the access time of this must be very short so as not to waste unacceptable amounts of time in storing and recalling the programs. There must be very effective means for protection of memory addresses to avoid errors [which would result from interference between programs]. There must be an adequate provision of consoles, display screens, and so on. And finally, the machine must be extremely reliable; if only one program is run at a time, a hardware error affects only that program and is easily located; but with multiprogramming the same fault can affect any number of programs, often in an unpredictable way, and thus can be difficult to correct.

Stretch was the first machine to provide multiprogramming proper; the majority of multiprogrammed machines have taken up its interrupt-handling system, involving the use of a mask, and its method of protection of memory addresses. Other machines of the second generation were designed for multiprogramming, some of which will be described in other parts of this study;[12] here I shall say a little about one machine, the Honeywell 800. This machine had a three-address instruction word that eased the task of multiprogramming by clearing its location after execution. It could deal simultaneously with 8 programs, the overlapping of which could be done at the level of the individual instructions; for this there were 8 sets of indexing operations, with 8 counters enabling the state of any program to be known at any instant. But the three-address structure turned out to be impractical. The instruction word was 48 bits long, but each address was only 8 bits; more than this would have been needed to refer to a large enough number of memory locations, but this would have made the word much too long. For this reason such a structure is seldom used in multiprogramming machines.[13]

As well as special architecture, a multiprogramming machine must have special software. The most difficult problem with which this has to deal is the supervision of the different programs. Such software did not exist until after 1964, when, using the experience of IOCS and IBSYS, IBM produced the unified *operating system* (OS) for the IBM 360 series of machines. This was for a long time the only system to have both wide scope and great power.

Limitations of Batch Processing

The possibility of executing several tasks at the same time on a single processor—or, what was still more difficult, on several processors— gave rise to a number of serious problems, in particular those arising from programming errors. A program behaving erratically could adversely affect others; it was more than twenty years before such difficulties were completely overcome and the conditions proposed by Codd completely fulfilled. However, with or without multiprogramming, batch processing and its corollary, concurrent processing, made possible a considerable increase in the throughput of computers; it became very quickly the way in which most computers were used.

But it was not without drawbacks, of which the most serious was undoubtedly the inevitable delay between submitting one's program, say at a reception point where the different jobs were batched together, and getting the results. This made the development of programs particularly difficult. Users of the computer centers of the early 1960s cannot recall their experiences without feelings of irritation. They would hand in a program, hoping that the operator would deal with it immediately and put it in the next batch to be run; filled with this hope, they would come back for their results several times during the day, until at last the program had been run. But alas! often there were no results, just a diagnostic message from the computer saying that there was an error in the program text — for example, a comma where there should have been a full stop. All the users could do then was to rush to the nearest card punch, correct the card with the error, and resubmit the program, hoping it would be run in the next batch; and so on, until the results appeared.

While batch processing is scarcely ever used now in program development, it does still find some application when response time is not very important. An example is the need, at a stated time, to carry out stated processes with large files of data, such as payroll, billing, monthly accounts. Making up and checking accounts would be more difficult to do by other systems of operation.

Batch processing led to the development of "service bureaus," companies that sold machine time or contracted to undertake particular processing tasks for their clients. By improving the throughput of the machine, batch processing reduced the average cost of individual tasks; thus users who needed to use a computer but who did not have enough work to justify machines of their own could get the work done at lower cost by sharing the bureau machine with other users.

3 Direct-Access Shared-Use Systems

The need to work through an operator in order to gain access to the computer was a step backward for users when compared with the way they had been able to work during the first generation. But starting in the early 1960s systems allowing the kinds of simultaneous operation just described also allowed users direct access once again, the economics of this now being justified by the sharing of resources among many users. This was first done (in, for example, controlling a number of experiments by a single machine) with real-time systems developed from the very first machines, such as Whirlwind. I shall not say any more about this type of use, even though it was found in some very prestigious applications, such as landing men on the moon; I shall focus, instead, on systems that followed soon afterward.

The early view of a computer was that it was a machine on which users could first develop and then run programs; but it soon became clear that the combination of computer and program could be an extremely powerful tool in the hands of users who need know nothing about computer science but who want simply to process their data with the aid of the program and are content to take on trust from the specialists all details of the method. Thus two classes of user appeared in these early 1960s. One was the class of computer specialists, a group of whom would share the machine for program development, each effectively unaware of the existence of all the others using the machine at the same time. The other was the class of users who were not computer specialists, a group of whom would share the use of application programs and data. We shall study these two types of use in turn, and afterward the means provided for communication between the user and the machine, because neither type of use would have been possible without these means.

Shared Use

What was so frustrating for the users of batch-processing systems was that it seemed to them that the machine's time was regarded as more valuable than theirs; and even so, the machine's time was not well used because for the most part a program used only a small fraction of the machine's resources. It was natural therefore to look for means by which several programmers could use the same machine at the same time, and for this to be made possible, special hardware and software would have to be designed, so that the several users need not be aware of each other's presence. This led to the development of what were called *time-sharing systems.*

John McCarthy and Marvin Minsky at MIT initiated proposals for several systems; some of these were aimed at making the best possible use of existing machines, such as those developed first for the IBM 704, then for the IBM 709 and IBM 7090; others involved completely new developments, such as that for the PDP 1.

One of the very first time-sharing systems was that developed under F. Corbato's direction at MIT in 1961, first for the IBM 709 and then for the IBM 7090; neither of these machines had been designed with this type of use in mind. This was the Compatible Time-Sharing System (CTSS), a software system that was held in the main memory. When a user asked to run a job, the system extracted the program from the backing store, executed it, sent the results to the user's terminal, and returned the program to the backing store; and during this time it was always ready to respond to another request coming from another terminal. Since most of the work consisted of students' exercises, which required only a few seconds of machine time, each student had the impression of monopolizing the machine's use. In addition to the normal advantages of a monitor system, CTSS in its final version provided its users with very powerful facilities for loading, editing, and developing their programs.

A system of this type can be called *conversational* because it enables a question-and-response type of dialogue to take place between the user and the machine, without undue delay between question and response, as in an ordinary conversation. It is also *interactive* because the programmer is able to intervene during the running of the program: for example, to halt it in order to change an instruction or the value of a data item.

If a user tried to develop a long-running program on a system such as that just described, the response time for other users would soon become unacceptably long. A time limit was therefore imposed, at the end of which the program was halted and control handed over to another. One of the first systems to include this feature was that developed for the PDP 1. Here, when a program had run for 140 milliseconds, as measured by an internal clock, it was halted, taken out of main memory, and copied on to one of the 22 tracks of a fast drum; the capacity of each track apparently corresponded to 4,096 words of main memory. The next user's program was then called in, as in fact happened if a program was interrupted for any other reason. The transfer to the drum and the recall each took 33 milliseconds.

It turned out in practice that exceeding the time limit was not a common reason for returning a program to the drum; this was because programmers would usually break down their programs into small sections and submit a new section only after studying the results of running those preceding it. Further, in the PDP 1 conversational system, as with all shared-use systems developed since then, each terminal had a buffer memory in which input and output messages were stored. When a message input on the terminal was complete, the contents of the buffer were added on to the end of the queue of programs waiting to be run. But often there was no queue; it was only occasionally that a program had to wait because, as we have seen, in the conversational mode of use the programs are usually short.

These early systems had their drawbacks, however. The main memory, for example, was used inefficiently, most of it being empty when a small program was running; it was the same for the central processor, which spent most of its time moving programs in and out of the main memory. These drawbacks were overcome to some extent with the aid of techniques developed in Manchester and used for the first time in the Ferranti Packard 6000 (FP 6000).[14] The FP 6000 had a main memory of from 4,096 to 32,768 words of 24 bits each with an access time of from 2 to 6 microseconds and could run four programs at the same time (Marcotty, Longstaff, and Williams [1963]). The memory was not organized in pages as in the Ferranti Atlas, but instead each program stated the amount of memory that it needed, and at an appropriate moment this amount was assigned to it. The difficulty clearly was to determine which program to move out of the main memory and into the backing store in order to leave room for the incoming program.

Time-sharing as the standard mode of use of the computer for program development had to await the arrival of the IBM 370 series. These machines incorporated the ideas of pagination and virtual memory found in the CTSS, study of which had been taken up by the IBM Scientific Center in Cambridge, Massachusetts, in 1964, which later collaborated in this work with the IBM France Scientific Centre in Grenoble after this had been formed in 1967.[b]

On-Line Systems

The second main type of direct-access system consisted of what were called *on-line systems*; these were shared-resource, conversational systems that were not necessarily interactive. Here users shared the same data and the same programs, which imposed certain constraints on the structure of the latter. In an MIT internal report of 1954 entitled "The Multi-Sequence Program Concept" (Fredkine [1963]). W. Clark showed how a subroutine could be written so that it could be used by any program without any change being necessary to meet the particular needs of the program using it. J. C. Licklider [1960] called such subroutines "pure procedures."

Very often the users of such systems not only shared the resources but dealt with exactly the same problem. The commonest instance of this was that employees of a single organization, without any technical knowledge of computer science, would use a terminal to enter data and questions to a machine that could be hundreds of miles away and would get their responses almost immediately: the mode of use here would be interactive. The first commercially produced machine to allow this type of use was the IBM 305, which could be accessed by four terminals at distances of up to 1,000 yards. As IBM said, management and staff could now for the first time use a terminal to a distant machine to pose a question concerning inventory, accounts, production, billing, sales statistics, and so on and get a response almost immediately on the same terminal. A rather amusing demonstration was given at the international exhibition in Brussels in 1956: questions on the main events in the history of the human race could be put to "Professor RAMAC" from any of the four terminals and in any of ten languages, and the reply was given in the same language.

The best known on-line system was that developed by IBM and the American Airlines company between 1956 and 1962, as a joint research project, for the handling of airline seat reservations; this was SABRE, Semi-Automatic Business-Related Environment. With this, American Airlines were able to tackle the problems associated with making reservations for passengers on their routes. Here is an illustration of the problems. In 1960 the company carried 8.615 million passengers, for whom the reservation of seats involved 26 million telephone calls covering the whole area of the United States. It had proved so difficult to keep manual daily flight records of which seats were taken and which were free that it had become the practice to leave a certain number of seats vacant on every flight up to the time of departure, so that if passengers arrived with reservations that as a result of an error had not been recorded, they could still be given a place on the flight. This resulted in a significant loss of revenue; and loading of the aircraft was often reduced still further as a result of lack of time to record likely cancellations. SABRE made it possible for everything concerning the sale and control of air travel to be done in real time, from the moment of the first telephone contacts with passengers to their arrivals at their destinations. The necessary data were supplied by means of a system of 1,200 terminals connected to a central computer and located in travel agencies; these latter were given all the information that the customer might need, such as flight number, times of departure and arrival, type of aircraft, meal service, likely delays, and so on.

The communications system for SABRE involved 12,000 miles of telephone lines, with multiplexors each controlling up to 10 long-distance lines.[15] Comprehensive control software had been developed specially to deal with the identification of the terminal, the requests made, the sending and receiving of messages, and so on. Multiprogramming was on a scale never before attained, with up to 30 programs being handled simultaneously at times.

SABRE ran 24 hours a day, 365 days a year; the necessary reliability was ensured by there being two IBM 7090s, one duplicating the other to guard against failures. Each had 32,768 words of main memory, in which the control programs and the messages in process of handling were held. The main programs were very large, over 100,000 words; they were held in the backing store and called into the main memory as needed. The secondary memory included a magnetic drum of 7.2 million characters capacity on which all the information relating to a flight—number of seats sold or still available, date, time, airport, type of aircraft, and so on—could be held temporarily. The total body of information was held on magnetic disks, a capacity of over 500 million characters being provided. Finally, a complete historical record was preserved by copying all the memories onto magnetic tape periodically and storing this in an archive.

The body of information available to the computer was organized as a data base, and users could get immediate access to the data they needed without having first to read through other records in order to locate these. This illustrates the point that a data base demands not only hardware with sufficient storage capacity to hold the large volumes of data that will be involved but also special software for its interrogation and for general handling of the data. SABRE provided one of the very first examples, and on a very large scale, of that association of a data base with a communication system that has since become a characteristic of modern information technology; it is referred to as data base/data communication, DB/DC.

The characteristic features of SABRE are found in the majority of present-day on-line systems. They are

1. dedicated hardware: when SABRE was running, the machine could not be used for any other purpose;

2. a supervisory program for the particular application, written specially in a low-level language (see chapter 4) in order to give fast responses to inquiries;

3. a comprehensive system for managing the data base;

4. a comprehensive system for managing the communications network;

5. orientation of the complete system to use by people with no knowledge of computers or computer science.

Features Common to On-Line and Time-Sharing Systems

From the start, these two classes of systems have had many points in common, the most obvious of these being that in both there are many users of a single machine, each effectively unaware of the presence of the others. The difference between the two systems has been decreasing, with time-sharing systems providing more and more in the way of shared data, files, and programs in order to lighten the task of the programmer. Nevertheless there are differences. The use of an on-line system [in contrast to that of a time-shared system] is characterized by the following:

1. The users never develop programs, and in fact know nothing about programming.

2. The tasks to be carried out by the machine are known in advance, and the times required are known, at least to a good approximation.

3. The resources required for any task are known in advance.

4. The response to an inquiry must be almost immediate; but users must accept that occasionally they will have to wait a few seconds.

5. All access is made via files, whose formats are fixed and which are relatively few in number.

6. There is a formal organization of the files, and the programs are written for real-time processing; this is not the case for time-sharing systems.

Data Communication

Time-sharing systems could not have developed as they did without improvements in the means for communication between users and distant machines. For such a system to be effective it must be possible for whatever information is relevant to a task to be input at the user's terminal and communicated to the machine with minimum delay and the results of the processing returned to the user, again with minimum delay.

The means first used for communication with computers were the existing telephone and telegraph lines; it was only later that special data-communication lines were provided. The basic problem with transmission of data is that the signal is discontinuous, in contrast with the continuous signal of, for example, voice communication over the telephone. As we have seen, data are usually represented in terms of a binary alphabet, which simplifies the receiver's task of detecting the signal in the presence of noise because it has only to distinguish between two possibilities.[16] Somewhat offsetting this advantage is the fact that in the methods of communication that we normally use, the voice, for example, there is a great deal of redundancy in the signal; there is much less in data communication between two computers because the need is only to overcome the noise on the lines. The speed of data communication can be much greater than that by voice because both transmitter and receiver are machines.

The numbers and types of channels used for data communication have increased steadily ever since the first computers appeared; the types of channel used include cables, radio aerial arrays, and satellites. One of the first transmissions across the Atlantic was made from the IBM Research Laboratory at La Gaude, near Nice in France, in September 1962, using the TELSTAR satellite that had been launched on 10 July 1962. But to make it possible for these channels to transmit data, the signal must first be put into a form that they can handle— for example, by modulating it in amplitude, frequency, or phase (with the inverse transformation being made at the receiver). These operations are carried out by two pieces of equipment: a *modulator* at the transmitting end and a *demodulator* at the receiver; the process is shown in figure 3.7. As the two are usually housed together in one box, the combined device is called a *modem*, short for modulator-demodulator. It seems that the first commercial modem was that built for the IBM Transceiver, described below. In the following discussion two types of data transmission are distinguished, according to the mode of use of the line. These are *point-to-point*, referring to transmission between two and only two stations, and *multipoint*, referring to transmission between a single master and two or more remote stations sharing a single line. In a multipoint system transmissions from the master are received by all stations, but transmissions from any one station are received only by the master.

Point-to-Point Transmission

In a data-communication system the data to be transmitted are sent out from some information-support device in the transmitter and go into a corresponding device in the receiver. In the majority of installations in the early 1950s the input/ouput buffer in the computer at the transmitting end acted this way, and thus the transmission process was supervised by the computer. There was therefore an imbalance between the speeds of the computer and of the transmission, particularly great because, on the one hand, the process took place almost always over the slow Teletype network, and, on the other, because the receiving device was a paper-tape punch, which was very slow. To overcome this disadvantage IBM in 1954 produced the Data Transceiver, an off-line device that for the first time enabled data to be transmitted directly from punched cards and to be punched directly onto cards at the receiving end. It was also the first device to use leased telephone lines. Use of this equipment speeded up the transmission and relieved the computer of the task of supervision. Then in 1960 IBM produced the IBM 7701 Synchronous Transmitter Receiver (STR), also an off-line device, with which data could be transferred between magnetic tapes at a speed comparable with that of reading the tape and thus of a different order from the speed of the Data Transceiver.

Multipoint Transmission

Clearly the off-line systems just described were ill-adapted to multipoint transmissions. Thanks to SAGE a leap forward in multipoint communication was achieved in the early 1950s. This system included about a million miles of communication lines and several thousand graphical terminals (Soffel and Spack [1959]), organized around a set

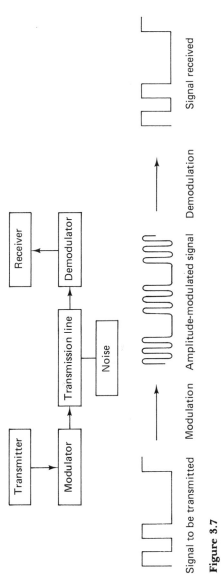

Figure 3.7
The classical communication channel.

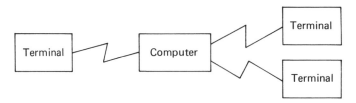

Figure 3.8
A second-generation communication system. The broken line signifies a transmission line.

of AN/FSQ7 computers built by IBM to the design of MIT. Each computer had a real-time data interface, and the results of processing the data were sent to a weapons system that itself was controlled by a specially designed computer, the AN/FSQ8; each of these latter communicated with the nearest AN/FSQ7. This represented the first true *computer network*—a term by which one understands a geographical distribution of terminals, often numbered in hundreds or thousands, spread over tens or hundreds of localities and linked to one or more computers (even if in SAGE there was at first only one master computer).

The development of communication systems was accompanied by that of terminals specially adapted to these needs of particular applications. An important example is the terminal for over-the-counter financial transactions, first put into service by the First National Bank of Chicago in 1962. The computer used was the IBM 1410, which, as we have seen, was a more powerful derivative of the IBM 1401 (see figure 3.8)

Management of a Data-Communication System
The efficiency of a data-communication system clearly depends upon the quality of the management of the communication links between its components. This involves a large number of activities, the essential features of which have already been indicated in discussing the closely related problems of input and output; the following are a few examples:

1. Interrogation of the terminals at regular intervals, to find whether they are ready to send or receive messages.

2. Assembling of messages in a buffer, first one bit at a time to form a character, then one character at a time to form the message; the processor deals only with complete messages.

3. Transformation between the code used by the transmission line and that used by the computer; it is possible to have different types of lines and of terminals in a single system, with the result that data may be transmitted in different formats and at different speeds.

4. Control of errors in transmission, and so on.

Throughout the first generation and for most of the second, the users themselves had to write the software to manage their communication systems; but at the start of the 1960s the manufacturers began to provide computers specially designed to undertake some of this work of management. These included *message switching machines*: the Control Data 8050/8090, the General Electric Datanet 30, and the IBM 7740. These machines could receive messages from distant terminals and perform such tasks as analyzing the information to determine th destinations to which these should be sent and making whatever code conversions were necessary in order to use the lines over which they were to be transmitted. Their scope was limited conpared with what is available today; few machines had been built at that time that provided a true interface between the computer and the network, what we now call a *front-end processor*, or to act as a *line concentrator*, the function of which is to receive incoming messages from a number of slow lines and dispatch them on a single fast line. There were nevertheless some machines that simplified the programming of these functions, for example, the Collins Data Central, made by the small Collins Radio Company in 1963.

To conclude, an important point is that these special, communications-oriented machines did not have enough memory capacity to deal with some of the tasks required by the messages they could receive. This processing possibility had to await the third computer generation; it is generally referred to as *distributed intelligence*.

4 Conclusion

We have seen in this chapter how the techniques of computer science came into general use during the period of the second generation. The most prestigious applications were certainly those of NASA in their use of large computers for the conquest of space, such as the Burroughs Atlas for the Atlas mission and the IBM 7094 for Gordon Cooper's 22 orbits around the earth in 1963. But it was the small machines that spread the new technology. It has been estimated that the total value of the installed equipment in 1964 was six times what it had been at the end of the first generation. Further, improvement in productivity was achieved partly by a broadening of the manufacturers' lines so as to make machines available that were better adapted to particular uses, and partly by the development of ever larger bodies of software for the control and exploitation of the machines' resources.

Table 3.2
Characteristics of some second-generation computers

	Type[a]	Word length (bits)	Number of words	Memory type	Access time (microseconds)
Gamma 60	O	24	8–32k	Ferrite	10
Burroughs 5000	B/D	13	4–32k	Ferrite	6
			32–65k	Drum	8,500
CDC 1604	B	48	8–32k	Ferrite	4.8
CDC 3600	B	48	32–262k	Ferrite	1
Honeywell 800	D	12	4–32	Ferrite	6
IBM 1401	D	Variable	1.4–16k	Ferrite	11.5
IBM 1620	D	Variable	20–60k	Ferrite	20
IBM 7030 (Stretch)	B	64	16–262k	Ferrite	2.2
IBM 7040	B	36	4–32k	Ferrite	8
IBM 7070	D	10	5–10k	Ferrite	6
IBM 7080	D	Variable	1k	Ferrite	1
			80–160k	Ferrite	2
IBM 7090	B	36	32k	Ferrite	2.18
IBM 7094	B	36	32k	Ferrite	2
PDP 1	B	18	4–65k	Ferrite	5
Philco 2000–210	D	8	8–32k	Ferrite	11.5
			32k	Drum	25,000
LARC	D	12	100	Ferrite	1
			10–97k	Ferrite	4
			6,000k	Drum	68

a. B = binary; D = decimal; O = octal.

Times for basic operations (microseconds)			Price in US dollars (millions)	Number of instructions in code	Number of addresses per instruction	Number of index registers	Indirect addressing?	Floating point?
+	×	÷						
200			1.5		1–3		Yes	Yes
10	37	63	0.5–2	115	Variable	0	Yes	Yes
7.2	25.2	65.2	0.750	62	1	6	Yes	Yes
2	6	14	1.4	92	1–2	6	Yes	Yes
24	150	312	0.980	51	3	64	Yes	Yes
230	2,100	2,600	0.125	43	1–2	3	No	No
56	496	1,686		32	2	0	Yes	Yes
1.5			5–7		1	16	Yes	Yes
16	33.5	18.5	0.625	73	1	3	Yes	Yes
72	924	792	1	200	1	99	Yes	Yes
11	100	253	2.1–3.8	106	1	0	Yes	Yes
4.36	4.36–30	6.54–30	2.9	227	1	3	Yes	Yes
4	4–10	6–18	3.1	268	1	7	Yes	Yes
10	20	30	0.120	28	1	0	Yes	Yes
14.8	69.9	73.8	1–2	225	1	8	No	Yes
4	8	28	7	76	1	99	Yes	Yes

The broadening of the line of machines is illustrated in table 3.2, which gives the basic characteristics of a selection of machines (Auerbach [1961]). We see that one indication of this broadening is the spread of prices, from about $100,000 to several millions, a ratio of nearly 110 : 1; another is the similar spread of speeds. The spread of the number of instructions in the codes for machines at the two ends of the range is less, from about 30 to a few hundreds; but this is no less important, and the smallness of the number of instructions provided in the bottom-of-the-line machines explains the interest that developed in microprogrammable machines. The variations in the amounts of main memory are much less important, because the mastery of the process of manufacture of ferrite-core memories had made it possible for small machines to be given quite large memories (for the time) if that were needed. The access times varied by less that 10 : 1. The need for adaptation to particular demands has resulted in a continual increase in this spread. Thus today it ranges from the microprocessors used for innumerable applications—digital watches, washing machines, personal chess-playing machines, and so on—to ever more powerful computers with speeds of several million instructions per second and main memories of several million bytes. Compared with these, Stretch and LARC are minicomputers.

At the same time as this development of basic hardware was going on, work was being directed toward improving the productivity of the computer by modifying the classical von Neumann architecture. Multi-processing appeared during this second generation, a mode of use now so common that it is difficult for us to recall that it took so long to develop, more than a decade. The channel also appeared and came into general use during this period for the handling of input and output; and also data-communication systems, forerunners of the huge computer networks of the 1980s. But the activity that most characterizes the period is the development of system software with the aim of improving the efficiency of use of machine resources. This led to the idea of batch processing and to its widespread use; and to the appearance of on-line systems, although these presented such difficulties that they did not come into general use until the 1970s.

These innovations made increasingly heavy demands on software; the amounts that became necessary would have been unimaginable a decade earlier. Two numbers will illustrate this (see figure 3.9): In 1955 the whole body of programs for the control of the IBM 650 comprised about 5,000 instructions; in 1959 the corresponding number for the IBM 7090 was little short of 1 million. The size continued to grow; in 1964 the operating system for the IBM 360 had several million

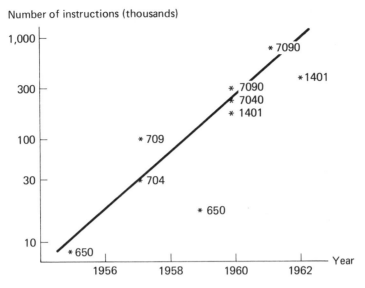

Number of instructions (thousands)

Figure 3.9
The increasing complexity of software, illustrated with second-generation IBM computers.

instructions, that for the IBM 370 at the beginning of the 1970s had over 10 million, and for the big machines of the 1980s the need was for about 20 million instructions. For the first time programs were produced that were too big for any one person to understand fully; the software for the SAGE system took 6,000 man-years to produce, the operating system for the IBM 360 took 5,000 man-years. Only an industrial organization could undertake a task of this magnitude, and in fact it became necessary for the computer manufacturers to produce their system software themselves, just as previously they had been led to produce the machines themselves.

As the technology has evolved, it has become possible for the processes of hardware construction to be increasingly automated; but there has been nothing corresponding to this in the case of software, which has always had to be written by hand, so that its cost has decreased very little. There was practically no decrease in cost in the few years before 1980, no method having been found that would lead to a significant increase in the speed with which correct programs can be written. Further, the fraction of the cost of a system attributable to the software has continued to increase ever since the start of the second generation; thus what was 15% in 1955 became an estimated 50% by the end of the second generation, rising to 80% by the end of 1979 (see figure 3.10)

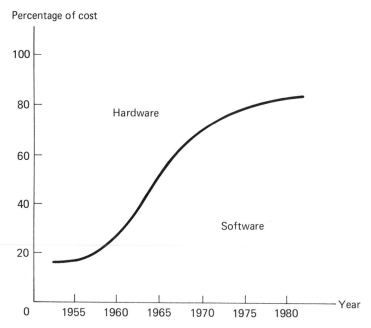

Figure 3.10
The changing relation over time between hardware costs and software costs.

The role of the universities changed during this period. Previously they had been the places where prototype machines had been built and their uses tested out, but this became too heavy a task. They therefore turned their attention to the new problems that, because of the lack of theoretical understanding, were delaying and defeating the programmers. For example: How should program construction be organized so as to cope with such large numbers of instructions? How can one make certain that a control program will do what it is supposed to do? How can one test it for correctness? As a result, they began to develop, among other things, abstract concepts that led to a better understanding of programs and operating systems and to a greater mastery of their construction. In the study of the evolution of programming languages in the next chapter, many examples will be given of this symbiosis of academic and industrial research.

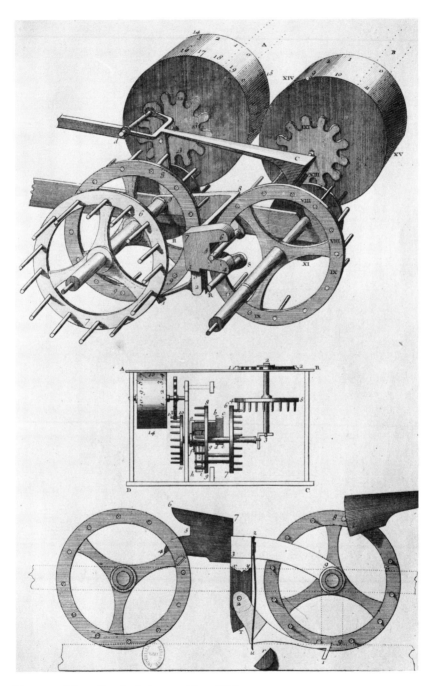

Diagram of Pascal's calculating machine, 1643.

Earliest example of a loom operated by perforated tape, 1728.

Business office with punched-card machinery, 1930.

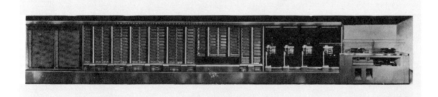

The IBM ASCC (Automatic Sequence-Controlled Calculator), better known as the Harvard-IBM MARK I, 1944: length, 51 feet; height, 8 feet; weight, 10,000 pounds.

The ENIAC (Electronic Numerical Integrator and Computer), 1946.

John Presper Eckert. (Courtesy IBM Archives)

John von Neumann. (Courtesy IBM Archives)

Thomas J. Watson, Sr. (Courtesy IBM Archives)

Wallace J. Eckert. (Courtesy IBM Archives)

Herman H. Goldstine. (Courtesy IBM Archives)

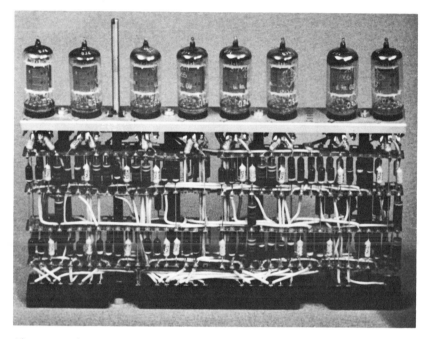

First-generation computer circuitry: tubes.

Second-generation computer circuitry: transistors.

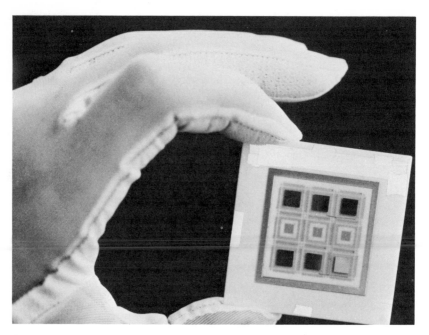

Current computer circuitry: chips.

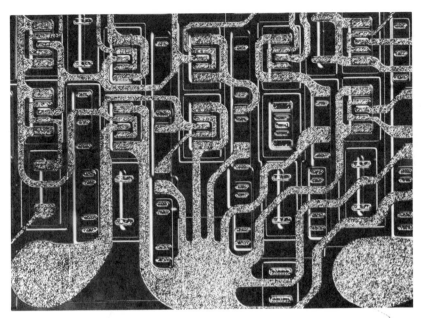

Chip under a microscope: area approximately one-hundredth of a square inch.

4

Programming Languages

The user communicates with the machine by means of a programming language. These are of two main types: those intended for systems programming, and therefore used for writing the software that controls the basic resources of the machine; and those intended for the solution of problems on the machine and called *problem-oriented languages* (*POL*). From the abstract point of view, the first type is only a special case of the second, and therefore only these latter will be considered.

As a generalization one may say that a language sets up a correspondence a set of concepts to be communicated to the machine, termed "signifieds" and "signifiers" by De Saussure, and here "sources" and "targets," respectively. The sources are the statements of operations required, and the targets are the corresponding instructions given to the machine. The set of the targets is said to be the "vocabulary" of the programming language. The writing of the instructions is built from alphabetical symbols that for a long time have been essentially binary. But a language, like Morse code, for example, which uses only two elementary symbols, makes communication a long and difficult process. On the other hand, a language without syntax is equally difficult to use because of the great variety of the concepts that have to be communicated. Thus one has to acknowledge that a language is more or less easy to use according to whether it possesses certain characteristics found in natural languages. I shall present four such characteristics.

1. The first characteristic may be illustrated by an example. Consider the word *chair*. This is a semantic unit of level $n+1$ made up of semantic units of level n, these being *leg, seat, back*. If we add another unit of level n, *armrest*, we get a new word, *armchair*, which is of level $n+2$. For ease of communication, the hierarchy of targets in a language

must correspond to the hierarchy of sources; it is easier to speak of an armchair than of a chair with armrests.

2. In order to express an unlimited variety of sources with a limited number of symbols, it is necessary to combine these symbols. If, for example, one needs only to interpret road signs, a dictionary of these is sufficient; but a dictionary alone is not sufficient if one needs to translate a statement in a natural language—this requires at least some syntactic analysis of greater or lesser complexity. A language that is easy to use cannot have a syntax so simple that a dictionary will suffice for its interpretation.

3. A language must not obstruct the thought process by requiring users to pay attention to constraints not relevant to the subjects of their communications. In particular, no preliminary coding should be necessary: we do not use the term "language" when describing a cryptographic system. For ease of use, it must be possible to express the concept to be conveyed without paying any regard to the means of communication. Thus in speaking to a friend we do not concern ourselves with the properties of the air around us; when telephoning we have to speak close to the microphone, but this is no impediment to the expression of our thoughts.

4. A natural language enables us to express any concept, any thought whatever. Can we know whether it is possible for a programming language to express any algorithm whatever, and thus to be a universal language in this sense? I shall try to answer this question at the end of this study.

The characteristics of a natural language are of increasing strength in the order given. A programming language that has none of them will clearly be more difficult to use than one having one or more. The machine languages are examples of languages having none of the characteristics; the assembly languages have only the first, some languages have the first three and some have all four. Programming languages are often put into two groups: in the first are the basic machine languages and the so-called assembly languages; in the second, the rest, described as evolved or high-level languages. These latter must have at least the first two of the above characteristics. I shall describe first the low-level languages and then the high-level languages, among the latter of which I shall distinguish three categories:

1. There are the earliest high-level languages, which appeared at a time when most people believed that it would not be possible to realize them. It would not have been reasonable to expect the designers of these languages to give abstract definitions of them; they had to build

small parts of the language they were planning, show that these could be used to write programs that could then be translated into efficient machine code, extend from this base to new areas, and so on. Thus these early high-level languages evolved in fact by a sort of trial-and-error process and were very closely dependent on the features of the machines on which they were developed. FORTRAN was the most typical and has had the greatest influence of these languages.

2. There are the high-level languages defined in the abstract. Once it was known that high-level languages were a practical possibility it became reasonable to hope that they could be defined formally, taking into account only their aptitude for expressing the source concepts and not being concerned with the properties of the machines on which they were likely to be run. ALGOL, COBOL, and PL/I are representative of this group. All languages of this type were modeled more or less faithfully on the machine architecture defined by von Neumann, and some writers, including John Backus, referred to them as von Neumann languages.

3. There are some languages, which appeared at the end of the 1950s, more functional in nature; LISP and APL are the most typical of these.

1 The Low-Level Languages

Among what I am calling the low-level languages are machine languages, which were the first to appear and were for a long time the only languages, and the assembly languages.

Machine Languages
I have already made some mention of these; they consist of instructions that are directly executable by the computer, and there is a correspondence between these instructions and the wiring of the machine. Here I shall be concerned only with the form taken by these instructions and with its historical development.

Machine-Language Instructions
The machine languages are made up of elementary instructions called the *code* of the machine. As I have said, a wired-in operation corresponds to each instruction. There are several parts to an instruction. One defines the operation to be performed. The achievement of the operation involves some transfer of information within the machine. Thus there must be one or more parts of the instruction that give the address(es) of the memory where the information is to be found and of the register(s) where it is to be put. Thus an instruction may refer

to one or more addresses, and the addresses can be of variable length; it follows that even on the same machine different instructions may have different lengths. We now consider this possibility and the problems to which it leads.

In the simplest form of address, there is a number in the instruction giving the location in the memory of whatever is the item to be used. There were many variations on this in the first-generation machines, and I have already mentioned the method of *indirect addressing* used on the IBM 709. Another was what is called *implicit addressing*, used, for example, on the IBM 705; in this machine the result of a multiplication was always placed in one specific register, so that there was no need for the instruction to refer to this address[1] — it was implicit in the operation. Another type was *content addressing*, in which the memory position was stated in terms of the item to be used by a statement of the form "the location containing X"; this clearly involved calling in a subroutine to find the location of X. Content-addressable memories are also called *associative memories* because of the possibility they provide of associating several locations together in a single parallel access.[a] This concept is probably of French origin; F. H. Raymond took out a patent relating to this[2] in 1956, and there was an associative memory in the CAB 500. Content addressing could be done on the RCA 301 by means of special instructions.

Whatever form of addressing is adopted, the problem arises of how many addresses should be used in an instruction, a number that clearly depends on the type of operation to which the instruction refers. Most of the operations that have to be performed in the course of an algorithmic process can be written symbolically as

$$A = B \; op \; C$$

where *op* refers to some operation to be performed with B and C, such as addition, transfer of B to C, and so on. Every instruction must therefore provide at least four pieces of information:

1. an operation code, telling the central processor what internal connections to set up;

2. the address of the memory location where the first operand is to be found, here written B;

3. the address for the second operand, here C;

4. the address for the result of the operation, here A.

When all three addresses are given explicitly, we have what is called a *3-address instruction*; this was the form used in all the first machines, for example, the Bell Labs machines and later SEAC and NORC. It was found again on the Honeywell 800, for which, as I have said, the instructions were of 48 bits, of which 12 were used for each of 3 addresses and 12 for the operation code and index registers. On scientific machines, however, the form most used up to 1963 was the *1-address instruction*, often called the von Neumann form because of its invention by the EDVAC team at the Moore School. It was used on LARC and on the IBM 700 and IBM 7000 machines, among others. Here the instruction states only the operation code and the address of one operand, the second address being implicit. This second address can be that of a fixed location in which the result of a previous operation will have been placed, so that all that needs to be done is to extract that result from that location; or of a fixed location in which the result of the current operation is to be placed. Thus the machine is organized around a small number of registers that act as sources or destinations for transfer operations; every machine operation results in a transfer between two points, and conversely every transfer requires an instruction.

Another possible form is the *2-address instruction*, in which the two addresses refer to the first and second operands, respectively, and the result is placed in the second address [that is, the form is C = B *op* C]. The machine's activity thus appears as a succession of movements of information from register to register. This form was used in the IBM SSEC and in the British ACE; it appeared again in the ERA 1103 and, most important, in the IBM 1401, IBM 1410, IBM 1440, and IBM 7010 machines, the large number of users of which made it a popular form.

A further possibility is the instuction with a variable number of addresses. This can arise in two ways. Either the manufacturer provides on the same machine instructions with 0, 1, or 2 addresses, as was done in the CDC 3600, the IBM 1460, and the CAB 500; or the choice of length and structure of the instruction is left to the programmer, as was done in the IBM 1401 (where the length could be from 1 to 8 characters and the number of addresses 0,1,2, or 3), the Burroughs B 5000, and the Gamma 60. Reductions in both programming and execution time can be achieved by suitable use of multiaddress in-structions, and memory can be economized by use of single or even zero address instructions. The constraints imposed by multiprocessing led the engineers to develop a very flexible addressing system for the Gamma 60; here an instruction could refer to any number of addresses whatever, the required length being formed simply by joining together the necessary number of machine words.

Although the programmer could decide the instruction length in some machines, in the great majority of cases this was fixed by the manufacturer. How then was it determined? We may recall that the process of locating data and elementary instructions in the memory is fundamental to the concept of the computer. The form of these instructions must fit therefore into the framework that has been decided for the data structure, whether word or character oriented, and this will determine the organization of the memory and the registers of the central processor.

Consider, for example, the scientific machines. During the first two generations these were word oriented—the longer the word, the greater the precision to which the machine could compute; very few had word lengths less than 32 bits. There were, however, particularly interesting machines having a word length of 48 bits. Why was that number chosen? The reason is that all scientific work involves handling not only figures but also characters, if only for the identification of variables. The word must therefore be a multiple of the length of the character. In many machines of the period the latter could be either 6 or 8 bits. Hence it was natural to choose a word length divisible by both, and as the smallest common multiple, 24, gave too short a word, the next, 48, was chosen.

Let us turn now to the instruction length in these 48-bit machines. Since 16 bits was too short, the choice was between 24-bit instructions placed two to a word and one 48-bit instruction occupying a whole word. The former was chosen for the CDC 1604, the instruction being made up of 6 bits for the operation code, 4 bits for auxiliary purposes, and only 14 bits for the address; this allowed direct reference to only 16,384 memory locations, which was already small for that period. There were, however, 48-bit machines with two types of instuction, "normal" and "long." "Normal" instructions were 1-address, 24 bits, and were held in pairs in 48-bit words; "long" were 2-address, 48 bits. The most typical of these was the CDC 3600, an improved version of the CDC 1604 launched in 1963; its long instructions were used for decimal arithmetic, channel control, and so on. The CDC 3600 was much faster than the CDC 1604 and it had adequate software; its great commercial success gave Control Data a firm base in the computer market.

Finally, for two computers to which reference has already been made, all the instructions were of 48 bits. The Ferranti Atlas, which appeared in 1961, used 1-address instructions with a 24-bit address, allowing direct reference to 16 million memory locations; and the

Honeywell 800, using 3-address instructions to simplify microprogramming.

Sequential Execution of Programs

An interesting instruction form, already mentioned, is that in which one of the addresses gives the location of the next instruction to be obeyed. In the first calculators the correct sequential execution of the instructions was guaranteed by feeding these one by one into the machine. Thus if, for example, the instructions were 24 bits long and were read in from cards, as soon as a group of 24 bits was received, the wiring of the central processor caused the relevant operation to be performed and the next group was then read. In the first computers the execution was in the order in which the instructions had been located in the memory, as in the MARK I and the IBM SSEC. Later the sequencing was controlled by means of an *instruction counter*; this was done in the IAS machine and the UNIVAC I, and the use of this method spread rapidly.

However, some machines were produced with what were called (1 + 1)-address instructions, in which one of the addresses referred to the next instruction in the program to be obeyed. An example was the IBM 650, the instructions of which were described as (1 + 1) address. By the end of 1963 almost all the types of instruction found in modern machines had been experimented with.

Limitations of Machine Languages

For a computer to be able to carry out the algorithmic procedure required for the solution of a problem, it must first have been given the necessary *competence* [represented by an appropriate program]. The process of communicating a program in machine language was first carried out in the same way as had been used for the early automatic looms and for Babbage's machine: in terms of a binary alphabet. This transformed the stating of even the simplest problem into a task requiring the closest attention to every detail, in the course of which, if only as a result of a momentary distraction, it was easy to make a mistake, such as writing a 0 instead of a 1 at some point in the long sequence of bits that represented an instruction. Further, the user had to know the binary codes for all the instructions, and the exact location in the memory, also in binary, where every item of data was to be found. This was an enormous labor of encipherment, undertaken to relieve the machine of this burden.

But most users wanted to see the machine as no more than a problem-solving tool whose use should distract them as little as possible. Use of machine language, however, required them to know every detail of the structure and working of the machine, and also often involved them more in programming than in problem solving. Among all the languages for communication between man and the machine, machine language is by nature the one furthest from the problems; computer use could not have developed had this remained the only language available.

Assembly Languages

Two extreme courses of action could be taken in order to bridge the gap between the language used by the machine and that used by humans in expressing the method of solution of a problem. One was to adapt the problem to the machine, which carried the risk, if one was not careful, of modifying the statement of the problem in the interests of simplifying the processing. The other was to adapt the communication language to the needs of the problems. The first is a matter of saying "how" a problem is to be solved, and in the greatest detail; the second, of saying "what" is the problem and leaving the machine to look after the details of the process of solution. As the *level* of a language rises, it moves steadily further from the "how" toward the "what." Languages for man/machine communication intermediate between the "how" and the "what" were developed during the first two computer generations and are those still most in use today. Use of these involved the development of a new type of program, the *translator program*, with the aid of which a machine-language program could be produced that was the equivalent of the same program written in a high-level language. The first such languages were the assembly languages.

Mnemonic Codes and Symbolic Addresses

The first step in this direction was the development of *mnemonic codes*. This occurred first in connection with the EDSAC, for which, for example, $S(n)$ meant the nth location in the memory (S for Store), C the content of this location, and so on. Similar codes were used in the instructions for UNIVAC I from 1951 onward, as the outcome of the work of a group of programmers at the Eckert-Mauchly Computer Corporation, led at that time by Grace Hopper.

Suppose a machine has instructions 30 bits long, and the elementary instruction

001110   000000   000000   000000   100000

means "Put into the Accumulator register the contents of Register 32." If the mnemonic code for the operation is CLA, the instruction can be written

CLA   000000   000000   000000   100000

The binary alphabet has been enriched by the addition of letters, but this has brought only a slight improvement. Use of mnemonic codes still leaves the programmer with the tasks, among others, of telling the machine exactly where the operands used in an instruction are to be found and where the result is to be placed. To reduce this labor the Cambridge (England) team invented and used on EDSAC what is now called *symbolic addressing* (Wilkes [1969]).[b] This allowed the programmer to define a location in the memory by means of a symbolic name, such as R or Toto or anything else. When this name was encountered during the reading-in of the program, the machine looked for a vacant location in the memory, recorded its address, and assigned the data item or the result, as appropriate, to that location. This was done at machine speed, and therefore orders of magnitude faster than manually.

Instructions made up of mnemonic codes and symbolic addresses are called *symbolic instructions*, and languages written in terms of these are called *assembly languages*. Programs that translate from assembly language to machine language, and therefore into a sequence of instructions that can be executed directly by the machine, are called *assemblers*. The name is due to the Cambridge team, which, according to Wilkes [1969], gave the programs for many subroutines and showed how these could be linked together to provide the program for the solution of a problem.

In addition, the Cambridge team took up and developed an idea first put into practice on the IBM Card Program Calculator (CPC) in 1947. Plug boards corresponding to subroutines could be used to control that machine, and each of these was given a name, which was often mnemonic, such as SIN for the board that calculated the sine function, EXP for exponential, and so on. The Cambridge team used such names for subroutines in their assembly language, thus providing a vocabulary by means of which they could be called when needed. The linking between the subroutines was organized by what is now called a *link editor*.

Translation into Machine Language

Instructions that differ in any way from those of the machine's code are incomprehensible to the computer and must therefore be translated into machine language. The program in the higher-level language is called the *source program*; the equivalent machine-language program into which it is translated is called the *object program*, or sometimes the *code*, in spite of the ambiguity in the term. The translation must

Figure 4.1
The translation process.

be done by means of a program because a human translator could not do the work quickly enough, so that the process may be called *automatic*. The term *automatic programming* was used in the early 1950s, but its meaning was never very clear, and it is no longer used; see figure 4.1.

There are two main types of translator programs, the *interpreters* and the *compilers*. Interpreters were the first to be used. An interpreter reads the instructions of the source program one by one in sequence and translates and executes each instruction as it is read; therefore partial results can be obtained at any stage during the execution of the source program. All the first assemblers, such as SPEEDCODE, were translated by interpreters. Interpretation has the serious drawback that each instruction in the source program has to be translated afresh into machine-code instructions every time it appears in the program [and every time the program is run]. For example, if a function has to be evaluated for 50 values of a parameter, the source-program instructions for the function have to be translated 50 times. It would be better if one could use some procedure by means of which the translation was done once only and the resulting machine-language instructions used as often as required. The first compilers were written partly to make this possible. A language which is translated by means of an interpreter is called an *interpretive* language.

Compilers are programs that translate from source to object program but that differ from interpreters in that the product of the translation is not the result of the calculation but the complete object program corresponding to the source. This is then used in a second phase to get the result required. A language translated in this way is called a *compiled* language. A compiler is not constrained like an interpreter to translating the source instructions one by one in sequence; it can, for example, translate a sequence, place the resulting machine-language instructions in the memory, and recall these whenever the same source sequence appears again in the program. It can also do a certain amount of optimization of the object program in order to reduce the running time; this was done, for example, by the Symbolic Addressing Optimiser and Assembly Program (SOAP) for the IBM 650, which placed in-

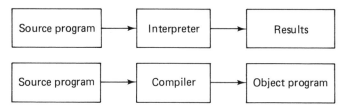

Figure 4.2
Interpretation and compilation.

structions and data on the drum in such a way as to minimize the retrieval time. Optimization was done also by the Symbolic Assembly Program (SAP), produced for the assembly language for the IBM 704 in 1956. See figure 4.2.

Thus an assembler can be either an interpreter or a compiler. With a compiler, the process involves four main phases:

1. reading the source-program text (to find the words it contains: mnemonic codes, symbolic addresses, and so on);

2. formation of a table giving the real addresses in the memory corresponding to the symbolic addresses of the program;

3. translation of the mnemonic codes into machine-language instructions;

4. production of the object program, using the results obtained in the previous phase together with library programs for subroutines.

The process can be reduced to a simple dictionary lookup and is almost trivial compared with the complexity of the task of the compilers developed for the more highly evolved languages to be considered. Assembly-program compilers are not in fact now regarded as true compilers.

Limitations of Assembly Languages
The arrival of these languages led to many innovations, the most important of which was probably automatic programming. We have already mentioned the related development of libraries of subroutines. In designing an algorithm, all the possible cases to which it may be applied must be foreseen and provided for in the finest detail; but it is so difficult for people to envisage all the possibilities that might be encountered in the solution of any one of an infinite class of problems that they soon forget those they may have encountered. A computer, however, can preserve the knowledge of the past, since that knowledge, once acquired, can be preserved in library programs.

But assembly languages were only one step on the way to higher-level languages. They still required the programmer to produce a sequence of instructions very closely related to the structure of the machine, and thus acted as a distraction from the essence of the problem. For this reason some writers (Sammet [1978]) regard neither assembly languages nor machine languages as programming languages. They have lost some of their importance in favor of the higher-level languages and are now little used except when it is necessary to make the best possible use of the machine's structure.

The way in which the machine's hardware works is not necessarily related to the expressions most frequently encountered in the course of applications: no machine, for example, can have circuits that will evaluate directly every arithmetical expression, but a programming language intended for scientific applications must enable any such expression to be easily communicated to the machine. One of the objectives of any high-level language is to ease this process of communication of the expressions most frequently encountered in its field of application.

2 The First High-Level Languages

To illustrate the types of difficulty that have to be overcome, consider the following very simple expression involving the four variables A,B,C,D:

$$A = B + (C \times D).$$

To evaluate this, one must first form the product of C and D and then add this to B; the sum is then placed in the memory in the location corresponding to A. This cannot be done until after a *syntactic analysis* has shown the order in which the operations are to be performed; such an analysis cannot be performed by the assembly process. Thus the third of the characteristics in the introduction to this chapter as typical of a good communication language is closely related to the second; it provides a criterion for distinguishing between high-level and low-level languages.

There were many computer specialists in the early 1950s who found it impossible to believe that even simple syntactic analysis could be done by the computer at adequate speed, and therefore that a compiler for a high-level language could be fast enough to be useful. This view did not change until John Backus gave, with FORTRAN, a striking demonstration to the contrary. According to Jean Sammet [1978], FORTRAN (FORmula TRANslator) was a *general-purpose language*, even though its use was confined to scientific applications—which, up to a point, simplified the translation [into machine language]. In fact, it was found that translation of some *special-purpose languages* required translator programs that were themselves extensions of high-level languages. This will be illustrated by describing, after FORTRAN, the APT language, used for controlling machine tools.

FORTRAN

This was the first true high-level language; one of its aims was "to enable a problem to be stated concisely in mathematical notation" (Backus [1978]). Although Rutishauser in Zurich in 1952 and J. H. Laning and W. Zierler in 1954 in connection with Whirlwind had devised methods for communicating mathematical expressions to a computer in fairly natural form, neither of these systems provided the same facilities as did FORTRAN. Laning and Zierler's language was interpretive, algebraic expressions being analyzed separately.[3] A program could involve only 26 variables, identified by the 26 letters of the alphabet; this is the origin of the requirement met by all modern programming languages that the character string used to name any object with which the program is concerned must always begin with a letter. Interpretation, however, slowed the process of getting the result of the calculation; only compilation could speed this up. But was this possible with such complexity? John Backus had written [1978], "In the early 1950s, because of the lack of high-level languages, the cost of programming was at least equal to that of the equipment, and this held back the development of computers." The only way to overcome this difficulty was to take up again the idea of "automatic programming" and to develop languages that were easy to use and above all had efficient translators. The majority of translators up to that time had been written for translating the mnemonic codes of assembly languages, organizing the use of library subroutines or, above all, for providing floating-point arithmetic and index operations.

The hardware of the IBM 704 provided both floating-point and index registers, so that with this machine software for these was of little interest. It seemed to Backus[4] that with these new hardware aids a language could be developed with a translator that would produce object programs as efficient as handwritten machine-code programs. Further, this language could be specially adapted to the communication of algorithms met in scientific applications. The odds against success in such an aim were clearly very heavy, for the general view in the computer community at the time was that one could not expect an object program [produced by a compiler] to be less than five times slower than the equivalent program written directly in machine language: this was so for almost every assembler then existing. In spite

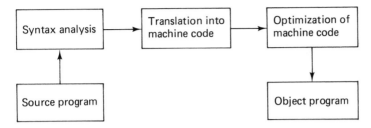

Figure 4.3
Compilation.

of this Backus was able to convince the IBM directors that success was possible, and in December he was given charge of a group that included David Sayre and P. B. Sheridan.

The FORTRAN compiler, the ancestor of all modern compilers, was the first to have such power and such breadth. Production of the first version (IBM [1954]) took about 25 man-years. Optimization of the results of the syntactic analysis was performed in various ways: elimination of some redundancies by reusing the translation of a statement every time it was reencountered and simply putting in the new values for the variables; rearranging the order of the operations to reduce the time taken; organizing the use of the registers and the memory locations so as to speed up the calculation; and so on. The quality of this optimization guaranteed the success of FORTRAN. It was the most striking achievement in the history of programming languages. The first versions of the FORTRAN compiler of 1955 were almost as efficient as the assemblers of the time, a fact that showed that the skepticism then current concerning compilers was without foundation[5] (see figure 4.3).

Definition of the Language
It had not been possible to give a definition of the language a priori because the validity of each stage had to be established as it was reached; the language evolved as time went on. From the start FORTRAN took up again the ideas of Laning and Zierler and those of Rutishauser, but added many new ones such as that of the conditional instruction, the IF;[6] a branch instruction, the GO TO; an instruction to set up an iteration, the DO; input/output instructions; and so on. FORTRAN also introduced a number of important new features, in particular subscripted variables, arithmetic and boolean expressions, tables for which the size was known at compilation time, and subroutines compiled independently of the main program.

Backus's group published a first version (IBM [1954]) of the language on 10 November 1954, which became known as FORTRAN I. In this the names of the objects figuring in a program could be of one or two characters, names of functions were of three or more characters, subscripted variables could have up to three subscripts, and arithmetical expressions could be written so as to be evaluated either in fixed or in floating point; input statements could specify the order in which data were to be read, but output statements could not specify the format in which the results were to be printed.

There were a number of obvious defects in this first version, made all the more irritating by the lack of any automatic process for checking syntax errors made by the programmer. Means for this were provided in the second version, FORTRAN II, developed by Backus in collaboration with R. A. Nelson and I. Ziller, work on which started at the beginning of 1955. Several changes were made to the original language: deletion of some features which had proved relatively difficult to translate into machine language; improvement of the input/output statements, in particular, inclusion of format specification in the output statement; extension of the GO TO instruction with the "computed GO TO"; increase of the permitted names for variables to six characters; and others.

Thus FORTRAN evolved along lines suggested by the experience gained in its use. The group decided to take advantage of this experience and to write a reference manual for programmers; the work was undertaken by David Sayres and the manual (IBM [1956]) was the first and for a long time the only one of its kind.[7] In April 1957 the compiler had proved sufficiently reliable to be distributed to all the IBM 704 customers, together with a *Preliminary Operator's Manual* describing how it was to be used; this manual also was the first of its kind.

As an example of programming in FORTRAN II, consider the summation of 100 numbers, the numbers to be read in to the machine from one of its input devices and the sum to be printed on an output device. The program is as follows:

```
        DIMENSION A(100)
        READ 2, A
        SUM = 0
        DO 7 I = 1, 100
7       SUM = SUM + A(I)
        PRINT 7, 1, SUM
        STOP
1       FORMAT (F 10,4)
2       FORMAT (E 10,3)
        END
```

In this program A is the name given to an ordered set of 100 numbers. The instruction DIMENSION A(100) tells the computer to reserve 100 locations in the memory for the elements of A. Before it can do this the machine must know whether these elements are letters, integers, real numbers (that is, numbers including a decimal point), or other; in FORTRAN a name beginning with any of the letters I, J, K, L, M represents an integer, and one beginning with any other letter represents a real number. The instruction READ 2, A tells the machine to read the 100 numbers that are the elements of A from the input unit, and it also tells it that the format in which these are given is specified in the line labeled 2. The format statement E 10,3 means that the numbers can be of up to 10 decimal digits, of which 3 are after the decimal point. Note that the numbers used to label the lines need not be in any particular order.

The meaning of the = sign is that the result of performing the process on the right of this is to be put in the memory in the location corresponding to the variable on the left; thus SUM = 0 means that the value zero is to be placed in the location of which the symbolic address is SUM. Instructions of this type are called *assignments* because they "assign" the result of the calculation specified on the right to the location defined by the variable on the left. The DO instruction says that all the following instructions down to and including line 7 (here there is only one) are to be executed a number of times, the first time with I given the value 1, the second time 2, and so on until the value 100. Thus in this case the same instruction is executed 100 times.

The PRINT instruction calls for no comment. STOP is the point at which the execution of the program is to finish; END is the end of the text.

Ziller developed a language, which he called FORTRAN III, that used the same variables as FORTRAN and in which symbolic instructions could be mixed with FORTRAN statements and instructions; it included other novelties, such as boolean expressions. It was used by about 20 IBM customers from 1958 onward but was never made a commercial product. FORTRAN IV appeared in 1962 and this, apart from a few details, is the version used today.

The Influence of FORTRAN

Although FORTRAN was at first looked on with distrust by the computer community, there is no doubt that it made writing and developing programs much easier. And although certain features of the IBM 704 had to be taken into account in using the first versions, from FORTRAN II onward programs could be written and results obtained without any attention being paid to the particular machine on which the work was done. FORTRAN II's success was such that by 1959 any manufacturer hoping to sell a scientific machine had to offer a high-level language at least as good; most of them adopted FORTRAN and offered a compiler rather than produce a new language. Thus for the first time, by the force of circumstances, one single language was used by many manufacturers for many different machines; and FORTRAN became the first *machine-independent language*. This independence of the machine is an aspect of the third of the characteristics given in the introduction because it is only in this case that an algorithm can be expressed without reference to either the machine or the means of communication.

This, however, is not to say that the same program written by different groups for the same machine will necessarily give the same results. Writing a compiler involves a number of compromises, such as between the location in the memory of the compiler instructions and the speed of the calculation; and the translations of the source program made by two different compilers will not be identical if the two do not make the identical compromises. The difficulty is even greater if two different makes of machine are involved, because it is most unlikely that they will have the same fundamental hardware organization. Thus programming languages have *dialects*. In the case of people, members of a single linguistic community can understand one another even if they speak different dialects of one language; but a computer cannot understand a program written in a different dialect from its own. If a program gives identical results when run with any acceptable data on two different machines, it is said to be *portable* between the two; the problem of achieving portability has still not been satisfactorily solved. Thus a language is defined completely not by the manual alone but by the manual and the compiler together.

Rivals and Descendants of FORTRAN

FORTRAN was not the only high-level language to be developed at that time. Several other compiled languages appeared during the period 1952–1957 having the aim of easing the problems of handling mathematical expressions; only two of these will be considered: MATHMATIC, also called AT3, and IT (Internal Translator).

MATHMATIC was implemented on the UNIVAC I by a group led by Grace Hopper,[8] and the first manual was produced in April 1957. While it had some interesting features, the language had little success; among other defects, it suffered from being written for a machine that had neither index registers nor built-in floating-point arithmetic.

IT was the name given by a group under Al Perlis at Carnegie-Mellon University[c] to a language that they wrote for the IBM 650

(Perlis, Smith, and van Zoeren [1967]) aimed at simplifying the process of communicating algorithms to the machine. It demonstrated that the compiler for a simple language can be written quickly, provided the work is done by programmers of exceptional ability and that full documentation is not required; here it was done in only 2 man-years. IT first did a syntax analysis and then translated the source program into the assembly language SOAP, which the SOAP assembler then translated into machine language. IT became very popular with users of the IBM 650, but later gave way to FORTRAN.

FORTRAN had many descendants, from among which I shall select for description PAF (Programmateur Automatique de Formules), developed by D. Starynkewitch in France in 1958 for the SEA machine CAB 500. The aim was to make it possible "to write in plain language, closely similar to spoken French, the instructions to be obeyed in the course of a calculation." Instructions like POSER (PUT) or CALCULER (COMPUTE) or SI A > B ALLER EN (IF A > B GO TO) where included in the language. PAF could be either interpreted or compiled. With the interpreter the machine could be used interactively, rather like a desk calculator. When working in this mode users did not have to wait until the whole of their programs had been read into the machine before getting any results; they could have these step by step and, if they wished, could modify the programs in the light of intermediate results. Each mathematical statement was written on a separate line, and its completion was signaled to the machine by the return of the carriage of the input typewriter; the line was then interpreted immediately. Any calculation could be halted at any chosen point and restarted later, for example, to evaluate more cases if that were needed. The PAF compiler produced very efficient object code. The CAB 500 was in fact one of the first machines on which a program could first be developed interactively, using the interpreter, and then compiled for execution.

PAF made a considerable impression in France. For one thing, its statements were in French, so that one could write, for example, IMPRIMER AVEC 2 DEC(imales) RC(racine carrée) (de) N—PRINT SQUARE ROOT of N to 2 DECIMALS. There was a view in France at that time that a programming language for France should use French words, and IBM translated FORTRAN instructions into French and sold two versions, English and French. Users, however, preferred the English form, on the grounds that this made a [scientific] program more easily understood by the entire international scientific community and more easily transferable from one center to another. It is for this reason that after the mid-1960s the terms used in high-level scientific languages were almost exclusively English.

PAF vanished with the CAB 500, but it had a famous descendant, BASIC, produced in 1965. Even if the authors of this language did not know of PAF, BASIC had the majority of its features.

The APT Language for Control of Machine Tools

FORTRAN influenced the development of not only general-purpose high-level languages but also special-purpose languages. Such languages must provide the same flexibility of expression as general-purpose languages; for example, if the problem is to instruct a machine tool to cut a piece of metal to a specified shape, the control language must make it possible to express the algebraic relations that define the required contours. It must also allow the incorporation of any special facilities required by the particular application, in this case subroutines for special tests, controlling the various movements of the machinery, and so on. I now describe the oldest of the languages still used for this particular application, APT—Automatic Programmed Tools.

In 1951 the US Air Force Air Material Command awarded a contract to the Servomechanisms Laboratory at MIT for the development of a system for computer control of machine tools. In 1955 the laboratory had produced a program by means of which the Whirlwind computer could punch the paper tapes used to control these machines. This led to the setting up of the APT project under D. T. Ross, who laid down the main lines in a letter written on 4 October 1956 (Ross [1978]). The project started from the MIT software by means of which shapes could be defined, provided they were made up of planes or parts of spherical surfaces, and extended this to include cones, cylinders, and other surfaces of revolution. The system was written in a language that was independent of the computer and included special features for the control of the tool.

The development of FORTRAN had generated the knowledge needed for the writing of a compiler, and consequently this control language allowed syntactically complex statements to be written: for example,

"TOOL RIGHT, GO RIGHT/BASE": telling the right-hand tool to move to the right along the base-line;

"C = POINT/1.5": defining C as the point with coordinate (1,5);

"CROU = CIRCLE/CENTER AT A THRU B": defining the curve CROU as the circle with center A and radius AB.

An extended version APT II was made available on the IBM 704 in 1957 and another, APT III, on the IBM 7090 in 1961.

This was a very novel application of computers. APT was more than just a simple language for man-machine communication; its use involved three phases: first the statement, in the language, of what was to be done and the translation of this into the object program for the computer; then the translation of this into the command language for the machine tool; and finally, the transmission of these commands to the tool by the computer, which supervised the actual operation. There was thus communication not only between man and computer but also between computer and machine tool; and it was with APT that the first steps were taken to apply computers in the field of automation.

Lack of space makes it necessary to forgo descriptions of other specialized languages. It would have been interesting to describe GPSS—General Purpose Simulation System—the first language for simulation by computer of discrete events, such as the arrivals of ships in ports and movement of traffic in towns. This was marketed by IBM in 1961 for the IBM 704, IBM 709, and IBM 7090 machines and is still in wide use today.

3 Formally Defined High-Level Languages

At the beginning of the 1950s there was no certainty that an efficient compiler could be written at all; and FORTRAN and APT were defined step by step as the translation into machine language progressed. But in 1957 there were no longer any such doubts, and the scientific community, going to the other extreme, fell into the habit of laying down formal definitions of programming languages, making the implicit assumption that a compiler can always be written if necessary. Several languages that had been proposed in the late 1970s were in fact never compiled.

Three languages that appeared during the period under discussion illustrate both the value and the drawbacks of the formal approach. The first was ALGOL, a language that has not been used very much in practice but that has provided a theoretical model on which much study has been based. The second was COBOL, defined under the aegis of the US Department of Defense, which, while independent of any computer, was adopted by all manufacturers in order to preserve their position as suppliers to the American government; consequently COBOL became very widely used. The third was PL/I, defined with the aim of combining the advantages of FORTRAN and COBOL while using the structure of ALGOL.

ALGOL

Definition of the Language

A mainly American school maintained that only specialized languages could meet the needs of users; this view was opposed by another school, originally mainly European but later more universal, which claimed also that such a view led to too many programming languages. A group was formed in Europe to define a multipurpose language[9] that should be completely independent of any computer and in which any algorithm could be clearly stated. The initiative for this came from F. L. Bauer of the University of Munich; he approached the American Association for Computing Machinery (ACM), which asked A. J. Perlis to form a committee to cooperate with the Europeans. A meeting was held in Zurich in the spring of 1958, in which the European participants were F. L. Bauer, H. Bottenbruch, H. Rutishauser, and K. Samelson; the American participants were J. Backus, C. Katz, A. J. Perlis, and J. H. Wegstein. A report was published in 1958 defining an International Algebraic Language, IAL (Perlis [1958]), which later was called ALGOL 58.

The language included instructions for assignments, loops (iterations), conditional branches and so on such as were already included in FORTRAN, IT, and MATHMATIC, but it was very different from these, and particularly from FORTRAN. Some of these differences were due to technical reasons. FORTRAN had been planned at the time when the problems presented by compilation were first beginning to be appreciated and the compiler was not free from defects; also, it was influenced by the features of the IBM 704.[10] Further, the designers of ALGOL 58 took the view that a programming language should be used not only for communication between man and machine but also for communication between people, and for this reason they paid little attention to the problems of input and output. Clearly the FORTRAN designers could not have taken such a view because they did not know, in advance, that a high-level language could actually exist. Some of these differences were of a more political nature; FORTRAN was viewed as the scientific language of IBM.

As I have said, Perlis described ALGOL 58 as a "single universal computer language"; but as will be seen, while it did allow any algorithm to be expressed, it did not have the flexibility of expression needed in business data-processing applications. Thus it is no longer considered as having the fourth of our stated characteristics.

At the beginning of 1959 IBM set up a group under R. Bemer and J. Green charged with writing an experimental compiler for ALGOL 58; they demonstrated a first version on an IBM 709 in May 1959 to a meeting of SHARE, the users' association for the large IBM machines. Some members of SHARE wrote to ACM asking them to lay down a standard for ALGOL, but there seems to have been no response, the members of their ALGOL group being then concerned with other languages (Sammet [1969]). Further, the ALGOL partisans in SHARE were only few in number, the use of FORTRAN having grown to an almost unbelievable extent. Users of IBM machines certainly did not want to see the development of FORTRAN halted in favor of a new language for which, while there was an attractive, though incomplete, definition, no compiler had yet been written that would enable its practical value to be judged. SHARE therefore asked IBM to continue with the development of FORTRAN. What this shows is that programming is not just a pure abstraction; in choosing a language, a user must consider things other than its formal elegance.

Some Characteristics of ALGOL 60

Nevertheless the ALGOL group continued with its work. As a result of Bauer's initiative and the financial support of IBM Europe, a meeting was held in Paris during the week of 11 January 1960 attended by Bauer, Rutishauser, and Samelson who had participated in the Zurich meeting, and P. Naur (Denmark), B. Vauquois (France), and M. Woodger (Britain). This group defined an improved language, the famous ALGOL 60 (Naur [1960]), which, mainly because of the strict definition of its syntax, served as a basis for the formal definition of programming languages for many years to come. For this they used a new notation, the famous Backus Normal Form, BNF, developed by John Backus, who had been seconded full-time to the American group by IBM and who had become one of its most active members.[11]

A subroutine in ALGOL may use its own specification in its text; in computer jargon, it may *call itself*. It often happens that the data needed by a subroutine are themselves the result of applying that subroutine to other data. For example, the factorial function of N, written N!, has the value $N \times (N-1) \times (N-2) \times \cdots 2 \times 1$ when N is a positive integer, and $1! = 1$; thus $4! = 4 \times 3 \times 2 \times 1$. This can be computed by a subroutine of the form IF $N > 1$ FACTORIAL $N = N \times$ FACTORIAL $(N-1)$ where the FACTORIAL subroutine is called repeatedly until the number on which it operates has been reduced to 1. Such a subroutine is said to be *recursive*. ALGOL 58 allowed such a process, while FORTRAN did not.

The main difference between ALGOL and FORTRAN was structural. Every ALGOL program is made up of *blocks*, sequences of instructions framed by the key words BEGIN and END. BEGIN is followed by the *declaration* of the objects to be found inside the block, and then the instructions to be executed.

An example of an ALGOL program, simply calculating the result of raising a number A to the power I, is

BEGIN

       REAL A,B;
       INTEGER I;
       B: = A ↑ I;
       WRITE (B);

END

REAL indicates that A and I are real numbers; : = has the same meaning as = in FORTRAN; ↑ indicates the operation of raising to a power (here A is to be raised to the power I). All instructions are terminated by ;.

An ALGOL block may contain other blocks, as shown schematically in the following:

BEGIN

       BEGIN

              BEGIN
              END

       END
       BEGIN
       END

END

Objects are declared only in the block within which they occur, and the declarations are not valid outside that block; this allows better use to be made of the memory by freeing the locations used by the declared objects on exit from the block.

Stack Machines

The theoretical work on which ALGOL was based had an influence on the logical design of the computer. I have already said that anything that can be done by software can be done equally by hardware and have discussed the relative advantages and disadvantages of the two approaches. It was only to be expected that computers would soon be built with internal structures corresponding to the instructions of some of the high-level languages, and the first attempt in this direction was the NCR 304 with hardware oriented toward programs written in a high-level language for commercial applications. Such an approach is attractive and has been copied in some modern machines, but it has the drawback of inflexibility. This became evident very quickly in the case of the NCR 304, when three years later the specialized structure was found to make it very difficult to write a COBOL compiler for the machine, a language having the same field of application.

Other attempts at the hardware solution concerned providing for recursion. There is no theoretical reason to limit this to any stated number of calls; but without any limit on this, an unlimited number of locations must be reserved in the memory for return addresses. The only practical solution is provided by what is called the *stack*, a group of contiguous locations identified by a single name, which is such that at any instant only one, the *top of the stack*, is accessible. Several manufacturers have produced machines with *hardware stacks* for which the addressing is determined by the wiring.

In 1952 Burroughs brought out their B 5000, a machine in which the arithmetical registers acted as though they were at the top of a stack; and the machine embodied also the ALGOL feature of dynamic allocation of memory. The compiler organized the program into segments corresponding to the ALGOL blocks, each of maximum size of 1,024 words; when the program needed to refer to information contained in a particular segment the segment was brought into the memory, after looking up a table in which its location was stored. The B 5000 had also one of the first forms of virtual memory and an advanced multiprogramming system, but it was relatively slow for its date, 1963, and had little success. A second version, the B 5500, had the same architecture, but three times the speed, and had enthusiastic supporters. The stack architecture was continued in subsequent Burroughs machines, the D 825, D 830, and D 850, which appeared at the end of the period under discussion.

Several American manufacturers after Burroughs produced machines with stacks that were partly realized in hardware: Digital Equipment in the PDP 6 and General Electric in the GEPAC 4000. In France, SEA went further with their CAB 1500, which had two stacks, one wholly and one partly in hardware.

A Descendant of ALGOL: JOVIAL

The founders of ALGOL had aimed at producing a truly universal language, but, as I have said, it was ill adapted to the problems of business data processing. Its direct descendant, JOVIAL, had a much wider field of application.

The US Air Force, needing a successor to the air-defense system SAGE, wanted to start afresh: new computers, a new system altogether and new techniques for writing operating systems and application programs. At the end of 1958 an engineer, Jules I. Schwartz, proposed a language derived from IAL, the first form of ALGOL, in which both types of program could be written; it was called JOVIAL, Jules's Own IAL. Schwartz formed a group that, according to him [1978], knew nothing about compilers and yet delivered a compiler for this multi-purpose language on the IBM 709 by the deadline; it was demonstrated in December 1960.

JOVIAL was the most "universal" language of its time. And as the Air Force wanted it to run on every machine in the system, whatever its make, compilers were written for several machines during the early 1960s; difficulties of maintenance, documentation, and so on, appeared later. It had a great initial success, but later became much less used, apparently suffering from the arrival of PL/I.

Limitations of ALGOL

In spite of its elegant formal definition ALGOL was not without ambiguities. A first modification to remove these was published by Naur in 1963 (Naur [1963]) and a second by D. Knuth in 1967 (Knuth [1967]). But the most serious drawback was the almost complete lack of concern with input and output. One reason—that its originators viewed it to a significant extent as a language for communication between people—has already been given; another doubtless was the view that scientific applications involved long calculations but little data. Together, these relegated the provision of input and output facilities to a matter of secondary importance.

ALGOL's limited commercial success was, as we have seen, that many computer users had just adopted FORTRAN and saw no reason why they should change. But neither this nor its drawbacks prevented ALGOL from having a strong influence on the development of programming languages generally. The block structure, in particular, was widely adopted. This was considered unfortunate by some, on the grounds that it was too restrictive and a step back from FORTRAN, in which the principle of modular structure of programs based on subroutines seemed more flexible in some circumstances. (I shall return to this point in section 4.)

ALGOL had an equally strong influence in Europe. In 1959 the majority of European computer manufacturers were at best producing only assemblers, and the European members of the ALGOL group felt that the language could be used in each of their countries. Although in the end their hopes remained largely unfulfilled, there is no doubt that the Zurich meeting marked the start of European research activity into programming, which has been of international value. The concepts of ALGOL 60 continued to be developed, mainly by the Europeans who played a leading role in the definition of ALGOL 68 (Winjgaarden

[1968]) and in adapting programming languages to the needs of teaching.[12] This last problem gave rise to the idea of the PASCAL language, another descendant of ALGOL 58 (Wirth and Hoare [1966]).

Why ALGOL with its many excellent qualities should not have been universally adopted is a question that has been debated often, and often with bitterness. It has given rise to what is often called the theology of languages. Some languages have their fanatical devotees. It is not necessarily the most used languages that inspire such infatuation; there have been fanatics for ALGOL 60, for example. Neither is fanaticism cliquish; there are fanatics for APL, a much used language about which I shall have something to say shortly. As there are never fanatics without corresponding detractors, the qualities and defects of various languages are often debated on a heroic scale—debates, however, that can enrich the subject because they may show how the theory and the practice of programming languages may be advanced. It is interesting that there are scarcely any fanatics for FORTRAN, one of the most widespread languages, or for COBOL, the business-applications language, which is certainly used more than any other language.

COBOL

Origin of the Language

At a meeting held in the Computation Center of the University of Pennsylvania on 8 April 1959, attended by computer users, members of various universities, and a few manufacturers, it was agreed that there was a need for a machine-independent language for business data processing corresponding to what was being provided for scientific work by ALGOL 58. This view was communicated to the US Department of Defense, which was known to be developing a commercial language AIMACO, Air Material Command. The proposal was welcomed by Charles A. Phillips of the Office of the Defense Secretary; subsequently, at the ACM (Association of Computing Machinery) annual conference on 1 September 1959, he said that he was only sorry that the idea had not come from the Department of Defense in the first place.

A second meeting was held in the Pentagon on 28–29 May 1959 under Phillips's chairmanship; there were about 40 participants of whom about 20 were from various branches of the US government, 15 from manufacturers, and the rest from universities. The discussions highlighted once again the need for programs to be transferable between machines, whatever their make, and the need also for a precisely defined language; at the same time they acknowledged that the creation of a new language would lead to inconveniences and loss of time resulting from the need to reprogram applications written in languages that had become obsolete. Two opposing views were voiced. One was that development should be pushed as quickly as possible, making all possible use of the experience already gained from existing commercial languages. The other was that there was no great urgency and that it would be better to start by studying the fundamental needs of business data processing and only then to propose the formal structure and standards of a new language, using the linguistic theory then being developed.[13]

Because no general agreement was reached, Phillips set up three subcommittees: A "short-range committee," chaired by J. Wegstein of the National Bureau of Standards—this later became the COBOL (Common Business-Oriented Language) Committee; a "medium-range committee," chaired by A. E. Smith of the US Navy; and a "long-range committee," which was never in fact constituted. On 4 June 1959 it was decided that there should be a general organization called the Committee on Data Systems Analysis, CODASYL, and that the work should be supervised by a group of experts chaired by Phillips. Two consultants were appointed, Grace Hopper of Sperry Rand and R. W. Bemer of IBM.

Characteristics of COBOL

The COBOL committee reviewed three existing business languages. The first was FLOWMATIC, developed by Grace Hopper's group at Univac (Sperry [1958]) and already in use on several installations; E. F. Somers of this group was a member of the committee. The second was AIMACO, developed by a group in the US Air Force directed by Colonel Alfred Asch; Asch, who had attended Grace Hopper's seminars, was also a member of the committee. The third was IBM's COMTRAN (Commercial Translator), the development of which was just completed and for which there was already a manual; the man responsible for this project was Roy Goldfinger, who joined the committee at the end of 1959.

The committee decided that a new language should be created, despite the known objections to this course, and that in order to make progress quickly, it should keep close to the three existing languages. They decided also that it should be called COBOL, like the committee. Jean Sammet, who was then an employee of Sylvania Electric Products and who was with the committee in that capacity, said later (Sammet [1978]) that if the majority of the members had known that their work would lead to so long-lived a language, they would have gone about things differently.

The main features of the new language, and especially the use of natural-language words, were taken from the FLOWMATIC language used widely on UNIVAC machines (Univac [1958]). Objects could be given code names of up to 12 characters, so that either their usual name could be used or, at worst, a close abbreviation. The extent of this quasi naturalness was increased by the use of English words for commands, such as COMPARE: a COBOL instruction could be as "natural" as this one:

IF A GREATER THAN B GO TO INSTRUCTION 3

COBOL represented an important step in the direction of using quasi-natural language for communication between man and machine. But the "medium-range" committee studied the language and apparently concluded that it did not have an adequate formal basis; its preference was for FACT, a formally defined business language that Honeywell was in the process of developing. The COBOL committee, fearing that the Department of Defense would be influenced by this, commented that following such a course would only waste time and that their language, while certainly not perfect as it stood, could be improved steadily. And this they proceeded to do, at a remarkable rate. The US government then threw all its weight into the balance and decreed that if a computer manufacturer did not offer COBOL with its machine, it would not be eligible as a supplier to the government unless it could demonstrate that it was offering a language that gave better performance. Comparisons between two languages being always partly subjective, this in effect imposed COBOL. The decree was announced just at the time when the first specification of COBOL 60 was published (Sammet [1961]). As a result, COBOL became, from 1963 onward, the first language to be "normalized"; and one of the reasons for its success is undoubtedly that users prefer a language for which there are norms, even if they are imperfect.

Such is the importance of the US government market that two companies, RCA and Remington Rand, made great efforts to have COBOL available by the end of 1960. Remington apparently built on FLOWMATIC as skeleton for its COBOL compiler. The RCA 501, produced in 1958, had quite good success in spite of being rather slow; this was probably thanks to its having a COBOL compiler. The two companies made an interesting experiment in order to meet the requirements of a government order; by modifying their compilers they were able to run the same COBOL program on the UNIVAC II and the RCA 501 and get the same results. This was one of the first actual examples of *program transferability*.

COBOL's Contribution

One of the contributions made by COBOL was the possibility it offered to programmers of using natural-language expressions. Another, probably the most important, was to give the description of data as much importance as other instructions. While COBOL was considered verbose and might have been behind the state of the art for its time in the clarity of its definition, it was clearly in advance in this matter of data. This attention to data was the forerunner of one of the concerns of modern theoretical work on programming languages, that the objects to which algorithmic processes are to be applied must be clearly defined. The same feature was retained in PL/I.

PL/I

While it is always possible to apply a programming language in a field for which it was not intended, it is clear that neither FORTRAN, ALGOL, nor COBOL can be rated a universal language. An important step toward such a language was made with PL/I.

By the end of the 1950s many users were complaining that with FORTRAN it was difficult to handle alphanumerical data and also to take advantage of newer operating systems and advances in computer technology. SHARE and IBM decided jointly in September 1963 to study these problems and, if necessary, to modify FORTRAN; this led to the SHARE-FORTRAN Committee. The committee quickly came to the conclusion that a new language, incompatible with FORTRAN, was needed and proposed such a language to SHARE in March 1964 in a report entitled "Report on the SHARE Advanced Language Development Committee." This, like every new language, had mixed reactions. IBM had made no commitment in this matter, but decided in 1964 to offer a version as a commercial product; it took up the ideas of the SHARE Advanced Language but also took into account the views expressed by members of SHARE and also those of members of GUIDE, the association of users of the small IBM machines. It called its language NPL for New Programming Language; but the British National Physical Laboratory, always known as NPL, asked IBM to change these initials, and the language became PL/I, for Programming Language number I.

PL/I was undoubtedly the most "universal" language produced in this period. Its field of application was extremely wide, covering those of FORTRAN, COBOL, and JOVIAL among others, and also that of a language to be described later, LISP.[14] But in order to cover such a wide field, it had to allow for many forms of expression and consequently is rather bulky.

PL/I is the world's most used language after FORTRAN and COBOL. It is often criticized, however, on the grounds that its definition allows a number of exceptions, with the result that it can be difficult to prove that a program will do what it is supposed to do. I shall take up this point at the end of this chapter; it was not appreciated at the time when PL/I was defined.[15]

Limitations of Formally Defined Languages
ALGOL, COBOL, and PL/I provide us with three examples of the consequences that are likely to follow when a language is formally defined by groups having different interests. In theory such an approach should result in a perfectly clear and unambiguous definition and an absence of verbosity. This was certainly true of ALGOL, defined by an academic group whose members came from a very small number of universities; but it took very little account of practical constraints. It was not the case with COBOL, defined by a group of users whose prime concern was the solving of down-to-earth problems of business data processing; but the formal definition certainly helped in defining norms for the language, whose existence was an important contributor to its success. It was true to quite a large extent in the case of PL/I, which, while also defined by users, profited from the other two languages; and if it did not have the formal purity of ALGOL, it was no less clearly defined.

The independence of the computer, which is a result of the formal definition, does, however, lead to some problems. For example, there are at least as many compilers as there are different machines, and any modification to the language entails changes to all these compilers—a task that is more or less difficult and costly. Consequently the more the language is used on different machines, the less it can be changed. Again, it is not possible for a machine-independent language to take full account of the features of any particular machine, as can be done with assemblers and machine languages. Ever since the arrival of FORTRAN there have been, and still are, heated discussions between the partisans of high-level languages and those of low-level languages. The first, basing their views on the experience now gained of the use of computer programs, maintain that a program has to be modified often in the course of its life and that therefore the accent should be on ease of expression rather than on processing time, provided that that is not too long in comparison with what can be achieved with an assembler. The second retort that this attitude sacrifices machine throughput to ease of use.

4 Functional Languages

Whether the languages are defined formally, and regardless of differences in detail between them, important though some of these are, programs written in any of the high-level languages just discussed consist mainly of assignment statements. By convention, the term on the left side of an assignment statement defines the memory location in which the result of the calculation defined by the expression on the right is to be placed. In some sense, therefore, the main role of the assignment statements is to manage the traffic between the memory and the arithmetical-logical unit. The amount of movement of items of information, one at a time, is made all the greater by the need to assign to the objects named in the expression on the right the values they must take at the moment of execution of the instruction and, moreover, to read these values from the memory. Thus this traffic is dominated by the computation of addresses rather than by the handling of useful items of data. The effect of this is to make it appear to the programmer using one of these languages that the store and the central processor are linked by what Backus [1978] has called a *von Neumann bottleneck*, through which everything has to go. This can result in the programmer losing sight at times of the functional nature of the process being used for the solution of a problem and becoming preoccupied with the problems of managing the traffic flow through this bottleneck.

It is to help in this that all high-level languages make a very clear distinction between the instructions that the program has to execute and the objects with which it has to deal. The objects are symbolized by names and are declared at the beginning of the program, so that their types are known to the computer. An algorithm is a function, and a programming language should therefore make it possible for functions to be expressed directly in mathematical terms without any concern for the extraneous features just described; that is, a programming language should be a *functional programming language* (Backus [1978]). It should of course have the third of our characteristics, but in a different form from the languages that have been described.

The first attempt to define such a language was made at the end of the 1950s, when FORTRAN had shown that it was possible to produce high-level languages. This was LISP, in which programs could be written in a notation very close to that of mathematics, but that was limited to a very special field of application. Shortly afterward, at the beginning of the 1960s, another language, APL, was defined, which was less wholly functional but of much more general application.

LISP

This was implemented by John McCarthy at MIT in 1958, on an IBM 704. The first versions could be used only on this machine, and some of the mnemonic codes, such as CAR—contents of the address part of the register number—reflect this. But the language evolved continually; a second version was implemented on an IBM 709, and gradually interpreters or compilers appeared on almost all scientific machines. Today LISP is defined independently of any machine.

The original aim of LISP was the handling of certain problems in artificial intelligence; it was therefore directed toward manipulating symbolic expressions and lists of objects; the name, in fact, comes from LISt Processor. Its field has since been extended: from manipulation of algebraic expressions to chess playing, from formal proofs of theorems to certain problems of automatic translation, and so on.

Data in LISP are *symbolic expressions*, or *S-expressions*. An S-expression can be either an *atomic symbol* or a pair of S-expressions. Thus the definition is recursive. If

B,   3.5,   CDA,   A,   C

are defined to be symbols, then

A,   (A,B),   (A,(B,C)),   ((A,B),CDA),   (((A,(B,C)),B)

are all S-expressions. Two operators that can be applied to S-expressions are CAR and CDR. The result of CAR(S) is the left part of S, and of CDR(S) is the right part:

CAR(A,(B,C)) = A,   CDR((A,(B,C)) = (B,C).

New S-expressions can be formed by means of the operator CONS:

CONS(A,B) = (A,B),   CONS(A,(B,A)) = (A,(B,A)).

The identity of two S-expressions can be tested by means of the operator EQ, the result of which is given by the atomic symbols T (true), F (false):

EQ(A,(B,C)) = F,   EQ((A,B),(A,B)) = T.

Another operator, ATOM, is used to test whether an S-expression is an atomic symbol:

ATOM((A,B)) = F,   ATOM(A) = T.

Conditions are expressed in the form:

p1→e1,   p2→e2,   · · · · ·   pn→en,

meaning that if p1 is true, then e1 is taken, or if p2 then e2,. . . .

These definitions give enough for us to show an example of a LISP program. The problem is to define a function FA that will give the leftmost symbol of a list to which it is applied, and the solution is

FA(x) = (ATOM(x)→x,   T→FA(CAR(x))).

For example, let x be the S-expression ((A,B),C). ATOM((A,B),C) = F, so that we apply the second condition indicated by T and calculate FA((A,B)). The result is again F, so that we continue and calculate FA(A), which is true and the result is therefore T. Thus FA((A,B),C) = A.

It is seen from the foregoing that in LISP every operation is written as a list, of which the first element is the operator and the others are the operands. Thus in CAR(A,B), CAR is the operator and A,B are the operands. This may remind the reader of Polish notation. More generally, a LISP program is simply a mathematical definition of a function, followed by the list of arguments of that function. In contrast to other high-level languages, there is no need in LISP to give a name to a function, provided that it does not need to call itself during its evaluation. The above example shows that LISP is a recursive language. There are no assignment statements; a LISP program is itself a list, with a large overlay of sublists.

Other contrasts to languages of the von Neumann type are these:

the concept of an "instruction" does not exist in LISP;

the running of the program is initiated directly by the specialized operators and their operands;

a LISP program has the same structure as LISP data, and there is no distinction between the two; thus one program can be used as a data item in another.

LISP is very popular with artificial-intelligence specialists. However, it has intrinsic defects. It is applicable mainly to problems concerned with manipulating symbolic expressions or lists. Also, LISP programs are very difficult to read and to write; much of this difficulty is due to the many parentheses, among which it is often difficult to decide which left parenthesis goes with which right parenthesis.

APL

It should be possible to produce a language for which the notation is much closer to that of mathematics as generally used, even if the mathematical notation has to be modified slightly so that the keyboards of existing input equipment can be used. Such a language for general use would certainly be less functional than LISP, and in the interests of making modifications easily possible, the objects that it manipulates should not need to be declared. APL, A Programming Language, is such a language.

Originally APL, due to Kenneth Iverson, was designed as a tool for the description and the formal analysis of a computer. It was used in 1962 to describe the IBM 7090, among other applications (Iverson [1962]), and in 1964 the IBM 360. Just as the design of a computer may be based on the form of a programming language, so a language may be used to describe a computer's design. I have already mentioned the letters between Ada, Countess of Lovelace, and Charles Babbage on this point; another reference which may be consulted is Hopper [1953].

At the end of the 1950s Iverson extended the work he had done for his doctoral thesis by developing subroutines with which he could test the relative merits of different methods for solving systems of differential equations. Experience with this work led him to the decision that an APL program should consist of a "central body" that could call any number of independent subroutines and that like FORTRAN it should not have a block structure. But in contrast to FORTRAN, in which the types of named objects apply throughout the whole of the subroutine in which they appear, or throughout the whole program, in APL they are taken into account only at the moment when the instruction in which they appear is obeyed.

Iverson convinced himself also that data items should be handled very dynamically during the running of a program and therefore should not be frozen by initial declarations; in APL, therefore, names are not declared at the start of a program. But this makes APL difficult to compile. In fact, one of the conditions that must be satisfied if a language is to be compilable is that all the information needed in order to determine the type of object to which a name refers be available before the instruction in which it occurs is executed. If the type is not declared, then, in particular, the object program cannot be optimized. We see, then, that not all high-level languages are compilable.

In addition, Iverson wanted it to be simple to express mathematical relations. APL therefore includes function expressions with explicitly stated arguments, and the results of evaluating these are given immediately; the relations $=$, $>$, $<$, . . . ,are treated as functions. There are also functional forms, including inner and outer products and reduction, very much in line with the ideas of functional programming.

The first interpreters for APL appeared about 1964, and a new religion grew up around them. APL, as I have said, is very different from other high-level languages; consequently one large body of programmers takes the view that nothing can be achieved, whatever the field of application, except by writing in APL, while another, equally large, body considers APL useless and of no importance.

Quasi-functional languages like APL and completely functional languages like LISP provide an approach to programming that is entirely different from that provided by what are called the von Neumann languages. Their special notation, and in some respects their complexity, make the former at one and the same time easy for specialists and difficult for nonspecialists; this is a consequence of our third characteristic. Altogether it seems likely that while there are only a few functional languages available at present, the number will increase in the near future in order to relieve the very strong restrictions on freedom of expression of algorithms imposed by the "von Neumann bottleneck."

5 Conclusion

Let us now assess the value of the characteristics given at the start of this chapter as a means of classifying the different languages.

1. According to some writers (Sammet [1978]) the essential difference between high-level and low-level languages is this. For the latter, the forms of the instructions and the data are very close; for the former, however, the two forms are different, and the instructions can be much more complex. But this criterion would lead to the conclusion that LISP, in which instructions and data have the same form, is a low-level language—a contradiction that has led some writers to say that LISP is not classifiable. The difficulty is avoided if we take our second characteristic as the criterion and say that a high-level language is distinguished by a nontrivial syntax and that translation into elementary instructions always requires a syntax analysis.

2. At what point does the application of the third characteristic provide programming languages with what Sammet calls a *conceptual form*, which to a certain extent may inhibit the expression of one's thoughts? It is clear, for example, that specialists in artificial intelligence will find it easier to express themselves in LISP than in a language less well adapted to their needs, in spite of difficulties that the LISP notation might present to a nonspecialist. Thus the form of a language will seem to users to be more or less well adapted, or more or less con-

straining, according to their levels of familiarity with the concepts with which it is concerned. The possible forms are very varied. In this historical period they have ranged from forms close to natural languages, of which COBOL was the most significant example, to forms corresponding to highly symbolic concepts, such as those of LISP. A way was opened either for communication between man and machine in terms of quasi-natural language, a very common feature of today's use of computers, or, in the opposite direction, for the use of functional forms. It follows that there is no objective criterion for the form of language that a user should choose when wishing to communicate with a machine.

3. There is the problem of deciding whether a language may be considered as universal—and therefore whether it has the fourth characteristic. Consider a few examples. When the Florentine monks of the fifteenth century discovered the method for solving the cubic equation, there was no algebraic language, and they had to express their method in a universal language—Latin. This required a book of 150 pages, whereas in a modern textbook on algebra it is given in a page or so and is easily understood. When Backus described FORTRAN to von Neumann, the latter, so it is said, asked what could be done in FORTRAN that could not be done in machine language. Clearly only machine language is truly universal. But universality may act against ease of use, as the monks found, and up to some point may diverge from the third characteristic by requiring new concepts to be expressed in terms that (as was implied in von Neumann's comment on FORTRAN) had been laid down without taking these into account. The only way in which a high-level language can be relatively universal is by having means for easy expression of the concepts of a large number of fields of application. But then it becomes very bulky, and even so it still may prove ill adapted to use in a new field.

Thus again there is no unequivocal answer to the problem. Programmers will doubtless prefer a language specifically adapted to the needs of a well-defined field if they need to solve problems in that field, and a more "universal" language if they are concerned with problems from several fields.

4. Up to 1960 the main effort in computer science went into achieving efficient translation of programming languages; thus the definitions of these languages were often arrived at as a compromise between the need, on the one hand, for conceptual forms to make the language easy to use in its field of application and, on the other, for simple structures that would be easy to compile. However, once the problems

of compilation were understood, there was a natural move (as in the case of ALGOL) toward the theoretical study of the form that the definition itself of a language should take. Consequently, by the end of this period the groundwork had been laid for a fundamental study of programming, to cover not only man-machine communication but also the objects of that communication, the algorithms.

The first thing to do when a problem is to be solved is to devise an algorithm; this is then communicated to the computer through the medium of a programming language. Unfortunately an error may occur at this stage. It is necessary, therefore, to make tests to determine whether the result obtained corresponds to the data supplied. But if the number of possible combinations of input data items is too great, the programmer will have to be satisfied with taking samples of these, hoping that they are well chosen and that if the program gives correct results in these cases, it will do so always. It is as if one went about proving that the sum of the squares of the two sides of a right-angled triangle is equal to the square of the hypotenuse by measuring the sides of a variety of triangles of different shapes and sizes; such a procedure could never give the absolute certainty of a mathematical proof. In 1962 methods for proving whether a program gave the solution to the problem for which it was written were proposed almost simultaneously by Goldstine and von Neumann [1963] and, in a more formal style, by McCarthy [1963]. I shall not discuss how this was achieved, but shall simply say, as seems obvious, that it requires that the programming language be formally and unambiguously defined.

This leads to the conclusion that a fifth characteristic of programming languages should be laid down:

5. A programming language should make it possible for a proof to be given that a program written in the language is correct. It must therefore be defined formally and unambiguously (Lecarme [1975]).

Much work has been done in the years since 1962 on the problem of proof of programs. It is now possible to prove or *verify*[16] that a program is correct if it is "small." This work has made it possible to use a methodology of programming unknown to the period with which this book is concerned. Programming is no longer done as it once was.

To finish, we must take up one last question: Why is it that the early languages FORTRAN, COBOL, PL/I, APT, with all their imperfections, are still those most used throughout the world, to the extent that they count for some 80% of all programs? The reason is that there is no automatic translator by means of which one can turn a program written in one high-level language into its equivalent in another. Consequently a computing center, having started by writing its programs in one language, cannot change to another without rewriting all the programs in its library. It is inertia, therefore, that holds back the spread of a new language.

5

Conclusions

The announcement of the IBM 360 series of computers in the United States in April 1964 marked the end of the period during which the foundations of computer science were laid. A number of stages had to be gone through in order to arrive at this state. There were first the several thousand years of development of the necessary concepts of mathematics; then the attempts to mechanize the operations of arithmetic, spread over the past four centuries; then the development of the first calculators, which, thanks to the advances in technology, took place over the last ten decades; and finally the appearance of the first computers thirty years ago. The computer has become commonplace. It is no longer an exceptionally expensive piece of equipment, even though it is still very dear, and its possession is no longer confined to a few richly endowed research centers. It has become reliable, fast, and effective and is manufactured on an industrial scale. By 1963 there were more than 20,000 installations in the western world; in the United States alone there were 16,000, with 9,000 more on order.

Europe is clearly behind America in this. According to a study made by the French computer bureau AFCALTI at that time, there were only a few hundred computers in France at the end of 1962. And France was not significantly behind the other western countries, nor behind Russia or the eastern countries, which had even fewer machines (see appendix). And yet, the first calculating machines originated in Europe, and during the 1950s Europe played a far from insignificant role in the development of science. But no European country had a big enough home market to enable it to compete with other computer manufacturers on a world scale. However, an even more important factor in Europe's failure to assume a leadership role in computers was World War II. The war brought an end to Europe's technological preeminence. The governments of Europe, fully occupied with the task of repairing the war's ravages, were neither able nor willing to help a new industry; in fact, even when this new idustry's future importance became quite clear, Europe's governments provided for it only halfheartedly. It was in the United States that the development of computers took off; and this was due to a small number of men, some of whom were scientists and some industrialists, and also to the drive of a small number of industrial companies, especially IBM, whose history seems inextricably mixed with that of the computer.

I have presented the successes of this industrial drive of the 1950s. As is always the case when progress is being made, some lines of development turn out to be dead ends. I did not deal with these in the preceding accounts so as not to overload the text, but here I give two examples, both concerned with novel ideas for building memories that raised great hopes in the early 1960s (Bowers [1977]): magnetic-tape cylinders and optical disks.

The idea behind the use of magnetic tape in the form of a cylinder (the "tape loop RAM") is simple. A magnetic drum is only a thin, virtually massless layer of magnetizable material that has been deposited on the surface of a cylindrical mass of metal so that it can be turned at high speed close to, but never touching, a reading/writing head. What is more natural than to seek to get rid of that mass of metal? And therefore why not make the cylinder from a loop of magnetic tape having about the same breadth as the height of the drum, getting the necessary rigidity as a result of centrifugal force when the loop is rotated rapidly? Further, it should be possible to have a series of concentric loops, one inside the other, and thus to have the equivalent of several drums in the same volume without the need for the supporting metal. A memory constructed thus should not be expensive — the first examples which were built cost about $15,000 — and should have a large capacity for the time, 50 million bits, and a low access time of about 90 milliseconds. The idea was attractive. But unfortunately such a device never worked satisfactorily for more than a few hours under practical conditions, and it was abandoned.

The proposal for the optical-disk memory arose in connection with attempts to use the computer to translate automatically between natural languages, the aim being to produce a memory large enough to hold very extensive dictionaries. The optical disk was a form of *read-only memory*, with a capacity of about 70 million bits. On some of these disks the information was written at a density of 2,000 bits per inch along a track, with 2,000 tracks per inch radially. Reading was done by means of a light spot at a rate of a few microseconds per word.

But only the prototype worked satisfactorily. It turned out that the slightest speck of dust falling on the disk at the time of either reading or writing made several hundreds of words of the dictionary inaccessible; it proved impossible to make a perfect disk, and the imperfections varied from one disk to another, so again the project was abandoned. But the idea of the optical disk was sufficiently attractive for it to be revived later; it has now been implemented in today's technology, using a laser in the read/write head to avoid these drawbacks.

While the way of progress may have been strewn with pitfalls, there is no doubt that there were some striking achievements during this historical period. This is well illustrated by the improvements in computer price and performance. (In this context, significance can be attached to performance, as to price, only in stated circcumstances.) Figure 5.1 shows the approximate time needed to compute the product of two numbers, each occupying a word in the memory, for each of the most powerful machines of its time between 1944 and 1962. This is a very inadequate measure, but the figure does show the 100-fold increase in speed every 10 years that is generally reckoned to be typical. This rate of increase has continued without any falling off and seems likely to do so until computing speeds come up against the limit imposed by the velocity of light. Achieving these speeds gives rise to various problems, and in fact, to increase their effective speeds, the largest computer systems of today make systematic use of multiprocessing.

The same figure gives also the corresponding times for several scientific machines that were produced in numbers that were large for the period. These show a similar rate of change, but with a slight delay in time, illustrating how the techniques developed for the fastest machine at any period become those used in what may be called the production machines. (The regression line in the figure shows only the average rate of change for the two types of machine.)

Even more remarkable than this increase in speed, and equally characteristic, is that it has been accompanied by a steady fall in price, a factor of about 100 every 10 years; and this has also continued until today and shows no signs of slackening. Figure 5.2 shows the results of some calculations made by Knight [1966] of the performance/price ratio for various IBM scientific machines. Again one can criticize the measure chosen for comparison. But to confirm the tendency that it reveals, figure 5.3 gives a performance/price ratio for a sequence of IBM machines that takes speed into account; the figures are taken from a paper written by L. M. Branscomb, IBM chief scientist. To see

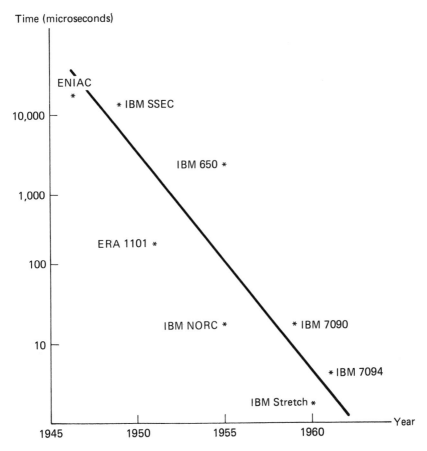

Figure 5.1
Reduction in multiplication time (approximate values).

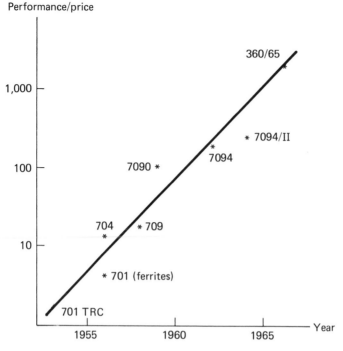

Figure 5.2
Improvement in the performance/price ratio (expressed as the number of operations performed at a price of $1,000) for some IBM scientific machines.

what the tendency shown by Knight's figures has led to in the field of small machines, one has only to go to one of the specialist shops or big stores, where one can buy for a few hundred dollars any of a number of microprocessors, which in spite of their small size are more powerful machines than the IBM SSEC or the ENIAC of only 30 years ago, each of which weighed many tons and filled a room of over 1,000 square feet.

It is a consequence of the development of microelectronics, which began at the end of the second generation of computers, that the computer has shrunk steadily in size with the same exponential tendency as the decrease in price and the increase in performance. The very small processing units called microprocessors have been put to a wide variety of uses since manufacturing facilities for very large-scale integration (VLSI) were set up in 1976. With this technology, which is still in full development, it has become possible, for example, to build the central units of the IBM 4300 with silicon chips 20 millimeters square, each carrying 704 logical circuits. We should note

Relative speed/relative price

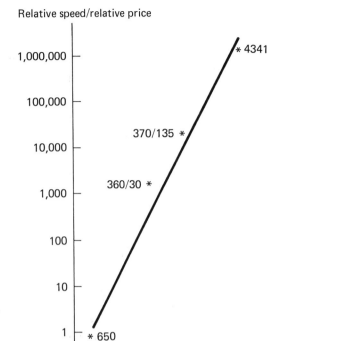

Figure 5.3

Improvement in the performance/price ratio when speed is taken into account (expressed as relative speed divided by relative price) for some IBM machines. The figure's entries are based on the following data:

IBM machine	Relative speed	Relative price[a]	Relative speed/relative price
650 (1953)	1	1	1
360/30 (1964)	43	0.025	1,700
370/135 (1971)	214	0.011	19,000
4341 (1979)	1,143	0.001	1,143,000

a. The cost to execute one instruction per second.

The numbers on the figure's vertical axis are evenly spaced powers of 10.

here that "microprocessor" and "microcomputer" should not be confused: a microcomputer is built around a microprocessor, but the input/output units, visual-display screens, typewriterlike keyboards, printers, and so on, cannot be miniaturized, and it is these that take up virtually all the space and, as pointed out when discussing printers, account for most of the cost.

The improvement in the performance/price ratio made it possible to produce machines that were better adapted to the users' needs, and thus to broaden the range of computers available. This broadening was shown by the development of ever more powerful machines, usually for general application, at one extreme and ever more specialized small machines like the CAB 500 and the IBM 1620 at the other; these latter were the forerunners of today's *personal computers*. Of course, the CAB 500 and the IBM 1620 were not as small as today's microcomputer, but they could easily be put in an ordinary room. If they needed some air conditioning, they did not require the elaborate environmental controls demanded by the top-of-the-line machines. If they did not have the visual-display screens of most of today's microcomputers, they did not differ fundamentally from them in either basic design or use. But their prices made it almost impossible for a private individual to own one, and they counted as "office" machines. The idea of the personal computer had to await the arrival of successors that were portable, needed no air conditioning, and cost only a few hundred dollars.

However, this broadening of manufacturers' computer lines brought some new problems. The manufacturers' tendency had been to build machines for particular types of application and not to give much attention either to compatibility with other machines in the same line or to any possible increase in the users' needs. Manufacturers therefore found themselves facing a triple challenge: to make machines that were general-purpose, mutually compatible, and modular (that is, structured as modules, so that users could adjust their systems in response to changing needs simply by adding or removing a module rather than having to replace the complete system).

At the end of 1961, in spite of the misgivings of those who feared that the decision would render obsolete all the machines already delivered, Thomas J. Watson, Jr., asked Frederick P. Brooks to design a series of modular, compatible, and general-purpose machines: this was to be called the IBM 360 series, by analogy with the 360 degrees of the compass. The main authors of the series were Gene Amdahl and Gerrit A. Blaauw. Six compatible models were announced in April 1964: IBM 360 Models 30, 40, 50, 60, 62, and 70. Their general-purpose character was due mainly to the use of the byte, or octet, taken from Stretch. The appearance of the IBM 360 series was another sign that the second generation of computers was coming to an end.

Another consequence of the improvement in the computer performance/price ratio was that it vastly increased the market for its buyers and users. No longer were the richest research establishments the only ones able to afford them, doubtless for use in their scientific work. In fact, this improvement made it possible for the computer to extend its field of application from the scientific world first into business and then into every field of human activity. Thomas J. Watson's predictions were fulfilled; the first computer to be manufactured in large numbers was a business machine, the IBM 1401, of which over 10,000 were made.

At the beginning of the 1950s business people were regarded as lower-class citizens so far as computer science was concerned, unable to appreciate such elegances as floating-point arithmetic or to comprehend a computational procedure. But this attitude changed drastically by 1963; as the dominant users, they were now given much more consideration. Since they were not comfortable with algebraic instructions, languages such as COBOL were developed so that they could express the solutions to their problems in terms more familiar to them. Since they needed to store enormous volumes of data, new technologies were developed to make this possible, such as the magnetic tapes of UNIVAC I and the magnetic disks of the IBM 305. Since they needed to issue extensive tables of results, high-speed printers were developed; the first of these was the printer on the UNIVAC I, which even then printed 600 lines a minute with 120 characters to a line. Indeed, by the end of the 1960s the boundary between scientific and business applications was becoming less and less definite because operations research, the scientists' tool for decision making, needed long calculations involving ever increasing volumes of data.

And then the computer entered into all fields of human activity. Several such fields have already been mentioned: payroll and billing in commercial companies, administration, banking, insurance, seat reservation in trains and airplanes, and so on. But there are other such fields, such as teaching and medicine, whose boundaries encompass everyone. The first experiments on the use of the computer to aid in teaching [an application now known as Computer-Assisted Education, CAE, or Computer-Based Training, CBT] were made at IBM's American research center in 1958 (Galanter [1959]). The first application to medicine seems to have been an experiment on computer-assisted diagnosis made in France in 1956 (Paycha [1957]); corresponding work in the United States has been described by Ledley [1959]. Many other medical applications were described at a conference on the subject organized by IBM at Poughkeepsie in 1958.

Mention must also be made of the important work done in artificial intelligence, of which the best-known example was the automatic translation of natural languages. Although the original purely syntactic approach has been abandoned in favor of more sophisticated methods, there is no doubt that the computer has made it impossible to discuss grammatical structures in the way this used to be done. Indeed, as work in this area shows, the very existence of the computer can stimulate intellectual progress. Interestingly enough, the work on language translation contributed to the development of compilers; this, of course, was not fortuitous, because translation from a programming language to machine language is a simple case of translation between natural languages. In addition to this application, and to others mentioned in the course of the book, such as proving theorems and playing chess or other games, there have been many others; an example is the processing of visual images with the aim of reproducing the power of the human eye to identify structures and other details. The first experiments along these lines seem to have been made by IBM in 1962.

In sum, by 1963 the range of applications of computers had become so wide that computer science was no longer the private territory of the mathematicians but had become a new science in its own right, with its own fields of research, its own applications, and an industry that both led and followed it.

The expansion of the range of applicability of the computer was the result of the development of technologies aimed at helping the users to solve their problems. The methods of attacking problems have changed fundamentally since the appearance of the computer, and especially since it has become possible to interact with the machine. Everything about the development of the computer has encouraged this change. The increase in calculating speeds and in the provision of other resources, especially memory, has led to the development of operating systems, the forerunners of those used today, for bridging the gap between machine and human speeds. And improvements in the means for input and output have made communication with the machine easier.

Actual interaction first appeared in the form of Stibitz's experiments in 1941 on communication with a machine from a distance. The technique was developed in the first networks of interconnected computers such as SAGE, which made possible the use of remotely stored files of information. Above all, the evolution of programming languages, either toward the more and more specialized or toward the more and more general, such as FORTRAN, COBOL, APL, and PL/I, made it easier for the machine to be given the "competence" needed for the solution of problems. The next step was to make it possible to use not only files stored in distant machines but also programs or other information stored by other users.

As a result of these advances, interactive working with the machine became possible. Now, relieved by the computer of routine tasks, incidental calculations, and other tedious and time-consuming activities, able to draw on the competence given to the machine by others, and enabled to get responses quickly and easily, users could make better use of their knowledge of the external world and of their subjective powers. The computer had become an intellectual amplifier.

If one were asked to sum up in a few words the evolution of computer science since the appearance of the first computers, one could begin by saying that the 1950s were the years during which it was shown that the computer could be manufactured, first on an industrial scale at all and then, because it was seen to meet a real need, in large numbers. I have dealt with the whole of this period. The 1960s were the years in which compatible families of computers appeared and the main types of operating systems. I have described the first achievements of this period; the developments which took place during the last years of the decade were essentially a continuation of those of its first years. The 1970s were the years during which the techniques and technologies of the computer and communications came together and were also the years when the personal computer appeared. The 1980s will undoubtedly be the years of the management of enormous data bases; we have seen that such problems were already appearing in the 1950s.

1963 marked the end of a crucial period in the history of the computer. By the end of that year, machine architecture, the main means for input and output, the main types of other resources and the means for exploiting them, and the main programming languages had all been defined. All the main fields of application had at least been studied. I have described only a few of the ideas and achievements that mark the later development of the subject. This may give the impression of a falling off during the last few years, when it seems that only technology has continued to advance at the old rate. It is a fact that during the first two decades after the end of World War II an immense fund of knowledge was exploited that had been accumulated over centuries in such fields as science, mathematics, logic, and linguistics. The symbiosis of these fields demonstrated by Chomsky in 1957 (Chomsky [1957]) is an excellent example; it lies at the roots of the main theories of programming languages and of the concepts of the syntax of natural languages.

It is no exaggeration to say that there has been no fundamental development in computer science since 1963. The years preceding had seen a real flowering of ideas, applications, and experiments, a richness that had impressed even the scientists. How, then, could the nonscientists be other than astonished? How could they avoid those feelings of spontaneous generation, rather mysterious and rather evil, about computers of which I spoke in the introduction to the book? Nevertheless this harvest of ideas gave rise to a number of [technical] problems, the most serious of which concern the architecture of the von Neumann machines. The bottleneck in this design has, as we have seen, become increasingly a brake on the development of both software and data bases (Flynn [1974]). Only new research will make progress possible.

APPENDIX
Early Work on Computers in the USSR

It is very difficult to identify the first developments in computer science in the USSR. The most reliable sources of information are a few papers published in the West, in particular, those by John W. Carr et al. [1959], H. C. Davies and S. E. Goodman [1978], which includes a detailed bibliography, and A. P. Ershov [1975].[a] Little effort seems to have been made in the Soviet Union before 1963 to build general-purpose computers in any large numbers. Nevertheless, a number of significant projects were undertaken. In 1947 S. A. Lebedev undertook to design a calculator, the MESM, which was built at Kiev and was put into service around 1950. Most of the Russian computers are derivatives of this: BESM1 and STRELA, which appeared around 1951; the M20 series, around 1956; and KIEV, around 1959. In parallel with the developments proceeding from MESM was a second line of developments proceeding from the M1, which first appeared in 1951. Let us deal with the two series[b] (see figure A.1).

Machines Derived from MESM

The BESM series   BESM1, as described in Lebedev [1956], was originally a machine with Williams-tube memory and, according to Russian statements, a speed of 7,000–8,000 operations per second; it seems that this refers to the average time for an arithmetic operation. Its only input medium, at least up to 1959 (Carr et al. [1959]), was punched paper tape, read at the very low speed of 20 characters per second. Output was printed at 1,200 lines per minute, but for one thing, this was really very slow because the line was of only 10 figures against the 120 characters of the printers on Western machines, and for another, this output, as well as the input data, was solely numerical. It seems that for a long time computer work in Russia was concerned

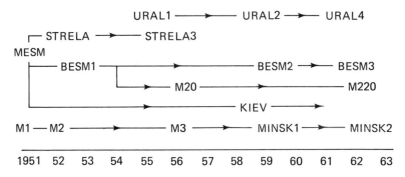

Figure A.1
Genealogy of the first Soviet computers.

only with numbers and very seldom with letters. BESM2, which replaced BESM1 in 1960, had a ferrite-core memory of 1,023 words with an access time of 6 microseconds.

The STRELA series   Another of the earliest machines derived from MESM was the STRELA, built by Y. Y. Vasilevsky of the Ministry of Automation and put into service in 1953. It too had Williams-tube memory. The STRELA3, derived from it, was built in 1956. But the series proved unsatisfactory and was abandoned.

SETUN and the URAL series   These machines replaced the STRELAs; they are shown in figure A.1 and table A.1, but I do no more than merely mention them. SETUN was an experimental machine.

The M20 series   M20 was a first-generation machine derived from BESM1, with a speed of 20,000 operations per second. It came into service in 1956 and was used for the top-priority work of the time, mainly in connection with the space program and military problems. The M20 series was designed at the Institute for Precision Mechanics in Moscow;[c] a transistorized version, the M220, was built at Kazan in 1963.

The KIEV   This machine was built at the Computing Center of the Ukranian Academy of Sciences in Kiev, reportedly for the nuclear research center at Dubna, and came into service in 1959. It was still a nontransistorized machine, with the added peculiarity of having no internal clock. There was a small core memory of 1,000 words, each of 41 bits, with an access time of 10 microseconds per word; and a secondary memory of three drums of 3,000 words each, running at 1,500 revolutions per minute. The extent to which the Soviet developments were behind those of the Western countries is shown by the comparison between the KIEV and Western machines of the same period, in particular, the LARC, which was aimed at the same types of application.

The MINSK Series

A second line of computers is derived from a prototype built at the Moscow Institute of Energy by I. S. Bruk, who built the M1 in 1951, the M2 in 1952, and the M3 in 1956. This was the MINSK22 series, the first of which appeared in 1964; the machines were built in Bye-lorussia to the order of the Ministry of Radio. MINSK2 and MINSK22 were the most used general-purpose computers in Russia; 2,000 of them and their derivatives were built between 1951 and 1976 (see table A.1).

MINSK2 and MINSK22 each had a set of 107 two-address instructions and a word length of 37 bits; the computing speed was 5,000 instructions per second and a floating-point addition took 72 microseconds. Main memory was on ferrite cores, with either 4,000 or 8,000 words; secondary memory was on magnetic tapes, although some MINSK22 machines had drums also. The MINSK22 was the first Russian machine to have input and output equipment that could handle letters as well as figures.

The different members of the MINSK series were not mutually compatible; compatability was provided only for some series of machines produced after 1963. The first experiments with multiprocessing seem to have been made in 1969 with a MINSK2 linked to a MINSK22 to give a machine called the MINSK222.

This appendix has mentioned only those Russian machines that seem to have been the most typical of the period. They were all intended for scientific applications—hence the choice of a long word, always greater than 36 bits, in the interests of high precision in the arithmetic, and the frequent use of binary arithmetic, and also perhaps the in-adequate input/output equipment. The long word made the machines unsuitable for business applications. Further, the secondary memories, which at best were provided by magnetic tapes and often by punched paper tapes, were of a very low standard. The actual magnetic tape was of such poor quality that the tape used on the MINSK22 had 16 tracks, of which 6 were for data and 2 for control, while the remaining 8 duplicated these as a safety measure. Disks did not appear until around 1973.

Development of practically useful software was made difficult by the lack of input and output equipment of the type common on

Table A.1
Characteristics of the first Soviet machines

	M2	STRELA	BESM1	URAL	KIEV	SETUN
Project leader	I. S. Bruk	Y. Y. Vasilevsky	S. A. Lebedev	B. I. Rameev		
Date	1952	1953	1953	1955	1959	1960
Word length (bits)	34	43	39	36	41	18
Multiplication time (fl = float, fx = fix)		fl 500 microseconds	fl 270 microseconds	fx 10 milliseconds	fx 290 microseconds	fl 360 microseconds
Main memory type	Williams tubes	Williams tubes	Williams tubes	drum	core	core
Main-memory capacity (number of words)	512	1,024 + 496 ROM	1,024 + 376 ROM	1,024	1,024 + 512 ROM	81
Main-memory access time	25 microseconds	20 microseconds	6 microseconds		10 microseconds	14 microseconds
Secondary-memory drum	512		5,120	1,024	3 × 3,000	4,000
Number of instructions per word		1	1	2	1	2
Number of addresses per instruction	3	3	3	1	3	1
Number of tubes	1,879	8,000	4,000	870	2,300	40
Input		Paper tape	Paper tape	Paper tape	Paper tape	
Output	Teletype	Punched card	Tabulator	Tabulator	Paper tape Tabulator	Paper tape Teletype

Western machines, the lack of visual display units, and the practice of not using letters in communicating with the machine. Also, while interesting work on the theory of programming languages was being done in the eastern European countries at this time, almost all programming was done in machine or assembly language. The first FORTRAN and COBOL compilers appeared only toward the end of the 1960s, and these languages were not used to any serious extent until the middle of the 1970s. Operating systems, often modeled on those produced in the West, did not appear until the late 1960s.

Altogether, the attitude toward computer science in the Soviet Union seems to have been that it was relevant only to high-priority scientific projects and did not merit attention beyond that. This is possibly the reason for there being only a few thousand computers installed there by the end of 1970 (Davis and Goodman [1978]). After that date it seems that the government decided to devote some effort to the design and production of computers for data-processing applications.

Author's Notes

Chapter 1

1. Consider, for example, "If I go on holiday, I take my car." The first elementary proposition, or *antecedent*, here is "(if) I go on holiday"; the second, or *consequent*, is "I take my car." The conditional proposition expressing a relation between two elementary propositions in such a way that the second follows from the first has formed an essential part of logic since the time of the Greek Stoics. Thus it is not surprising that conditional statements form part of the structure of algorithms.

2. Shannon's sampling theorem states that if a continuous function $f(t)$ of time t has

(1) a frequency spectrum with an upper limit f_m and

(2) a period k_1 such that $f(t)$ takes nonzero values between $t = 0$ and k and is zero between $t = k$ and k_1,

then it can be reconstructed from samples taken at intervals $1/2f_m$, provided that k and k_1 are sufficiently great.

3. According to Goldstine [1972] the word "bit" was invented by John Tukey during some discussions on ENIAC (see section 4 in this chapter).

4. There is a copy of this machine at the Musée des Arts et Techniques, Conservatoire des Arts et Métiers, in Paris.

5. In this, Leibniz was not influenced by either Schickard, whom he probably did not know, or Pascal, whom he certainly did know.

6. Many of these machines are at museums: the Museum of History and Technology in Washington, the Science Museum in London, the Musée des Techniques in Paris.

7. Augusta Ada Byron (1816–1852) was the only daughter of Lord and Lady Byron; she became Countess of Lovelace by her marriage in 1835.

8. Many types of analog calculation make use of electric circuits; the commonest are those using direct current; others use alternating current. Both are "continuous processes."

9. It should not be inferred from this that analog calculation is no longer of interest or importance; it is, in fact, still very much in use, particularly for performing calculations in parallel and for simulating complex phenomena. While the speed of analog calculation can be limited by the time constants of the components from which the calculator is built, it is usually independent of the complexity of the process.

10. Combinations of the two types of calculator, analogical and digital, called *hybrid calculators*, have been built, which to some extent give the advantages of both.

11. Léon Bollée was the son of Amédée Bollée, who built a steam car, La Mancelle, which in 1873 completed the Le Mans-Paris run. Léon and his brother Amédée became famous after World War I for their achievements in perfecting the motor car. It was they who organized the first Le Mans race.

12. One of Bollée's machines is now at the Musée des Techniques in Paris.

13. Felt called his machine the "macaroni box" because he built the first model using the wood of just such a box. There is a model at the Musée des Techniques in Paris.

14. In 1920 Watson, as president of CTR, went to Paris to form a new company, Société Internationale de Machines Commerciales; this was to sell American-made Hollerith machines in France and is the origin of IBM France. In 1922 he assembled together all the French staff in Paris: a total of 12 people. (It is more than 20,000 today.)

15. It is interesting that right to the end, Powers Samas made almost nothing but entirely mechanical machines.

16. The machine was demonstrated in 1914 at the Laboratoire de Mécanique at the Sorbonne, Paris.

17. The Z3 performed a multiplication in 3 to 4 seconds.

18. This system is often called FIFO, which in English stands for First In, First Out. [A better rendering in this context is First Come, First Served.]

19. Later Aiken and Grace Hopper were drafted into the US Navy, which assigned both to duty at Harvard.

20. The calculator unit is displayed in the entrance hall of the Howard Hathaway Aiken Computation Laboratory at Harvard. Large parts are at the Museum of History and Technology in Washington, DC.

21. The laboratory did not take this name until 1938.

22. In 1944 the Bell Labs machine took 40 minutes for one calculation of this size; in 1944 the MARK I took 15 minutes.

23. With this in mind Mauchly had visited John V. Atanasoff (Atanasoff [1940]), of Bulgarian origin and a professor at Iowa State University, who had published papers giving his ideas on the same question. Atanasoff claimed later that the Moore School machines were only implementations of his ideas.

24. Note also the use of the recently published theoretical work of Shannon on circuit design.

25. Some modules of ENIAC are displayed at the Museum of History and Technology in Washington, DC.

26. Similarly the logician Kleene gave the name *neuronal automata* to the finite-state automata that he had just defined, seeing these as modeling neurons and synapses (Kleene [1956]).

27. Mauchly [1979] has described the role played by Eckert and himself in the development of the stored-program principle; Goldstine did not object to my referring to that article.

28. The term used in the French edition, *ordinateur*, was invented by Jacques Perret in 1956, at the request of IBM France, which wanted a French equivalent for the

English/American *data-processing machine*. The new word had such success that IBM waived its claim to its use.

29. Thomas J. Watson, Jr., became president of IBM in 1952.

30. The program had been written by Kenneth Clark, who was undoubtedly one of the first full-time programmers in the industry.

31. In 1947 IBM had a worldwide total of 23,000 employees, less than one-tenth the staff in 1977 and about the same as IBM France in 1980.

32. The US Army had allowed universities free use of ENIAC.

33. Einstein also was then at Princeton.

Chapter 2

1. This, of course, is only a statement of the principle. The instructions belonging to the operating system or, possibly, to a language compiler are often held in a part of the main memory not accessible to users.

2. If a *flip-flop* circuit is used, then in principle two tubes per bit are needed; but the two can be contained in a single glass envelope.

3. The ones most used [in computers] were *mercury delay lines*.

4. The main units of Whirlwind are displayed at the Museum of History and Technology in Washington, DC.

5. Magnetic tape and a very fast printer made the machine especially well adapted to the handling of the census data, which consisted of very large volumes of both input data to be processed and output results to be printed. Some of the main units of UNIVAC I are displayed at the Museum of History and Technology in Washington, DC.

6. In Williams's tubes the same electron gun was used for both creating and regenerating the charges. This gave it a decisive advantage over the similar tubes made by Forrester and Haeff at MIT, in which two guns were used, one for reading or writing and one for regeneration.

7. Williams tubes can be seen at many museums—for example, the Museum of Science in Boston or the Museum of History and Technology in Washington, DC [and the Science Museum in London].

8. The IAS is displayed at the Museum of History and Technology in Washington, DC.

9. These two special bits are still used in modern punched cards.

10. 5 bits would have allowed only 32 different characters to be represented.

11. 6-bit codes had in fact been used before this, notably by the international comunications body CCITT (Comité Consultif Télégraphique et Téléphonique). But this was for an alphabet of 58 characters, and the codes had a different structure.

12. The MARK III (see section 3 in chapter 1) had a drum memory, but was a universal calculator rather than a computer.

13. Personal communication from P. Dreyfus.

14. GE withdrew from computer manufacturing in 1970 and sold that side of its business to Honeywell.

15. In 1953 Whirlwind had a core memory of 2,048 words of 8 bits, with an access time of 9 microseconds.

16. Amdahl was the father also of the IBM 360 series. He left IBM to form his own company, Amdahl, Inc., for the manufacture of very powerful computers, and left this in turn to form a new company, ACSYS, which in March 1981 became linked with CII (Compagnie Internationale pour l'Informatique) Honeywell Bull.

17. As was noted in chapter 1, two calculators, the Bell Labs relay machine and the MARK II, had floating-point arithmetic.

18. An interesting attempt at a very fast memory was made with the UNIVAC 1107 in 1962, in the period of the second generation. The main memory was of ferrite cores, but control instructions were held in a supplemnetary memory made of thin magnetic film and having an access time on the order of nanoseconds. But the UNIVAC 1107 arrived too late on the scene and had little success.

19. I am grateful to Dimitri Starynkevitch, a former project leader at SEA, for some of the information given here.

20. Almost all manufacturers have adopted the IBM code for punching.

21. Several of the early machines were given names relating to storms—Whirlwind, Hurricane, and so on. This doubtless expressed the feeling that in the computer one had a truly revolutionary tool. [Translator's note: But the group under Zemanek in Vienna gave the name Mailufterl—a nice spring breeze—to the machine that they built between 1956 and 1958.]

22. The IBM 705 did not have floating-point arithmetic: it was thought that this was too sophisticated a concept to be handled by business people.

23. RCA also, taking the idea from RAMAC, used stacks of disks with their RCA 301 and RCA 601 computers.

24. As a mass memory, RAMAC was followed in the early 1960s by two other products that had similar capacities but did not use disks: the RANDEX from Univac and the CRAM from NCR. CRAM (Card Random Access Memory) comprised magnetic cards, which, when called for by the machine, were wrapped round a drum [and there read or written]; it was thus in a sense an improved form of magnetic drum. CRAM was very successful and continued well after RAMAC.

25. This machine is displayed at the Museum of History and Technology in Washington, DC.

Chapter 3

1. This computer is displayed at the Museum of History and Technology, Washington, DC.

2. Seymour Cray left Control Data later to form his own company, which in 1981 marketed an exceptionally powerful scientific computer, the Cray 1.

3. For IBM the second generation was signalized by the building at its Poughkeepsie plant of the world's first fully automatic production line for transistors. In 1959 this produced 1,800 transistors an hour, which then seemed remarkable, and which now seems ridiculously small.

4. The contract for this machine was between Univac and the Lawrence Radiation Laboratory in Livermore, California; hence the name.

5. There had already been diagnostic program on Whirlwind.

6. These were produced in collaboration with A. Perlis.

7. Among the reasons for the success of the IBM 1401 were the remarkable IBM 1403 printer and the easily used programming language, to be discussed.

8. This information was supplied by DEC's museum, open to the public in Marlborough, Massachusetts.

9. Microprogramming came into general use only with the appearance of the IBM 360 series; its use here made it possible for the different machines of the series to be made mutually compatible. The microprograms in these machines were held in what was called Read Only Memory (ROM), the contents of which could not be altered by the user.

10. There was the possibility of providing a multibranched switch for the selection of the peripheral. By analogy with the switching systems used in telecommunications, this type of equipment is called a *multiplexor*, and the activity *multiplexing*.

11. This switching from one program to another, and back again as required, is done automatically.

12. I shall not deal with the CDC 6000, an exceptionally powerful machine for its time, because the first deliveries of this were made in 1964, after the end of the period with which I am dealing. This was a multiprocessing system, with two central processors and 10 peripheral processors sharing the same memory.

13. The Honeywell 800 had considerable success, but mainly because of other features. We have already mentioned its emulation of the IBM 1401. Its low price also made it very attractive, although its financial success is open to question.

14. This was one of the last computers to be made by the Ferranti Company, the computer division of which became part of ICT in 1963 in the course of the regrouping of the British computer industry. It was in continuation of this policy of regrouping that in 1968 International Computers Ltd. (ICL) was formed by the merger of ICT and English Electric LEO Computers Ltd., which finally brought all the British mainframe companies together.

15. These were known as MULCOMS (multiplexor communications devices).

16. Actually, the receiver has to distinguish between three possibilities: the two signals and the silent interval between signals.

Chapter 4

1. In contrast, the location of the result of an addition had to specified.

2. "Mémoires d'information à dualité de sélection de données" ["Dual-selection data memories"], patent no. 1 155 548 G 06K, 5-07-1956. The same patent was registered shortly afterwards in the United States.

3. This was done with the aid of a precedence grammar that was very powerful for its period.

4. Backus had already produced SPEEDCODE.

5. Producing an assembler has become almost a science and can be automated; but producing a compiler has remained an art.

6. Rutishauser had already proposed a method for controlling conditional branching. Backus [1978] confirms that he did not know of this when he was planning FORTRAN.

7. It was of 51 pages, of which 21 were for a description of the language, 11 dealt with input and output, and the remaining 19 gave examples of programs written in the language.

8. The members were almost all former employees of the Eckert-Mauchly Corporation.

9. In Perlis [1958] ALGOL was described as a "single universal computer language."

10. Especially in the limitations on the DO and IF statements.

11. The definition of ALGOL 60 could be expressed in BNF because its syntax was a context-free grammar in the sense of Chomsky. The reader wishing to know more of this may consult Moreau [1975].

12. When they were not developing languages with aims between programming and teaching, like ALGOL W.

13. Chomsky had just published his *Syntactic Structures* [1957].

14. To make this universal coverage possible, PL/I has a structure that, up to a point, allows it to dispense with reserved names.

15. For a good description of the language see Dorn [1969].

16. R. W. Floyd [1967] suggested that the term verification should be used rather than proof.

Translator's Notes

Chapter 1

a. Any operation of this last type can be, and almost invariably is, constructed as a sequence of binary operations.

b. I have chosen to translate *informatique* in various ways, depending on the context. Among the translations possible are *computer, computer science, programming, programming language*, and *information processing*, as well as *data processing*.

c. The author says Heidelberg, but Tübingen is correct. The University of Tübingen held a Festkolloquium in 1973 to celebrate the 350th anniversary of Schickard's machine, at which I gave a short paper on Babbage.

d. Babbage was undoubtedly as genius, and one of many sides; but while he contributed both to astronomy and to mathematics, it would not be fair to call him either an astronomer or a great mathematician; Babbage [1864/1969].

e. Babbage's own words (Babbage [1837]) are these: "The barrels are upright cylinders divided into about seventy rings, the circumference of each ring being divided into about eighty parts. A stud may be fixed on any one or more of these portions of each ring. Thus each barrel presents about eighty vertical columns, every one of which contains a different combination of fixed studs."

f. This was certainly so in the early days of computer development, but "memory" is now almost the standard term, at least for the internal storage of the machine.

g. The author says that Burroughs threw them out of the window; and according to Eames [1973] this is literally what he did—one by one.

h. In the mathematical sense, that is, the arithmetic of complex numbers $a + ib$, where $i^2 = -1$.

i. This is IBM terminology.

j. Comrie, 1893–1950, was born in New Zealand and worked most of his life in Britain; he was an expert in computation and table making. "He was the most influential champion of the calculating machine's use in science" (Eames [1973]).

k. A vacuum tube is used here as a two-state device, conducting ("on") or nonconducting ("off"), switchable by a pulse from one to the other; thus it can represent a binary digit.

l. Meaning the system of 20 vacuum-tube ring counters.

m. "First Draft of a Report on the EDVAC" by John von Neumann, Philadelphia, 1945. Details are in Goldstine [1972] and von Neumann [1945].

n. Crossfooting was a term used in accounting to indicate the addition of numbers across a row, rather than up a column.

o. In the case of the SSEC, the reference is to vacuum-tube memory; in the case of ENIAC, to ring-counter memory.

p. The idea of a page address first appeared with this machine, but automatic paging, making the virtual-store technique possible, first appeared on Atlas in 1960; see section 2 in chapter 2.

Chapter 2

a. The interesting history of ERA and the 1100 series of computers is recounted by Erwin Tomash [1980].

b. By convention, K means "binary thousand," that is, $2^{10} = 1,024$, while k, a standard abbreviation for kilo, means 1,000.

c. Alternatively, and very commonly, the required number n of repeats is placed in the index register and reduced by 1 after every cycle; the process is stopped when the number in the register is zero. This was the original Manchester scheme.

d. The Atlas paging system worked very well indeed. The original Manchester term for the arrangement was "one-level store," the later term "virtual store" being due to IBM. The ICT company (later ICL), which took over the Ferranti computer business, did in fact continue, and develop, the concept, in the 1900 series, for example.

e. The original edition gives 10.24 revolutions per *milli*second, which is surely a misprint.

f. I have translated the French word *tri* by *sorting*, but the author may have something of more general meaning in mind.

Chapter 3

a. Often called end-of-record mark.

b. Very effective, and much used, systems were provided on the ICT 1900 series.

Chapter 4

a. My understanding of the term "associative memory" is that it refers to the process of associating a memory location with a stated item of information, in contrast to stating its address.

b. Wilkes's original name for this was "floating address." On EDSAC this was purely numerical.

c. At that time it was called the Carnegie Institute of Technology.

Appendix

a. A more up-to-date reference is Ershov and Shura-Bura [1980].

b. Ershov and Shura-Bura [1980] give the meanings of some of these names: STRELA means arrow; MESM and BESM are the transliterated initials of the Russian for Small Electronic Computing Machine and High-Speed Electronic Computing Machine, respectively.

c. Ershov and Shura-Bura [1980] give the name Institute of Precise Mechanics and Computing Machinery, Academy of Sciences.

Bibliography

Agrawai, Ashok K., and Rauscher, Tomlinson G., *Foundations of Microprogramming*, Academic Press, 1976.

Aiken, Howard H., and Hopper, Grace M., "The Automatic Sequence Controlled Calculator," *Electrical Engineering*, 1946. (Reproduced in Randell [1973].)

Aiken, Howard H., Oettinger, Anthony G., and Bartee, John C., "Proposed Automatic Calculating Machine," *IEEE Spectrum*, August 1964.

Amdahl, Gene M., and Backus, John W., "The System Design of the IBM Type 704," IBM Engineering Laboratory, Poughkeepsie, 1955.

Arsac, Jacques, *La Science informatique*, Dunod, 1970.

Arsac, Jacques, *La Construction des programmes structurés*, Dunod, 1977.

Ash, R., et al., "Preliminary Manual for MATHMATIC and Arithmetic Systems," Remington Rand Univac, 1957.

Atanasoff, John V., "Computing Machines for the Solution of Large Systems of Linear Algebraic Equations," Iowa State University, 1940. (Reproduced in Randell [1973].)

Auerbach, Isaac L., "European Electronic Data Processing. A Report on the Industry and the State of the Art," *Proceedings of the IRE* (Special Issue on Computers), January 1961.

Babbage, Charles, "On the Mathematical Powers of the Calculating Engine," 1837. (Reproduced in Randell [1973].)

Babbage, Charles, "Letter to Arago," 1839. (Reproduced in Randell [1973].)

Babbage, Charles, *Passages from the Life of a Philosopher*, 1864. (Reprinted in 1969, Augustus M. Kelly, editor.)

Backus, John W., "The IBM Speedcoding System," *Journal of the ACM*, January 1954

Backus, John W., "The Syntax and Semantics of the International Algebraic Language of the Zurich ACM—GAMM Conference," *Proceedings of IFIP, UNESCO, Paris*, 1959.

Backus, John W., "The History of FORTRAN I, II, III," *ACM SIGPLAN Notices* (ACM SIGPLAN History of Programming Languages Conference, June 1978), August 1978.

Backus, John W., "Can Programming Be Liberated from the von Neumann Style? A Functional Style and Its Algebra of Programs," *Communications of the ACM*, August 1978.

Bashe, Charles J., Buchholz, Werner, and Rochester, Nathaniel, "The IBM 702: An Electronic Data Processing Machine for Business," *Journal of the ACM*, 1954.

Beckmann, Frank S., and Brooks, Frederick P., "Developments in the Logical Organization of Computer Arithmetic and Control Units," *Proceedings of the IRE* (Special Issue on Computers), January 1961.

Bollée, Leon, "Sur une nouvelle machine à calculer," *Compte Rendu, Académie des Sciences, Paris*, 1889.

Bosset, J., "Sur certains aspects de la conception logique du Gamma 60," *Proceedings of the International Conference on Information Processing, UNESCO, Paris*, 1959.

Boucher, Henri, "Machines informatiques," École Nationale du Génie Maritime, 1966.

Bowden, B. Vivien (Lord Bowden), editor, *Faster Than Thought*, Pitman, 1953.

Bowers, Dan M., "The Rough Road to Today's Technology," *Datamation*, September 1977.

Burks, Arthur W., Goldstine, Hermann H., and Neumann, John von, "Preliminary Discussion of the Logical Design of an Electronic Computing Instrument," Princeton Institute for Advanced Studies, 28 June 1946. (Reproduced in Randell [1973].)

Carr, John W., Perlis, Alan J., Robertson, S. E., and Scott, N. R., "A Visit to Computation Centers in the Soviet Union," *Communications of the ACM*, June 1959.

Chapuis, A., and Droz, E., "Les Automates, figures artificielles d'hommes et d'animaux," *Histoire et techniques*, Griffon, 1969.

Chase, George C., "History of Mechanical Computing Machinery," *Annals of the History of Computing*, July 1980.

Cheysson, E., "La Machine électrique à recensement," *La Science Moderne*, July 1883.

Chomsky, Noam, *Syntactic Structures*, Mouton, 1957.

Cocke, John, and Kolsky, H., "The Virtual Memory in the Stretch Computer," *Eastern Joint Computer Conference*, December 1959.

Codd, E. F., *Multiprogramming. Advances in Computers*, Academic Press, 1962.

Codd, E. F., Lowry, E. S., McDonough, E., and Scalzi, C. A., "Multiprogramming the Stretch: Feasibility Considerations," *Communications of the ACM*, November 1959.

Couffignal, Louis, *Les Machines à calculer, leur principe, leur évolution*, Gauthier-Villars, 1933.

Couffignal, Louis, *Sur l'analyse mécanique. Application aux machines à calculer et aux calculs de la mecanique celeste*, Gauthier-Villars, 1938.

Dahl, Aubrey, "The Last of the First," *Datamation*, June 1978.

Datamation ("The Zuse Z3"), September 1966. (See Desmonde and Berkling [1966].)

Datamation ("Fragments of Computer History"), September 1976. (See Yasaki [1976].)

Davis, N. C., and Goodman, S. E., "The Soviet Bloc's Unified System of Computers," *Computing Surveys*, June 1978.

Davous, Bataille, and Harrand, "Le Gamma 60," *L'Onde Électrique*, December 1960.

de Butts, John D., "What Happened to the Computer Revolution?" *Computers and People*, November 1974.

Demarne, Pierre, and Rouquerol, M., *Les Ordinateurs*, Presses Universitaires de France, 1958.

Denning, Peter J., "Virtual Memory," *Computing Surveys*, September 1970.

Desmonde, W. H., and Berkling, K. J., "The Zuse Z3," *Datamation*, September 1966.

d'Ocagne, Maurice, *Le Calcul simplifié*, Gauthier-Villars, 1905.

d'Ocagne, Maurice, "Vue ensemble sur les machines à calculer," *Bulletin des sciences mathématiques*, Ser. 2, 1922.

Dorn, Philip H., "Obsolescence of Systems Software," *Datamation*, January 1969.

Dornbusch, Marcus, *Le Langage PL/1*, Dunod, 1971.

Eames, Charles and Ray, *A Computer Perspective*, Harvard University Press, 1973.

Eckert, Wallace J., "The Computation of Special Perturbations by the Punched Cards Method," *Astronomical Journal*, October 1935.

Eckert, Wallace J., "Electrons and Computation," *The Scientific Monthly*, November 1948. (Reproduced in Randell [1973].)

Eckert, Wallace J., "The Significance of the New Computer NORC," *Computers and Automation*, February 1955.

Ershov, Andrei P., "A History of Computing in the USSR," *Datamation*, September 1975.

Ershov, Andrei P., and Shura-Bura, Mikhail R., "The Early Development of Programming Languages in the USSR," in *A History of Computing in the Twentieth Century* (N. Metropolis, J. Howlett, and G.-C. Rota, editors), Academic Press, 1980.

Falkoff, A. D., Iverson, K. E., and Sussenguth, E. H., "A Formal Description of System 360," *IBM Systems Journal*, October 1964.

Flatt, J. P., "Les Trois premières machines à calculer," Palais de la Découverte, 1963.

Floyd, Robert W., "Assigning Meanings to Programmes," *Proceedings of Symposia in Applied Mathematics*, Vol. 19, American Mathematical Society, 1967.

Flynn, Robert L., "A Brief History of Data Base Management," *Datamation*, August 1974.

Frank, Werner L., "The Second Half of the Computer Age," *Datamation*, May 1976.

Fredkine, E., "The Time Sharing of Computers," *Computers and Automation*, November 1963.

Galanter, Eugene, *Automated Teaching*, Wiley, 1959.

Ganzhorn, Karl, and Walter, W., "Die geschichtliche Entwicklung der Datenverarbeitung," IBM Germany, 1975.

Goldstine, Hermann H., *The Computer from Pascal to von Neumann*, Princeton University Press, 1972.

Goldstine, Hermann, H., and Goldstine, Adele, "The Electronic Numerical Integrator and Computer (ENIAC): Mathematical Tables and Other Aids to Computation," 1946. (Reproduced in Randell [1973].)

Goldstine, Hermann H., and Neumann, John von, "Planning and Coding of Problems for an Electronic Computing Instrument," Princeton Instiute for Advanced Studies, 1947–1948. (In von Neumann, John, *Collected Works*, Pergamon Press, 1963.)

Graef, Martin, editor, *350 Jahre Rechenmaschinen*, Carl Hanser Verlag, 1973. [A collection of papers, in German and in English, on various topics in the history of computing, given at a one-day colloquium at the University of Tübingen to celebrate the 350th anniversary of Schickard's completion of his calculating machine in 1623.]

Hanks, Dale, "Programming Considerations for Minicomputers," *Computers and People*, January 1974.

Hanks, Dale, "A Keynote Address on Concurrent Programming," *Computers*, May 1979.

Hopper, Grace M., "The Education of a Computer," *Proceedings of the ACM Conference, Pittsburgh*, 1952.

Hopper, Grace M., "Compiling Routines," *Computers and Automation*, May 1953.

Hopper, Grace M., and Mauchly, John W., "Influence of Programming Techniques on the Design of Computers," *Proceedings of the IRE*, October 1953.

Hsiao, David K., "Data Base Machines Are Coming," *Computers*, March 1979.

IBM Applied Science Division, "Preliminary Report: Specifications for the IBM Mathematical FORmula TRANslating system FORTRAN," Programming Research Group, 10 November 1954.

IBM Corporation, "Speedcoding System for the Type 701 Electronic Data Processing Machine," Reference Manual 24-6059-0, September 1953.

IBM Corporation, "The FORTRAN Automatic Coding System for the IBM 704," Programmers Reference Manual 32-7026, October 1956.

IBM Corporation, "FORTRAN II for the IBM 704 Data Processing System," Reference Manual 28-6000, 1958.

IBM France, "A propos," September 1980.

Iverson, Kenneth E., *A Programming Language*, Wiley, 1962.

Kilburn, Tom, Edwards, David B. G., Larrigan, Michael J., and Sumner, Frank S., "One-Level Storage System," *IRE Transactions on Electronic Computers*, April 1962.

Kleene, Stephen C., "Representation of Events in Nerve Sets and Finite Automata," in *Automata Studies*, Princeton University Press, 1956.

Knight, Kenneth E., "Changes in Computer Performance, " *Datamation*, September 1966.

Knuth, Donald E., "The Remaining Trouble Spots in ALGOL 60," *Communications of the ACM*, October 1967.

Knuth, Donald E., "The Early Development of Programming Languages," in *A History of Computing in the Twentieth Century* (N. Metropolis, J. Howlett, and G.-C. Rota, editors), Academic Press, 1980.

Lamond, F., "La Convergence des minis et des ordinateurs universals," *Informatique*, December 1977–January 1978.

Lebedev, Sergei A., "The High-Speed Calculating Machine of the Academy of Sciences of the USSR," *Journal of the ACM*, July 1956.

Lecarme, Olivier, "Reliability, Portability, Teachability: Three Issues for Programming Languages," In *New Directions in Programming Languages*, IRIA, 1975.

Ledgard, Henry F., *Proverbes de programming*, Dunod, 1978.

Ledley, A., "Reasoning Foundations of Medical Diagnosis," *Science*, 1959.

Leiner, Alan L., "System Specification for DYSEAC," *Journal of the ACM*, 1954.

Licklider, J. C., "Man-Computer Symbiosis," *IRE Transactions on Human Factors in Electronics*, March 1960.

Livercy, C., *Théorie des programmes*, Dunod, 1978.

Loveday, Evelyn, "George Stibitz and the Bell Labs Relay Computer," *Datamation*, September 1977.

Lynch, J., and Johnson, C. E., "Programming Principles for the IBM Relay Calculators," Report 705, Ballistic Research Laboratory, Aberdeen, MD, October 1949.

McCarthy, John, "Towards a Mathematical Science of Computation," *Proceedings of IPIP Congress 1962*, North-Holland, 1963.

McCarthy, John, Boileu, S., Fredlein, E., and Licklider, J. C., "A Time Sharing Debugging System for a Small Computer," *Proceedings of AFIPS Conference*, 1963.

McDonald, N. D., "Descriptions of Digital Computers," *Computers and Automation*, June 1963.

Mackenzie, Charles E., *Coded Character Sets*, Addison-Wesley, 1980.

McLaughlin, Richard A., "The IBM 704: 36 Bits Floating-Point Moneymaker," *Datamation*, August 1975.

McWhorter, E. W., "The Small Electronic Calculator," *Scientific American*, May 1976.

Marcotty, M. J., Longstaff, F. M., and Williams, A. P. M., "Time Sharing on the Ferranti-Packard FP 6000 Computer System," *AFIPS Computer Conference*, 1963.

Masson, J., "L'Industrie et les calculateurs electroniques," *L'Onde Électrique*, December 1960.

Mauchly, John W., "Amending the ENIAC Story," *Datamation*, October 1979.

Mauchly, John W., "The ENIAC," in *A History of Computing in the Twentieth Century* (N. Metropolis, J. Howlett, and G.-C. Rota, editors), Academic Press, 1980.

Metropolis, N., Howlett, J., and Rota, G.-C., editors, *A History of Computing in the Twentieth Century*, Academic Press, 1980. [A collection of essays, mostly based on papers given at the International Research Conference on the History of Computing, Los Alamos Scientific Laboratory, June 1976.]

Moreau, René P., "Les Langages de l'informatique," *Sciences et Avenir* (Numéro Spécial Informatique), 1969.

Moreau, René P., *Introduction à la théorie des langages*, Hachette, 1975.

Naur, Peter, editor, "Report on the Algorithmic Language ALGOL 60," *Communications of the ACM*, May 1960.

Naur, Peter, "Revised Report on the Algorithmic Language ALGOL 60," *Communications of the ACM*, January 1963.

Neumann, John von, "First Draft of a Report on the EDVAC," University of Pennsylvania, Moore School of Electrical Engineering, 30 June 1945.

Newell, Alan, Shaw, John C., and Simon, Herbert A., "Empirical Explorations of the Logic Theory Machine," *Proceedings of the Western Joint Computer Conference*, 1957. (Reproduced in Feigenbaum and Feldman, *Computers and Thought*, McGraw-Hill, 1963.)

Nora, Simon, and Minc, Alain, *L'Informatisation de la société*, La documentation Française, 1978.

Orchard-Hays, William, "The Evolution of Programming Systems," *Proceedings of the IRE* (Special Issue on Computers), January 1961.

Pair, Claude, "Some Proposals for a Very High Level Language on a Variable Universe," in *New Directions in Algorithmic Languages*, IRIA, 1975.

Paycha, R., *Aide au diagnostic des affections rétiniennes*, La Presse Médicale, 1957.

Perlis, Alan J., and Samelson, Kurt, "Preliminary Report—International Algebraic Language," *Communications of the ACM*, December 1958.

Perlis, Alan J., Smith, J. W., and van Zoeren, H. R., "Internal Translator IT: A Compiler for the 650," Michigan University, Statistical Research Laboratory, January 1957.

Perrier, L., *Gilberte Pascal*, Bibliographie de Pascal, 1963.

Phelps, Byron E., "Dual Trigger Circuits," *Electronics*, July 1942.

Phelps, Byron E., "Early Electronic Computer Development at IBM," *Annals of the History of Computing*, July 1980.

Plugge, W. R., and Perry, M. N., "American Airlines Electronic SABRE Reservation System," *Western Joint Computer Conference*, May 1961.

Rachjman, Jan, "The Selectron, a Tube for Selective Electrostatic Storage," *Symposium on Large Scale Digital Calculating Machinery, Cambridge, Mass.*, 1948.

Randell, Brian, *The Origins of Digital Computers: Selected Papers*, Springer-Verlag, 1973.

Randell, Brian, and Kuehner, C. J., "Dynamic Storage Allocation Systems," *Communications of the ACM*, May 1968.

Raymond, François H., "Deux calculatrices S. E. A.," *L'Onde Électrique*, December 1960.

Raymond, François H., *Les Principes des ordinateurs*, Presses Universitaires de France, 1969.

Rochester, Nathaniel, "The Computer and Its Peripheral Equipment," *Proceeding of the Eastern Joint Computer Conference, Boston, Mass.*, 1 November 1955.

Rosen, Saul, "Programming Systems and Languages. A Historical Survey," in *AFIPS Conference Proceedings*, Spartan Books, 1964.

Rosen, Saul, "Electronic Computers. A Historical Survey," *Computing Surveys*, March 1969.

Rosen, Saul, "Programming Systems and Languages 1965–1975," *Communications of the ACM*, July 1972.

Rosenberg, Jerry M., *The Computer Prophets*, Macmillan, 1969.

Rosin, Robert F., "Contemporary Concepts of Microprogramming and Emulation," *Computer Surveys*, December 1969.

Ross, Douglas T., "Origins of the APT Language for Automatic Programmed Tools, *ACM SIGPLAN Notices* (ACM SIGPLAN History of Programming Languages Conference, June 1978), August 1978.

Sammet, Jean E., "A method of combining ALGOL and COBOL," *Proceedings of the Western Joint Computer Conference*, Vol. 19, 1961.

Sammet, Jean E., *Programming Languages: History and Fundamentals*, Prentice-Hall, 1969.

Sammet, Jean E., "Programming Languages: History and Future," *Communications of the ACM*, July 1972.

Sammet, Jean E., "The Early History of COBOL," *SIGPLAN Notices*, August 1978.

Schwarz, Jules L., "The Development of JOVIAL," *ACM SIGPLAN Notices*, June 1978.

Soffel, R. O., and Spack, E. G., "SAGE Data Terminals," *AIEE Transactions*, January 1959.

Sperry-Rand Corporation, "FLOWMATIC Programming," Document V 1518, 1958.

Stern, Nancy, "From ENIAC to UNIVAC," *IEEE Spectrum*, December 1981.

Stevens, Louis D., "Engineering Organization of Input and Output for the IBM 701 Electronic Data Processing Machine," *Joint AIEE-IRE Computer Conference*, March 1953.

Testa, Charles J., "The Evolution of Man-Computer Symbiosis," *Computers and Automation*, May 1973.

Tomash, Erwin, "The Start of an ERA: Engineering Research Associates Inc. 1946–1955," in *A History of Computing in the Twentieth Century* (N. Metropolis, J. Howlett, and G.-C. Rota, editors), Academic Press, 1980.

Torres y Quevedo, Leonardo, "Essais sur l'automation. Sa définition. Étendue théoretique de ses applications," *Revue de l'Academie Royale de Madrid*, 1914.

Totaro, J. Burt, "Communication Processor Survey," *Datamation*, May 1976.

Traub, Joe F., "The Influence of Algorithms and Heuristics," Carnegie Mellon University, Department of Computer Sciences, January 1979.

UNIVAC, "FLOWMATIC programming." (See Sperry-Rand [1958].)

Wegner, Peter, "Programming Languages—the First 25 Years," *IEEE Transactions on Computers*, December 1976.

Weik, Martin H., "A Survey of Domestic Electronic Computing Systems," *Reports*, 1955.

Wier, J. M., "Digital Data Communication Techniques," *Proceedings of the IRE* (Special Issue on Computers), January 1961.

Wijngaarden, Ard van, editor, "Draft Report on the Algorithmic Language ALGOL 68," Matematische Centrum Amsterdam MR 93, January 1968.

Wilkes, Maurice V., "The Growth of Interest in Microprogramming: A Literature Survey," *Computing Surveys*, September 1969.

Wilkes, Maurice V., Wheeler, David J., and Gill, Stanley, *The Preparation of Programs for an Electronic Digital Computer*, Addison-Wesley, 1961 (first edition 1957).

Williams, Frederick C., and Kilburn, Tom, "Electronic Digital Computers," *Nature*, September 1948.

Williams, Frederick C., Kilburn, Tom, and Toothill, Geoffrey C., "Universal High Speed Computers: A Small Experimental Machine," *Proceedings of the IEEE*, 1951.

Wirth, Nicholas, "The Programming Language Pascal," *Acta Informatica*, 1971.

Wirth, Nicholas, and Hoare, C. A. R., "A Contribution to the Development of ALGOL," *Communications of the ACM*, June 1966.

Withington, Frederick G., *The Environment for Systems Programs*, Addison-Wesley, 1978.

Yasaki, Edward K., "Fragments of Computer History," *Datamation*, September 1976.

Index

Access devices, 73–86
Access systems, direct. *See* Direct access systems
Access time, definition of, 50
Accounting and Tabulating Machines Company, 24
Accumulator (A-register), 31, 47
ACE. *See* Automatic Computing Engine
Adams, Charles W., 52
Ada programming language, 17
Addressable support equipment, 73, 74–82
Addresses
 definition of, 50
 IBM Stretch and, 95
 indirect, 67
 of memory location, 37
 symbolic, 156
 variable length and number of, 151–153
Aiken, Howard H., 30, 31, 54
AIMACO (Air Material Command), 173, 174
ALGOL, 60, 94, 99, 150, 168–173
 definition of, 172–173
 difference from FORTRAN, 168
 JOVIAL as descendent of, 171–172
 limitations of, 172–173
Algorithmic procedure, 4, 5–6
Algorithms, 6–10
Alpha-numeric alphabet, 59
Amdahl, Gene, 65, 192
American Airlines, 125–126
American Arithmometer Company, 20
American Association for Computing Machinery (ACM), 168
American computers, first, 38–41
Analog machine, 18–19

Analytic Engine, 12, 15, 16, 17, 26, 41
Anderson, Harland, 105
AN/FSQ7, 96, 116, 130
APL (A Programming Language), 150, 180–182
Applications programs, definition of, 38, 51
APT (Automatic Programmed Tools), 166–167
A-register. *See* Accumulator
Arithmetic
 floating-point, 29, 32
 stages in mechanization of, 21
Arithmetical-logical unit (ALU), 8, 10, 15, 41, 47
Artificial intelligence, 11, 26, 194. *See also* LISP
Asch, Alfred, 174
Assemblers, 156, 157, 158
Assembly languages, 149, 155–159
 limitations of, 158–159
 mnemonic codes and, 155
 symbolic addresses and, 156
 translation into machine language and, 156–158
Atlas computer
 Burroughs, 131
 Ferranti, 72, 123
 Guidance Model 1, 91
Atomic Energy Commission (AEC), 92
Automata, 12–13
Automatic Computing Engine (ACE), 43
Automatic programming, 157, 158, 160

Babbage, Charles, 4, 12, 181
 machine of, 12–19, 26
Backus, John, 159, 160, 161, 162, 168

Backus Normal Form (BNF), 169
Ballistics Research Laboratory (BRL),
    33, 34, 42
Bardeen, J., 89
Bashe, C. J., 59
BASIC, 166. *See also* PAF
Batch processing, 108–121, 134
    concurrency and, 110–112
    input/output in, 113–118
    and interrupt control, 112–113
    limitations of, 120–121
    monitors for, 109, 110
    multiprocessing and, 118–120
Bauer, F. L., 168, 169
Bell Laboratories, 9, 27–29
Bemer, R. W., 168, 174
Bergfors, C. A., 39
BESM series, 197–198
B5000, 171
BINAC (Binary Automatic Computer),
    46, 51–52
Binary calculator, 27–29
Binary coded decimal (BCD), 32
Binary coding, 9
Binary machine, first, 27
Binary-to-decimal conversion, 75
Binary vs. decimal bases, 93–94
Bit, origin of term, 9
BIZMAC, 65, 77–79
Blaauw, Gerrit A., 192
BMEWS (Ballistic Missile Early
    Warning System), 101
Bollée, Léon, 19, 21
Bolt, Beranek & Newman Company,
    105
Boole, George, 27
Bottenbruch, H., 168, 169
Bouchon, Basile, 13
Branscomb, L. M., 188
Brattain, W., 89
B-register. *See* Index registers
British computers, first, 41–44, 46
British Tabulating Machines Company
    (BTM), 24
BRL. *See* Ballistics Research Laboratory
Brooks, Frederick P., 192
Brown, T. J., 30
BTL (Bell Telephone Labs) Models (1,
    2, 3, 5), 28–29
Buffer memory, 54, 55, 115–116
Bull, Frederick, 25
Bull Company, 25, 63, 64. *See also*
    Gamma 60
Burroughs, W. S., 20

Burroughs Atlas, 131
Burroughs B200, 62
Burroughs B5000, 171
Business data processing, 49, 58–59.
    See also COBOL
Business machines, definition of, 49.
    See also IBM 1401 business machine
Byte, definition of, 94, 193

CAB (Calculatrices Arithmetiques
    Binaires) series, 71–72
CAB 500, 106–108, 165
CAB 1500, 73, 171
CAB 2000, 70
CADAC, 61, 62
Calculating machines. *See* Computers;
    Electromechanical machines;
    Electronic machines; Mechanical
    machines
Carnegie-Mellon University, 164
Carr, John W., 197
Cathode ray tube (CRT), 44, 80
CDC (Control Data Corporation), 91
CDC 1604, 91–92
CDC 3600, 91
CDC 8050/8090, 131
CEC 201, 62
Census, computer development and,
    21, 24, 54
Central processing unit (CPU), function
    of, 50
Channels, 134
    of classical communication, 129
    development of, 115–116
    early use of, 99
    high-speed, 105
Character machines, 59–60
Charge-coupled device (CCD), 60
Chenus, Pierre, 63
Chess-playing programs, 53, 88
Cheysson, E., 21
Chips, 146, 147
Church, Alonzo, 43
Clark, W., 124
Clarke, Wesley, 113
COBOL (Common Business-Oriented
    Language), 99, 150, 174, 183
    origin and characteristics of, 173–176
CODASYL (Committee on Data
    Systems Analysis), 174
Codd, E. F., 111, 120
Code
    ambiguous use of, 156
    definition of, 107

machine, 150
Coding data, 8–9
Collins Data Central, 131
Colossus project, 43, 44
Columbia University, 26, 30
Compatible Time-Sharing System
　(CTSS), 122, 124
Compilers, 157, 158, 161
Computation Center, University of
　Pennsylvania, 173
Computer-aided design (CAD), first
　example of, 95
Computer-assisted diagnosis, 193
Computer-Assisted Education (CAE),
　193
Computer networks, 130, 134
Computer Research Association (CRA),
　61
Computers, 70. *See also* Specific
　computers
　birth date of, 41
　characteristics of, 46–47, 139–140
　circuitry of, 144, 145, 146
　compatibility between, 76–77
　definition of, 37–38
　early powerful, 93–101
　first American, 38–41
　first British, 41–44, 46
　first business, 54
　first French, 63–64
　first in USSR, 197–201
　interactions and, 194–195
　languages of (*see* Programming
　　languages)
　large-scale, 193
　main events in history of, 45
　memory development in, 49–69
　organization of, 46
　performance/price improvements in,
　　188, 189, 190–192
　programs, 38 (*see also* Programs)
　software development for, 69–88
　speed of, 87–88
　transistors in, 89–92
Computer system, definition of,
　115
Computing Scale Company of
　America, 24
Computing Tabulating Recording
　Company (CTR), 24
Comrie, L. J., 32
COMTRAN (Commercial Translator),
　174
Concurrency, 110–112

Console, operators' and engineers',
　95–96
Consolidated Engineering Corporation,
　62
Control Data Corporation. *See* CDC
Control programs, definition of, 38
Control unit, 47
　Babbage's, 17
　simplification of, 107
Conversational mode, definition of,
　106
Conversational systems, 123, 124–127
Corbato, F., 122
Core-memory machine, 65–67, 69
Couffignal, Louis, 27
Counter, ring, 34–35
Cray, Seymour, 91
CRT. *See* Cathode ray tube
CTSS. *See* Compatible Time-Sharing
　System
CUBA (Calculateur Universal Binaire
　de l'Armement), 63
CXPQ, 91
Cycle time, definition of, 50

Data base, development of, 79
Data base/data communication (DB/
　DC), 126
Data communication, 127–131
Datamatic Corporation, 75
Datamatic 1000, 70, 76
Data processing, 9, 49. *See also* Business
　data processing
Data Transceiver, 128
Data transmission. *See* Transmission,
　types of
Datatron, 62, 66
Davies, H. C., 197
DEC. *See* Digital Equipment
　Corporation
Decimal machine, 59, 62. *See also*
　Business data processing
de Colmar, Thomas, 12, 21
Delay lines, 51–56
Department of Defense (DOD), 93
　COBOL and, 167, 173–174
　IBM and, 58
　IBM 7090 series and, 101
DEUCE, 43
Diamond Ordnance Fuze Laboratory,
　88
Difference Tabulator, 26–27
Digital Equipment Corporation (DEC),
　104, 171

Digital machine, 17
Direct access systems, 121–131
  data communications and, 127–131
  on-line, 124–127
  and shared use, 122–124
Direct coupled system (DCS), 118
Disks, first fixed, 81
Dispacs, 81–82
Dreyfus, Philippe, 63
Drum memories, 32
Dynamic memory, 51, 52

E 101, 62
Eckert, John Presper, 33, 34, 42, 53,
  54, 140
Eckert, Wallace J., 26, 40, 142
Eckert-Mauchly Computer
  Corporation, and UNIVAC I, 53, 54
EDSAC (Electronic Delay Storage
  Automatic Computer), 44, 46, 52
  loader for, 109
  memory of, 51
  video display and, 86
EDVAC (Electronic Discrete Variable
  Computer), 36, 40, 42
  magnetic disks and, 80
  memory of, 51
Egli, Hans W., 19, 25
Egli-Bull Company, 25
ELECOM 100, 61
Electro Data Corporation, 62
Electromechanical machines, 21–32
Electronic calculator, 33, 39
Electronic Computer Corporation, 61
Electronic Control Company, 51
Electronic machines, 33–56
Electronics Research Associates (ERA),
  61
Electrostatic tubes, 56–60
Emulators, 108
ENIAC (Electronic Numerical
  Integrator and Computer), 33–35,
  38, 41, 42, 140
  memory of, 51
ERA 1101, speed of, 88
ERA 1103, interrupt control and, 112
ERMA (Electronic Recording Method
  for Accounting), 64
Ershov, A. P., 197
Evans, Bob, 116
Everett, Robert, 52
Exceptions, in a program, 112

FACT, 175

Feissel, Henri, 63
Felt, D. E., 20
Fem, Louis, 75
Ferranti Atlas, 72, 123
Ferranti Mark I, 53
Ferranti Packard 6000 (FP 6000), 123
Ferrite-core memories, 32
  IBM 704 and, 65–67, 69
Floating-point arithmetic, 29, 32
FLOWMATIC, 174, 175
Ford Motor Company, 91
Forrester, Jay, 52
FORTRAN (FORmula TRANslator),
  150, 159, 160–166
  compiler for, 161
  definition of, 161–163
  example of programming in, 162–163
  first use of, 67
  influence of, 163–166
French computers, first, 63–64
Function, definition of computable, 43
Functional languages, 178–182

Gamma ET, 63, 64
Gamma 60, 93, 94, 97, 99–101
  block diagram for, 100
  coordination in, 99, 101
  main memory of, 97
  multiprocessing and, 97, 99
  number sold of, 101
GE (General Electric Company), 64,
  171
  Datanet, 30, 31
GE 210, 64, 92
General Motors, 67
GEPAC 4000, 171
Germanium transistors, 89–90
Goldfinger, Roy, 174
Goldstine, Adele, 34, 42
Goldstine, Herman H., 33, 34, 36, 41,
  42, 47, 143, 184
Good, I. J., 44
Goodman, S. E., 197
GO TO instruction, 161, 162
GPSS (General Purpose Simulation
  System), 167
Graphical display screen, first, 105
Graphic terminals, 86
Green, J., 168
GUIDE, 176
Gurley, Benjamin, 105

Haddad, J. A., 56, 58
Hamilton, Frank, 39

Hardware, definition of, 38
Harvard-IBM machine, 21, 30–32, 39, 40, 41. *See also* MARK I
memory of, 31
programming system of, 109
High-level languages
first, 159–167
three categories of, 149–150
Hollerith, Hermann, 21
Hollerith machine, 21–24
Honeywell, Computer Division of, 75
Honeywell 800, 108
machine instructions in, 152
multiprogramming and, 120
Hopper, Grace, 164, 174
Hurricane computer, and magnetic tapes, 75

IAL (International Algebraic Language). *See* ALGOL
IAS. *See* Institute for Advanced Study
IBM (International Business Machines), creation of, 24
IBM Automatic Sequence-Controlled Calculator (ASCC), 30, 31
IBM Card Programmed Calculator (CPC), 57
IBM computers, 24. *See also* Harvard-IBM machine; Specific IBM computers
associations for users of (*see* GUIDE; SHARE)
compatibility among, 76–77
first commercial, 56–58
magnetic disk technology and, 83
IBM 305, 79, 81, 96, 124
IBM 360, 94
operating system for design of, 192–193
programs of, 134–135
IBM 370, programs of, 135
IBM 402 accounting machine, 57
IBM 603 electronic calculator, 39, 56
IBM 604 Electronic Calculating Punch, 56–57
IBM 650, 57, 62–63
characteristics of, 70
IT and, 164–165
magnetic drums in, 64, 65
optimization of, 157–158
programs of, 134
speed of, 88
transistors and, 92
IBM 700, machine instructions for, 152

IBM 701, 57–58, 75, 88
IBM 702, 58–60, 75, 76
IBM 704
characteristics of, 70
ferrite-core memories and, 65–67, 69
optimization of, 158
IBM 705
characteristics of, 70
and magnetic tapes, 75–77
IBM 709, 67
channels in, 116
time-sharing and, 122
IBM 709TX, 101–102
IBM 1311 dispac, 82
IBM 1401 business machine, 92, 103–104, 108
IBM 1403 printer, 85
IBM 1410, 104
IBM 1440, 82, 104
IBM 1460, 104
IBM 1620, 92
IBM 7000, machine instructions for, 152
IBM 7030. *See* IBM Stretch
IBM 7040, 102–103
IBM 7044, 102–103
IBM 7070, interrupt control and, 113
IBM 7079, 92, 93
interrupt control and, 113
programs of, 134
SABRE and, 125–126
IBM 7090, series, 101–103
IBM 7094, 91, 131
IBM 7701 Synchronous Transmitter Receiver (STR), 128
IBM 7740, 131. *See also* GUIDE; SHARE
IBM Selective Sequence-Controlled Electronic Calculator (IBM SSEC), 39–41, 111
IBM Stretch, 75, 79, 93–94, 95
local concurrency and, 111
multiprogramming and, 119
number sold of, 101
IBM System IBSYS, 117, 120
IBM Transceiver, 128
IBM TRC, input/output on, 116
IBSYS. *See* IBM System IBSYS
Ichbiah, Jean, 17
Impact printing, 84–85
Index cards, Babbage's, 15. *See also* Perforated tapes
Index registers, 30–31, 44, 66
Industrial companies, 24–25

Information-support equipment,
definition of, 16
Information supports, 69–86
Informatique, 9, 63
Input/output controller (IOC), 95,
117–118
Input/output Control System (IOCS),
116–118, 120
Input/output processing systems,
113–118
Input/output (I/O) units, 9, 47
Institute for Advanced Study (IAS), at
Princeton, 42, 57, 61, 65, 91
Instruction
concept of, 37
FORTRAN and, 162–163
and machine language, 150–154 (*see
also* Assembly languages)
symbolic, 156
variable-length, 104
Instruction unit, 41
Interactional systems, 123, 124
International Business Machines. *See*
IBM
International Computers and
Tabulators (ICT), 25
International Time Recording
Company, 24
Interpreters, definition of, 157
Interrupt control, 112–113
IOCS. *See* Input/output control systems
IT (Internal Translator), 164, 165
Iverson, Kenneth, 181

Jacquard, Joseph M., 13
Jacquard loom, 13–14, 41. *See also*
Perforated tapes
Jacquemarts, 12–13
JOVIAL, 171–172. *See also* ALGOL

Katz, C., 168
KIEV, 197, 198–199
Kilburn, Tom, 44
Knuth, D., 172
Kruesen, Knut, 25

Laboratoire de Calcul de l'Armement,
63
Laboratory for Electronics, 80
Lake, Clair D., 30
Language for control of machine tools,
APT, 166–167
Languages. *See* Programming languages
Language translation, automatic, 194

Laning, J. H., 160, 161
LARC (Livermore Automatic Research
Computer), 93, 95–96
block diagram for, 98
input/output controller and, 95, 119
local concurrency and, 111
machine instructions for, 152
multiprocessing in, 96–97
number sold of, 101
Lebedev, S. A., 197
Leclerc, Bruno, 63
Leibniz, Gottfried Wilhelm, 11, 21, 41
Licklider, J. C., 124
Lincoln Laboratory, 113
Link editor, 156
LISP (LIST Processor), 150, 179–180,
182, 183
Loader program, 109
Logic theory machine, 88
Lovelace, Countess Ada, 17, 181
Low-level languages, 150–159

McCarthy, John, 105, 122, 179, 184
Machine languages, 150–155
definition of, 106
limitations of, 154–155
translation into, 156–158
Magnetic-bubble memory, 56
Magnetic disks, development and use
of, 80–82
Magnetic drums, 61–65
Magnetic-tape cylinders, proposal for,
187
Magnetic tapes, 54, 55, 74–80. *See also*
TRACTOR
BIZMAC and, 77–79
first scientific machine using, 57, 58
IBM 705 and, 75–77
limitations of, 80
Manchester Automatic Digital Machine
(MADM), 44, 51, 66
MARK I, 31, 88, 114, 139. *See also*
Harvard-IBM machine
MARK II, 31–32
Mask, definition of, 113
Massachusetts Institute of Technology
(MIT), Servomechanisms Laboratory
of, 52, 166
Mass memory, 82
MATHMATIC, 164
Matrix printer, 85
Mauchly, John W., 33, 42, 53, 54
Maurice, Franklin, 63
Mechanical machines, 10–21

Memory
associative, 151
in Babbage's machine, 16
buffer, 54, 55
of calculators, 31
capacity of, 49-50, 87
cathode ray tubes and, 44
characteristics of, 47
definition of, 49
drum and ferrite-core, 32
dynamic, 51, 52
in ENIAC, 35
holding program in, 36-37
magnetic-bubble, 56
magnetic drum for main, 61
mass, 82
read-only, 187-188
secondary, 82
static vs. dynamic, 51, 52
technology used in main, 51-69
virtual, 72-73
Memory hierarchies, characteristics of,
  50-51. *See also* Information supports;
  Paging
Memory position, definition of, 50
MESM, machines derived from,
  197-199
Message switching machines, 131
Microcode, definition of, 107
Microcomputer, definition of, 192
Microprograms, early use of, 107-108
Millionaire machine, 19
Minicomputer, first, 106
MINSK series, 199-201
Minsky, Marvin, 122
Mnemonic codes, 155-156
Modem, 128
Monitor program, 67
Monitor systems, for batch processing,
  109
Monroe, J. R., 19, 21
Moore School of Electrical Engineering,
  33-34, 35-36, 42, 44
M20 series, 198
Multipoint transmission, 128, 130
Multiprocessing, 96-97, 134
in Gamma 60, 97, 99
meaning of, 118, 119
Multiprogramming, 118-120

NASA (National Aeronautics and Space
  Administration), 131
National Bureau of Standards (NBS),
  54, 63, 88, 96

National Cash Register. *See* NCR
National Physical Laboratory (NPL), 43
National Security Agency, 91
Naur, P., 169, 172
NCR, 39
  CADAC and, 61
  GE and, 64
NCR 102A, 61
NCR 102D, 61
NCR 304, 92, 170, 171
Nelson, R. A., 162
Newell, Allen, 88
Newman, M. H. A., 43, 44
NORC (Naval Ordnance Research
  Calculator), 86, 88, 151
Norris, William C., 91
Northrup Aircraft Company, 51
NPL. *See* National Physical Laboratory
Numerograph, 86

Object program, 156
Office machine mode, 106
Office-size computers. *See* CAB 500;
  IBM 1620
Olson, Ken, 52, 105
Olson, Sam, 105
On-line systems, 124-127, 134
Operand, 7
Optical-disk memory, 187-188
Optimization, and FORTRAN, 161
Output, printed-paper, 20. *See also*
  Input/output processing systems

PAF (Programmateur Automatique de
  Formules), 106, 165-166
Paging, 44, 69, 71-73
Palmer, R. L., 56
Pascal, Blaise, 11, 21, 41, 137
PASCAL, 173
Patrick, Bob, 67
PDP (Programmed Digital Processor)
  computer, 104-106, 123
PDP 6, 171
Perforated tapes, 13-15, 138
Peripherals, connecting. *See* Input/
  output processing systems
Perlis, A. J., 164, 168
Personal computers, 192, 195
Phelps, Byron E., 39, 56, 59
Philco 212, 91, 111
Philco 2000, 91
Phillips, Charles A., 173, 174
Planar technology, beginnings of, 90
PL/I (Programming Language I), 150,
  176-177

Point-to-point transmission, 128
Pottin, H., 20
Powers, James, 24
Powers Samas Company, 24, 25
Printing, impact and nonimpact, 84–86
Problem-oriented language (POL), 148
Problem solving, mechanization of,
    4–10
Processing, data, 9, 49
Processing systems, input/output,
    113–118
Programming languages. *See also* (e.g.)
    Ada; ALGOL; BASIC; COBOL;
    FORTRAN; PL/I
  characteristics of natural, 148–149
  classifying, 182–185
  compiled and interpretive, 157
  conceptual form of, 182–183
  first high-level, 159–167
  first machine-independent (*see*
    FORTRAN)
  formally defined high-level, 167–177
  functional, 178–182
  high-level, 159–167
  low-level, 150–159
  most frequently used, 184–185
  quasi-natural (*see* COBOL)
  universal (*see* PL/I)
  universality of, 183
Programs, 46
  basic, 109
  competence of, 154
  control of, 38
  sequential execution of, 154
  storage of first, 36–37
  on tape, 77
  transferability of, 175
  translation to machine language via,
    156–158
Punched cards and punched-card
    machinery, 21–25, 73–74, 139
Punched paper tape, 74

Quevedo, Leonardo Torres y, 26, 27

Rabinowitz, Jack, 88
Radar, and delay lines, 51
RAMAC (Random Access Method of
    Accounting and Control), 81, 96, 124
Rand, James, 24
RAYDAC, 75
Raymond, F. H., 63, 71, 151
Raytheon Corporation, 75
RCA (Radio Corporation of America),
    39, 65, 78, 92

RCA 501, 92
Real time, definition of, 52–53
Real-time computer, 104–106
Register, index, 44
  first use of term, 30–31
  IBM 704 and, 66
Relay Interpolator, 28
Remington Rand, 24, 54
Remote job entry, first use of, 29
Rimalho, Colonel, 25
Ring counter, 34–35
Rochester, N., 58, 118
Ross, D. T., 166
Rutishauser, H., 160, 161, 168, 169

SABRE (Semi-Automatic Business-
    Related Environment), 125–126
SAGE air-defense system, 53, 96, 116
  software for, 135
  video display and, 86
Samelson, K., 168, 169
Sammet, Jean, 159, 174
Sayres, David, 161, 162
Schwartz, Jules I., 171, 172
Scientific computer, 49, 62
SEA (Societé d'Electronique et
    d'Automatisme), 63, 71–72, 106. *See
    also* CAB
  numerograph and, 86
  stack machines and, 171
SEAC (Standards Eastern Automatic
    Computer), 63
  machine instructions in, 151
  transistors and, 91
SEA CAB 1500, 73
Secondary memories, development of,
    82
Semiconductors, definition of, 87
Sequential-access memory, 74
Servomechanisms Laboratory, at MIT,
    52, 166
SETUN series, 198
S-expression. *See* Symbolic expressions
SHARE, 169, 176
SHARE-FORTRAN committee, 176
Shaw, J. C., 88
Sheeber, Rex, 39
Sheridan, P. B., 161
Shickard, Wilhelm, 10, 21, 41
Shockley, W., 89
Simon, Herbert A., 88
Smith, A. E., 174
SOAP assembly language, 165
Societé d'Electronique et
    d'Automatisme. *See* SEA

Societé des Machines Bull, 25
Software
  definition of, 38
  development of, 69–88
  increasing complexity of, 134–135
Somers, E. F., 174
Sorting box, 22, 23
Source program, 156, 157
Space program, computers and, 131
SPEEDCODE, 157
Sperry Rand, 24
SSEC. *See* IBM Selective Sequence-
  Controlled Electronic Calculator
Stack machines, 170–171
Stanford Research Institute, 64
Starynkevitch, D., 106, 165
Statements (conditional, unconditional,
  logical), 5–7
Static memory, 51
Steiger, O., 19
Stibitz, George, 27, 29, 54
Stifler, W. W., Jr., 61
Stored programs, 15–16, 41
STRELA series, 197, 198
Stretch. *See* IBM Stretch
Support equipment, development of,
  73–86
Symbolic addressing, 156
Symbolic expressions, 179
Syntactic analysis, 159

Tabulating Machine Company, 24
Tabulator, difference, 26–27
Tape Processing Machine (TPM), 59
Tape Record Coordinator (TRC), 76
TELSTAR satellite, 127
Thomas J. Watson Astronomical
  Computing Bureau, 26, 30
Time-sharing systems, 122–127
Tompkins, C. B., 61
TRACTOR, and IBM Stretch, 95
TRANSAC S-1000, 91
TRANSAC 2000, 91
Transistorized computers, 91–92
Transistors, 89–90, 145
Translator program, 155, 156–158
Transmission, types of, 128, 130
Turing, Alan M., 43, 44
Turing machine, 43
TX2, 113

UNIVAC (Universal Automatic
  Computer), 54
UNIVAC I, 53–55

buffer memories and, 115
magnetic tapes and, 75
MATHMATIC and, 164
printer on, 84
speed of, 88
UNIVAC II, characteristics of, 70
UNIVAC III, speed of, 88
UNIVAC 1103, transistors and, 92
UNIVAC 1103A, 65, 66
Universal calculator, 14, 21
  first (*see* Harvard-IBM machine)
  first electronic, 33–35
University of Manchester, 69, 72
University of Pennsylvania, 33
URAL series, 198
Ursinus College, 33
USSR, first computers in, 197–201

Vacuum-tube technology, 48
Vauquois, B., 169
Virtual memory, 72–73
Visual display screens, 86
Von Neumann, John, 33, 36, 41, 42,
  54, 57, 141, 184
Von Neumann languages, 150
Von Neumann machines, 42

Wakelin, J. H., 61
Watson, Thomas J., Jr., 39, 41, 56, 57,
  192
Watson, Thomas J., Sr., 24, 26, 30, 142
Wegstein, J. H., 168, 174
Whirlwind computer, 46, 52–53, 65,
  86, 160, 161
Wilkes, Maurice, 43, 44
Williams, F. C., 44
Williams, Sam, 28
Williams electrostatic tubes, 56
Wood, Benjamin D., 26
Woodger, M., 169
Word machines, 59–60
Word mark, 103

Zeroth-generation computers, 48
Zierler, W., 160, 161
Ziller, I., 162
Zuse, Konrad, 28

DATE			

Ⓑ THE BAKER & TAYLOR CO.